Table of Contents

INTRODUCTION

ON-PREMISES PRODUCTS

ONLINE SERVICES

OVERVIEW

What is our Body of Knowledge?

Microsoft sell a wide range of products across traditional software, Online Services and Azure, and there are a substantial number of agreements that customers can purchase them through. The rules for how you acquire licenses for the different products are diverse, often complicated, and can differ dependent on how the licenses are purchased. The licensing information for all of these different products and agreements is spread across many documents and websites, and this makes it really difficult to learn the rules or even find them when you need them.

All this is why we've created our Microsoft Licensing Body of Knowledge – to gather together licensing information across all of the products across all of the ways to buy them. We've chosen the content carefully – we wanted to make it as complete as possible without making it overwhelming by including every single licensing detail about every single product. Overall, it's about 90% of the full set of licensing information, and we think that's probably the right amount for the vast majority of people.

Useful reference resources

The intention of this book is not to replace Microsoft's official documentation, rather to explain it. You should always reference Microsoft's own resources, rather than this book, for example, when you document your licensing decisions, and it's the Product Terms site and Microsoft's Licensing Guides that you'll probably find most useful.

Product Terms site

Until February 2021 Microsoft released monthly Product Terms and Online Services Terms documents which, together, gave detail on the licensing of its products. From March 2021, however, these documents are replaced by the Product Terms website. This site has sections for each product, as well as separate sections for Software Assurance benefits and CAL Equivalency Licenses, and a useful Glossary of terms.

You can find the Product Terms site here: https://bit.ly/BOKProductTerms.

Licensing Guides

Microsoft release on an ad-hoc schedule a variety of Licensing Guides and Licensing Briefs which usually aim to give more clarity on complicated areas of licensing. Microsoft don't have a single place where you can find all of these rather useful documents, so we've gathered them together and you can find them on our site here: http://bit.ly/MSLicensingGuides.

Using the Body of Knowledge

The book has two main purposes. Firstly, it's a reference book. There's an extensive index to help you to look something up or to answer a question that crops up.

Secondly, each section stands alone, so if you want to learn about Microsoft licensing then you can do that. If you're new to licensing, read the **Introduction to Microsoft licensing** section to get an overview of what Microsoft sells and how customers purchase licenses. Then, read the section introduction of the product you're interested in – **Licensing on-premises products**, **Licensing Online Services**, or **Licensing Azure**. After that, read the section for the particular product or program you're interested in – **Windows Server 2019**, or **Buying Online Services: EA**, or **Licensing Azure virtual machines**, for example.

Changes to Microsoft licensing

Of course, there are always changes in Microsoft licensing, and any that have been implemented after May 2021 are not included in this book. However, it's our intention to issue the Microsoft Licensing Body of Knowledge every year so that you've always got a complete and up-to-date reference.

INTRODUCTION TO MICROSOFT LICENSING

Use this section to get an introduction to the types of products that Microsoft sell, and for an overview of each of the different agreements and programs through which customers can buy them.

What does Microsoft sell?

Microsoft sells three different types of products: on-premises software such as Windows Server or SQL Server; Online Services such as Office 365 or Dynamics 365; and Azure services such as virtual machines or cloud storage.

For the on-premises products you buy a license which allows you to install and use the software. For the Online Services you buy a subscription which allows you to access the cloud services while the subscription is active, and most of the Azure services are sold on a consumption basis where you just pay for the service while it's up and running – while you're consuming it.

How do customers buy Microsoft products?

Microsoft have historically sold licenses for their software products through Volume Licensing agreements such as the Enterprise Agreement or an Open Value agreement. When Online Services and the Azure services became available many of the agreements were extended to allow customers to pay for these new services through their existing agreements. Today there are six main Volume Licensing agreements aimed at commercial customers – that is customers who are not government, academic or nonprofit customers.

This wide range of Volume Licensing agreements caters for different sizes of customers, whether they want to buy in a committed or transactional way, and whether they want to own licenses for the on-premises products. This flexibility does bring complexity, and many customers end up with multiple agreements. So, Microsoft have decided to offer a simpler solution in the future, and the goal is that over (a long) time the variety of Volume Licensing agreements will disappear, to be replaced be a single agreement: the Microsoft Customer Agreement. Clearly this cannot happen overnight, but the Microsoft Customer Agreement has already started to be introduced to ease the transition, as part of an initiative Microsoft call the New Commerce Experience.

Today the Microsoft Customer Agreement governs purchases made through a partner via the Cloud Solution Partner program, when a customer engages directly with an internal Microsoft salesperson, and when purchases are made direct from Microsoft's websites – through azure.com for example.

Here's a summary of the ways that customers can buy the three different types of products that Microsoft sell today:

Volume Licensing agreements

	On-premises software	Online Services	Azure services
Enterprise Agreement	✔	✔	✔
MPSA	✔	✔	
Select Plus	✔		
Open License program	✔	✔	✔
Open Value	✔	✔	✔
Open Value Subscription	✔	✔	✔

Figure 1: availability of products through the Volume Licensing agreements

Microsoft Customer Agreement

	On-premises software	Online Services	Azure services
CSP	✔	✔	✔
Direct from a Microsoft salesperson			✔
Direct from the Microsoft website		✔	✔

Figure 2: availability of products through the Microsoft Customer Agreement

Enterprise Agreement basics

An Enterprise Agreement is aimed at larger customers who have more than 500 devices or users. It is known as a committed agreement since a customer can't sign an Enterprise Agreement without making some sort of commitment based on the Enrollment type they choose. There are three types of enrollment, as shown below, dependent on whether the customer wants to commit to desktop products or server products:

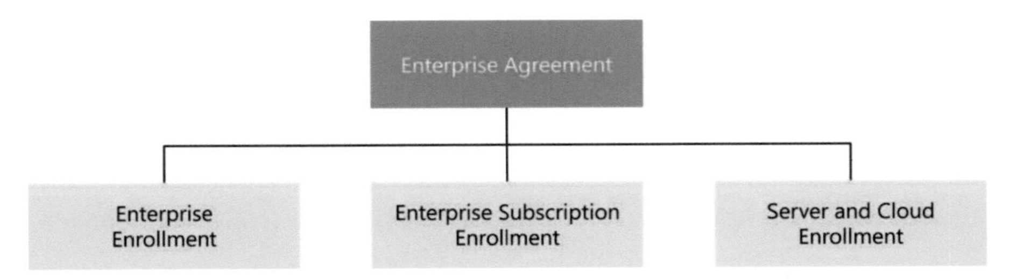

Figure 3: Enterprise Agreement structure

Enterprise Enrollment

An Enterprise Enrollment requires a customer to commit to the desktop products – they count all of their devices and commit to buying certain software for all of those devices, and this is known as an enterprise-wide commitment. They must also commit to Software Assurance which is an additional purchase and gives them additional ways to use their licenses for the greatest deployment flexibility (see page 15 for more detail). The licenses for software products acquired through an Enterprise Enrollment are perpetual licenses which means that the customer owns them forever, regardless of whether they renew the Enrollment at the end of the 3-year term. Detailed information on how the rules work for customers buying software licenses through an Enterprise Enrollment can be found on page 125. Once a customer has made the initial commitment to the software products they can then acquire Online Services (page 293) and Azure services (page 383) through that same enrollment.

Enterprise Subscription Enrollment

An Enterprise Subscription Enrollment is almost identical to an Enterprise Enrollment in that a customer needs to make the same commitment to buying software for all of their devices and to Software Assurance. However, the licenses for the software products are subscription licenses rather than perpetual licenses. Subscription licenses are cheaper than perpetual licenses since customers are, in effect, just leasing the software rather than owning it. At the end of the 3-year enrollment term the customer must decide if they want to renew the enrollment or to deinstall the software that they have been using. Detailed information on how the rules work for customers acquiring software licenses through an Enterprise Subscription Enrollment can be found on page 131. Once a customer has made the initial commitment to the software products they can then acquire Online Services (page 293) and Azure services (page 383) through that same enrollment.

Server and Cloud Enrollment

The Server and Cloud Enrollment (SCE) is the third enrollment that is available to be signed under the Enterprise Agreement. The Enterprise Enrollments cover the desktop products and the SCE focuses on the server products and Azure. A customer may choose to have an Enterprise Enrollment and/or an SCE – they're absolutely not dependent on each other. The SCE does share some characteristics with the Enterprise Enrollment: the term is 3 years, there's a level of commitment required, and Software Assurance is mandatory. SCE customers can choose to commit to the server products (see page 133) or to the Azure services, the rules of which are detailed on page 387.

Enterprise Agreement affiliates

Affiliates may also buy under an organization's Enterprise Agreement, where an affiliate is defined to be a separate legal entity controlled by the organization signing the Enterprise Agreement, where control means ownership of more than a 50% interest of voting securities in an entity, or the power to direct the management and policies of an entity. Affiliate organizations can be located anywhere in the world and thus the EA is ideally suited to an organization with a more complicated structure.

Direct and Indirect Enterprise Agreements

If you've heard the terms Direct or Indirect Enterprise Agreement, this just indicates how Microsoft invoice the end customer: either directly, or indirectly through a partner. The invoicing model varies by geography and customer type. There were some rule changes in November 2019 for commercial customers in direct markets and those are covered on page 383.

MPSA and Select Plus basics

If a larger customer is able to, and wants to, make a commitment to Microsoft products then they will probably buy through an Enterprise Agreement. If they would prefer to buy licenses on a more ad hoc basis then they will choose one of the transactional agreements which are the MPSA and Select Plus agreements. Many organizations have both a committed and a transactional agreement for maximum purchasing flexibility.

Microsoft Products and Services Agreement (MPSA)

The MPSA is aimed at the larger customer who has more than 250 users or devices. The agreement is considered to be an evergreen agreement since it doesn't need re-signing every three years as an Enterprise Agreement does. Software Assurance is a completely optional purchase in an MPSA; on a license-by-license basis, customers can choose whether or not they buy SA. All licenses for on-premises products are perpetual licenses, and the purchasing rules are covered on page 141.

Similar to the Enterprise Agreement the MPSA enables affiliates to buy under it, but there's more flexibility than the Enterprise Agreement since an MPSA affiliate may be a business unit, division, or subsidiary as well as a more-than-50%-owned legal entity. Purchasing Accounts can be set up for each affiliate which means that they can buy exactly what they need when they need it, separate to the needs of the other affiliates, but the overall purchasing is combined so that the best possible price levels are achieved.

Customers can also purchase Online Services through their MPSA, and these are covered on page 303, but the Azure services are not available through an MPSA.

Select Plus

In July 2014 the retirement of Select Plus was announced and although this process has not yet been completed there has been no new innovation in this licensing program since then, and new customers cannot sign a Select Plus agreement. This is an older agreement where customers with more than 250 PCs can only purchase perpetual licenses for on-premises products with optional Software Assurance on those licenses. The rules are very similar to the MPSA, so find out more detail in that section on page 141, and in the Select Plus section on page 148.

Open Programs basics

Microsoft use the term **Open Programs** to mean a collection of three licensing agreements aimed at smaller organizations. Between them, they offer similar purchasing frameworks for these smaller organizations as the Enterprise Agreement and MPSA offer larger companies.

Customers and their affiliates within one of a set of predetermined geographic territories can share one of these agreements. An affiliate is defined as a legal entity that the customer signing the agreement owns, which owns them, or which is under common ownership, where "ownership" is defined as more than 50% ownership.

Open License program

Often just called "Open", this licensing agreement is like the MPSA in that it allows customers to purchase perpetual licenses for on-premises products on an ad hoc basis, with or without Software Assurance during the 2-year term of the agreement – see page 149 for details. Both Online Services (page 306) and the Azure services (page 389) are also available through this agreement.

In October 2020 Microsoft announced that the Open License program would be retired at the end of December 2021. Nothing will happen to customers' existing licenses purchased through this agreement, but they won't be able to buy further licenses after that date. You can find more details on customers' options in the individual product sections.

Open Value

The Open Value agreement is a 3-year agreement where Software Assurance is mandatory on all purchases of licenses for on-premises products, which are perpetual licenses. When the agreement is signed customers decide if they want the agreement to be an organization-wide one, or not. If they choose the organization-wide option they need to commit to the desktop products (page 156), otherwise the only commitment they need to make is to Software Assurance (page 152). Customers can also buy Online Services (page 306) and the Azure services (page 389) through the Open Value agreements.

Open Value Subscription

The Open Value Subscription agreement is also a 3-year agreement and is most similar to the Enterprise Subscription Enrollment since a customer needs to commit to the desktop products organization-wide. Software Assurance is included, and licenses for the on-premises products are non-perpetual, or subscription, licenses – see page 158. Once the initial commitment has been made customers can also buy Online Services (page 306) and the Azure services (page 389) through their Open Value Subscription agreement.

Microsoft Customer Agreement

The Microsoft Customer Agreement is an evergreen agreement that is digitally accepted by a customer through the Microsoft 365 Admin Center. Any customer can preview the terms of the Microsoft Customer Agreement here: https://bit.ly/BOKMCA.

As I said at the beginning of this section, Microsoft plan to make the Microsoft Customer Agreement the single agreement that customers sign as part of the New Commerce Experience initiative which supports purchasing through CSP, direct from a Microsoft salesperson, or from a Microsoft website.

Cloud Solution Provider (CSP) program basics

The Cloud Solution Provider, or CSP, program is designed to enable partners to sell licenses for Microsoft software, Online Services, or Azure services, along with their own services, to customers. As a purchasing framework it's much more flexible than a Volume Licensing agreement and a partner is free to set the purchasing rules for customers. For example, they could set any payment terms for Online Services that suit the customer: upfront annually, monthly in arrears, upfront quarterly, best prices for upfront payment for 3 years etc.

There are some geographical restrictions within CSP, namely that a partner can only sell to a customer within the territory that they are authorized as a partner. The US and Canada are each separate territories and many European countries form another. This means that a partner based in the UK, for example, couldn't sell directly to the subsidiary of a UK customer based in the US.

Buying licenses for software products is covered on page 162, for Online Services on page 313, and for the Azure services on page 392.

Buying direct from a Microsoft salesperson

The Microsoft Customer Agreement is also used when a larger, more strategic customer buys direct from Microsoft. This was introduced in March 2019 and, so far, only supports customers who are buying the Azure services. You can find the purchasing rules for this on page 395.

Microsoft call this way of buying through the New Commerce Experience the **Enterprise motion**. Just to add extra clarity that this does refer to the Microsoft Customer Agreement we've called this way of buying the **Enterprise MCA** in this book. Note that this doesn't imply that it's governed by a different flavor of the MCA – the Microsoft Customer Agreement is the same whether customers are buying through this channel or CSP.

Buying direct from the Microsoft website

Any business can buy licenses for Online Services or pay for the Azure services directly through Microsoft's websites. Individuals can also buy licenses for certain Online Services using their business credentials if that is allowed by their IT department.

We haven't made this way to buy licenses and services a focus of this book.

Availability of licenses

To find out exactly which licenses are available through all of the different ways to buy, you should use the Product Terms website. If you look at the picture below you'll see that I've navigated to the Windows Server entry but I haven't chosen a program, and that means I can see which licenses are available where.

This is the link that takes you to this page: https://bit.ly/BOKWSAvailability:

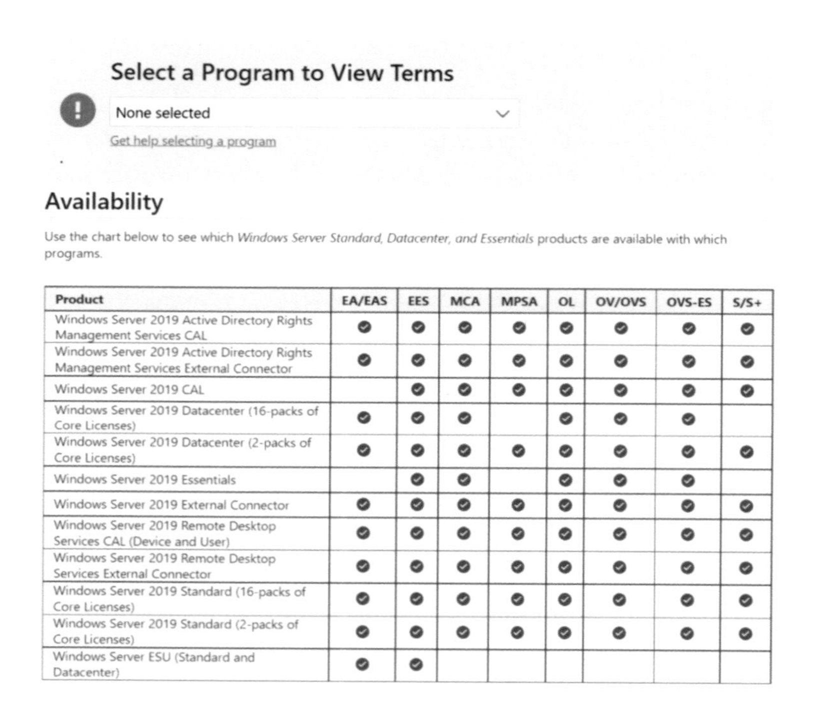

Windows Server Standard, Datacenter, and Essentials

Select a Program to View Terms

None selected

Get help selecting a program

Availability

Use the chart below to see which *Windows Server Standard, Datacenter, and Essentials* products are available with which programs.

Product	EA/EAS	EES	MCA	MPSA	OL	OV/OVS	OVS-ES	S/S+
Windows Server 2019 Active Directory Rights Management Services CAL	✓	✓	✓	✓	✓	✓	✓	✓
Windows Server 2019 Active Directory Rights Management Services External Connector	✓	✓	✓	✓	✓	✓	✓	✓
Windows Server 2019 CAL		✓	✓	✓	✓	✓	✓	✓
Windows Server 2019 Datacenter (16-packs of Core Licenses)	✓	✓	✓		✓	✓	✓	
Windows Server 2019 Datacenter (2-packs of Core Licenses)	✓	✓	✓	✓	✓	✓	✓	✓
Windows Server 2019 Essentials		✓	✓		✓	✓	✓	
Windows Server 2019 External Connector	✓	✓	✓	✓	✓	✓	✓	✓
Windows Server 2019 Remote Desktop Services CAL (Device and User)	✓	✓	✓	✓	✓	✓	✓	✓
Windows Server 2019 Remote Desktop Services External Connector	✓	✓	✓	✓	✓	✓	✓	✓
Windows Server 2019 Standard (16-packs of Core Licenses)	✓	✓	✓	✓	✓	✓	✓	✓
Windows Server 2019 Standard (2-packs of Core Licenses)	✓	✓	✓	✓	✓	✓	✓	✓
Windows Server ESU (Standard and Datacenter)	✓	✓						

Figure 4: Windows Server license availability

LICENSING ON-PREMISES PRODUCTS

Use this section to get some general information on how the on-premises products are licensed, and then get more detail in the individual product sections that follow.

Licenses for on-premises products

A Microsoft license for the traditional software products gives a customer the rights to install the software (where needed) and to use it. There are a number of different licensing models that govern the individual products and the sections of the book that follow cover each of the products and their specific licensing rules.

In general terms, for a product installed on a user's machine such as Windows or Office it's a device licensing model, where a license is assigned to each device. For server products such as Windows Server, you typically license the server device to allow you to install the software on that device, and then also license users or devices to allow them to access the services of the server.

Perpetual and subscription licenses

Dependent on the agreement or program they are purchasing through, customers may acquire perpetual licenses or subscription licenses for the traditional software products. A perpetual license is owned forever by the customer while a subscription license allows the customer to install and use the software only while the subscription is active.

License reassignment rights

As mentioned above, many of the licenses for the software products follow some sort of device licensing model where licenses are assigned to a physical device. Licenses may be reassigned to a different physical device, but no more frequently than every 90 days. The only exception to this "90-day rule" is if there is permanent hardware failure.

Versions and editions

A version is a particular release of a piece of software and it often corresponds to a year – Office 2019, for example. An edition is a way of differentiating between different sets of functionality that are included in the product – Office Standard 2019 does not include as many components as Office Professional Plus 2019, for example.

Downgrade and down-edition rights

New licenses are always sold for the latest version of a product. However, sometimes customers want to deploy further instances of an older version and so need to acquire additional licenses for that deployment. Most products give downgrade rights allowing you to install an earlier version of a product.

Some products also include down-edition rights. If you buy a Windows Server Datacenter license, for example, you can choose to install the Standard edition if you want to. Not all products include down-edition rights so always check the Product Terms site for confirmation if you need to make use of these rights. The diagram below shows the entry for Windows Server where you can see that both Standard and Datacenter editions also include the rights to install the Essentials edition (see page 30) as an alternative:

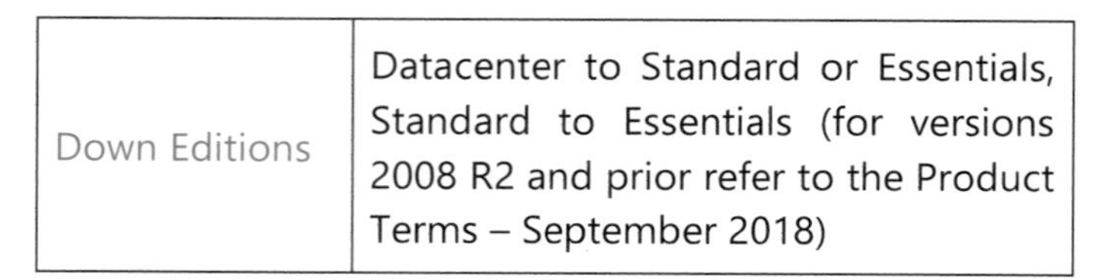

Down Editions	Datacenter to Standard or Essentials, Standard to Essentials (for versions 2008 R2 and prior refer to the Product Terms – September 2018)

Figure 5: Windows Server 2019 down-edition rights

Product use rights

If you do exercise either downgrade rights, then you need to understand which product use rights govern your deployment of the product. In other words, if you've purchased SQL Server 2019 licenses, but chosen to deploy

SQL Server 2008, which licensing rules should you follow – those for SQL Server 2019 or those for SQL Server 2008?

The rules state that it's the product use rights of the license purchased that prevail, not the use rights of the version deployed. So, in this case, since you've purchased SQL Server 2019 licenses, those are the licensing rules that you need to follow, regardless of what version you deploy.

Note that if you had purchased SQL Server 2008 and continued to deploy that, you continue to follow the licensing rules for SQL Server 2008.

Software Assurance

Software Assurance is an additional purchase that can be made when a license is purchased. A license gives a certain set of rights and Software Assurance typically gives an additional set of rights and benefits. For instance, a Windows 10 Enterprise device license allows you to install the software on a user's device, but if you want to deploy Windows 10 in virtual desktops for your users then you need Software Assurance to have the right to do that.

New Version rights are probably the most well-known of all the SA benefits: if an organization buys, for example, an Office Professional Plus 2019 license with SA then they're entitled to use any newer versions of Office released during the term of their Volume Licensing agreement. If they haven't installed that newer version of Office by the time their agreement ends, even if they don't renew the agreement, they are still licensed for that version – as long as they have purchased perpetual Office licenses of course.

When organizations buy licenses through their Volume Licensing agreement they must decide at the point of purchase if they want to include Software Assurance or not; there is no option to add on SA to a license purchase at a later date.

Customers who do purchase licenses with Software Assurance pay an annual fee for the SA – it's between 25% and 29% of the cost of the license each year. So, if an organization is purchasing through an agreement which lasts three years they will pay for the license and 3 x SA. When they come to the end of the agreement they can choose to renew the SA and that means that for the next term of the agreement they just pay for 3 x SA and, if they continue to renew the SA, then they will never need to purchase another license for that product again.

Step-up licenses

Customers with Software Assurance on their licenses for many of the products are eligible to purchase Step-up licenses. A Step-up license allows a customer to move from a lower edition of a product to a higher edition by just paying the difference in the license with SA price – this is the Step-up license price. In all of the Volume Licensing agreements apart from the Open License agreement, customers with active Software Assurance can purchase a Step-up license.

As an example, if a customer has SQL Server Standard Core licenses and later needs to deploy SQL Server Enterprise, they need to acquire Enterprise Core licenses. If they have no SA on the SQL Server Standard Core licenses, then they need to purchase new Enterprise Core licenses in the usual way. However, if they do have SA on the SQL Server Standard Core licenses then they can just purchase Step-up licenses and thus will just pay the difference in license with SA prices, potentially saving a significant amount of money.

External users

An organization licensing a server infrastructure will license its servers and its users who are known as internal users. They then potentially need to license their external users. An external user is someone who isn't an employee of the organization buying the licenses but does need to access an internal solution.

Assigning server licenses to dedicated hardware

The majority of the on-premises products are licensed with device licenses. In the case of the server products this means that licenses are assigned to a server device which must be dedicated to a customer's use. As an alternative to owning and managing hardware themselves, customers can choose to use hardware that is dedicated to them but is owned and managed by a third party. Microsoft categorize partners that offer this type of solution either as Listed Providers or Authorized Outsourcers, and the licensing rules differ dependent on the partner type.

The Listed Providers, at May 2021, are the following organizations:

- Alibaba
- Amazon
- Google
- Microsoft

All other organizations offering dedicated hardware solutions are known as Authorized Outsourcers. If there were to be changes to the list of Listed Providers you can always find the up-to-date list here: http://aka.ms/listedproviders.

Customers may assign their licenses, with or without Software Assurance, to servers owned and managed by Authorized Outsourcers and the licensing rules are exactly the same as for the customer-owned servers. Customers may sometimes assign their licenses to dedicated hardware solutions offered by Listed Providers and the rules are covered in the **License deployment options** section on page 358.

Using Online Services licenses to access on-premises servers

The on-premises servers are typically licensed by assigning licenses to the server and then licensing users or devices to access the services of the server. Many of the User Subscription Licenses for Online Services products such as Office 365 E3 also include rights to access licensed on-premises servers. These are known as CAL Equivalency rights and are covered in the Online Services section of this book. You can use the index to find the on-premises use rights for the particular product you're interested in.

WINDOWS SERVER 2019

Windows Server 2019 is Microsoft's server operating system and there are two editions used by most commercial customers: Standard and Datacenter editions. The main part of this section focuses on the licensing of these editions, and then we look at the licensing of the third edition, Essentials, on page 30.

Licensing Windows Server 2019

The diagram below shows a typical client server network: there's a server in the center where the server products are installed, and then there are users who use a variety of devices to access the services of the server.

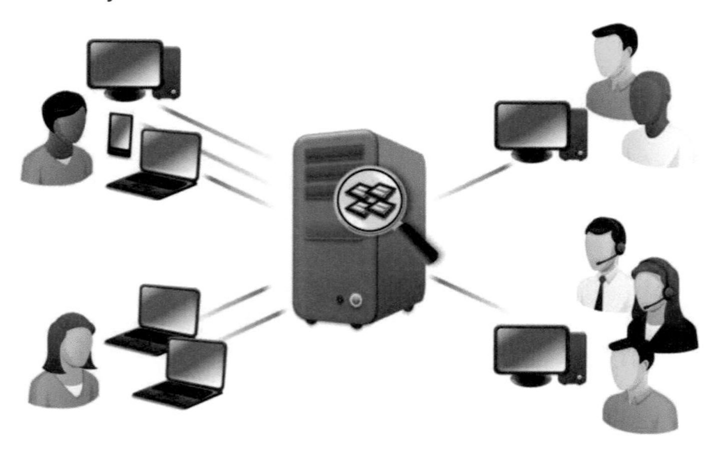

Figure 6: client server network

Both Windows Server 2019 Standard and Datacenter editions are licensed with the Per Core and CAL model. Licenses are assigned to a server based on the number of physical cores in the server, and then Client Access Licenses, or CALs, are assigned to either users or devices.

Windows Server Core licenses

The licenses assigned to the server are called Core licenses, and you need to assign a minimum of 8 Core licenses to each processor, and a minimum of

16 Core licenses to each server. Therefore, a single processor machine with 4 cores would need 16 licenses assigned to it, and a server with 4 x 2-core processors would need 4 x 8 = 32 licenses. All cores in the server must always be licensed. The diagram below shows the required licenses assigned to the servers in the examples we've just looked at, with the licenses in groups of 8 for easy counting.

Figure 7: Windows Server 2019 Per Core licensing

Across a network with several servers you can have different editions of Windows Server running – a mix of Windows Server 2019 Standard and Datacenter, for example. However, you can't mix licenses on a single server; a single physical server needs to be licensed entirely with Standard or entirely with Datacenter Core licenses.

You can imagine that if you have several servers that you need to acquire licenses for, the number of Core licenses required is likely to be large: 10 servers with 2 x 10-core processors will add 200 Core licenses to your shopping list for example. To make things a bit simpler, Windows Server 2019 Core licenses are purchased in 2-packs or 16-packs. Thus, for these 10 servers you could acquire 100 x 2-packs or 12 x 16-packs and 4 x 2-packs, for example. It doesn't matter how you combine the packs – it's only a way of purchasing licenses – and the licenses aren't joined together in any way. When buying the licenses, you don't have to be extraordinarily precise and buy 1 x 16 pack and 2 x 2-packs for each server, you just calculate the total licenses required and then buy that number of licenses combining the packs in any way that's convenient to you.

Client Access Licenses

Any clients accessing the services of the server need to be licensed with a Client Access License – a CAL, as shown in the following diagram:

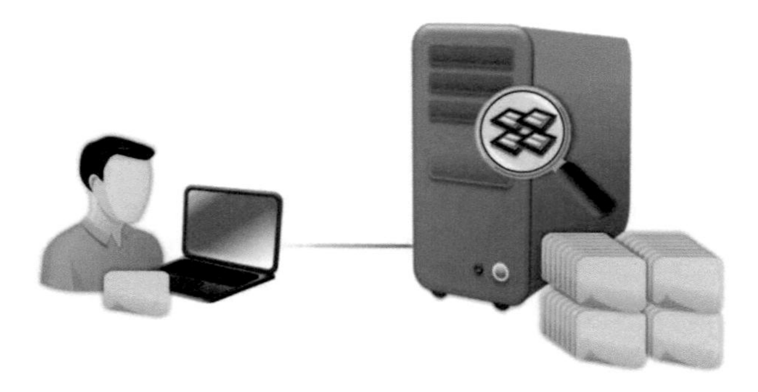

Figure 8: Windows Server 2019 Per Core and CAL licensing

CALs are available in two types for most products – a User CAL or a Device CAL – and both are available for Windows Server 2019.

Organizations buy User CALs when a single user will use multiple devices to access the services of the server. The CAL is assigned to the user, and that user may use any device to access the services of the server as shown in the diagram below:

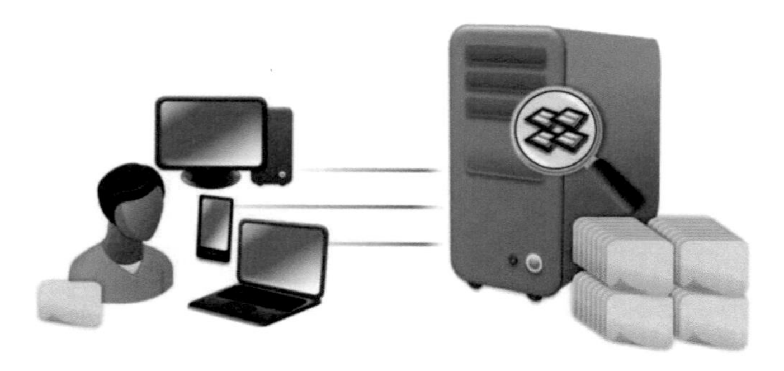

Figure 9: Windows Server 2019 User CAL

Organizations buy Device CALs when a single device will be used by several users to access the services of the server. The CAL is assigned to a device, and any user may use that device to access the services of the server as shown in the diagram below:

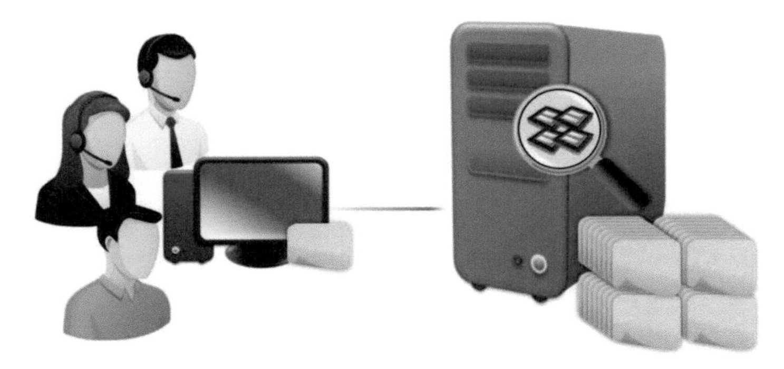

Figure 10: Windows Server 2019 Device CAL

Organizations can generally mix and match these CALs if required, but it does become more difficult to ensure compliance, and you'd need to check that an unlicensed user never uses an unlicensed device to access the server. If a business has bought their CALs with Software Assurance, then they are allowed to switch between User and Device CALs when they renew the SA.

Once users or devices have been assigned CALs, they may access any of the servers on the network; for example, if an organization has purchased Windows Server CALs for all users, then those users may access any licensed Windows Server on the network. The caveat to this is that the version of the CAL must be the same or higher than the version of the server. In other words, a Windows Server 2019 CAL may access a Windows 2019 server and/or a Windows 2016 server, but a Windows Server 2016 CAL may only access the Windows 2016 server, not the Windows 2019 server.

Per Server mode

There's an alternative way to use CALs and that's to assign them to a specific server rather than to specific users or devices. For example, if you had a particular server and assigned 100 User CALs to it then 100 users would be licensed to access the server at any one time. This is one of the rare examples of concurrent licensing in Microsoft's products. It's not a particularly widely used option and you can imagine that it wouldn't suit all scenarios where compliance would be too hard to prove.

Licensing external users

For Windows Server 2019, the organization can choose to buy CALs for its external users or the devices they use, but it's generally more cost-effective to buy an External Connector license. It's easier to manage too, since an External Connector license is a single license that allows an unlimited number of external users to access a server. It's assigned to a server which is already licensed with the regular Windows Server Standard or Datacenter Core licenses and there's just one edition – you don't need to choose a Standard or Datacenter External Connector license, for example.

The diagram below shows a network infrastructure with three servers, all of which have the required number of Windows Server Core licenses assigned to them. The shaded server at the top also has an External Connector license assigned to it allowing any number of external users to access that single server:

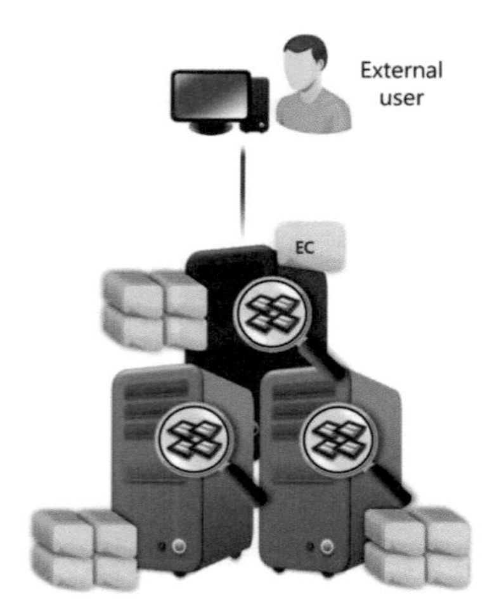

Figure 11: Windows Server 2019 External Connector license

Note that if there were virtual machines running on the server covered by the External Connector license then the external users would be licensed to access any or all of those virtual machines as required.

Licensing virtual machines

Let's take a look at how the licensing for Windows Server 2019 works in a virtualized environment by considering a physical server with 2 x 4-core processors on which 6 virtual machines need to be run:

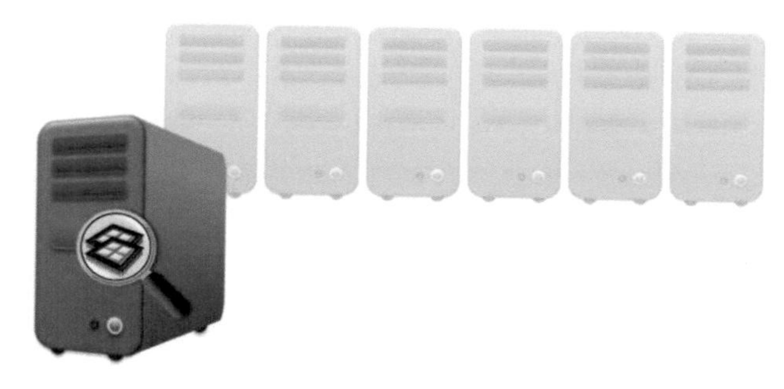

Figure 12: Windows Server 2019 virtual machines

Windows Server licensing doesn't change with virtual machines – you must still license all the physical cores of the server. So, starting with the Datacenter edition, we would need to assign 16 licenses to this device, following the minimums of assigning 8 licenses for each processor. Having assigned the licenses to the server the customer then receives rights to run a certain number of virtual machines, and in the case of the Datacenter edition, it's an unlimited number.

The licensing of Standard edition in a virtualized environment works in a similar way in that you have to license the physical server completely, but that just gives rights to run up to 2 virtual machines. In our example we'd assign 16 licenses to the physical server to run the first 2 virtual machines and then you license the server again to run the next 2 virtual machines and so on. This means that to license Windows Server 2019 Standard to run 6 virtual machines on this server with its 2 x 4-core processors you would need to assign a total of 48 Core licenses to the server.

Note that with both editions you can also run Windows Server in the physical operating system environment if it is solely being used to host and manage the virtual machines.

So how do you decide between using Standard and Datacenter licenses? From a cost perspective, Standard licenses are about 15% of the price of a Datacenter license but of course there's a point when it's more cost-effective to assign Datacenter licenses rather than Standard licenses. This varies dependent on the specification of the physical server, but even running as few as 8 virtual machines means it's generally worth comparing pricing between the two editions. However, it's much easier to ensure compliance if you license with Datacenter edition since you can run an unlimited number of virtual machines without having to worry about specifically assigning additional licenses as additional virtual machines are added to the infrastructure. Generally, customers will weigh up the costs against the convenience in the context of their plans for their server farms.

Licensing Windows Server Containers

Organizations might choose to deploy apps in containers rather than virtual machines so let's take a look at the licensing of Windows Server Containers, and Microsoft define two types of containers in the Product Terms.

Firstly, there's a **Windows Server Container with Hyper-V isolation** which, from a licensing perspective, is considered to be a virtual operating system environment and thus follows the licensing rules for virtual machines which are covered in the previous section.

Then there's a **Windows Server Container without Hyper-V isolation** which is a feature of the Windows Server software itself, and thus a customer may use as many of these containers as required as long as, of course, the physical server is completely licensed.

Licensing a server farm

So far we've just used one physical server in our scenarios as we've learned about the licensing of Windows Server 2019. In reality, of course, organizations will have several servers within a server farm. The diagram below shows three servers in a server farm which will run 8 virtual machines, all of which are currently running on the first server.

Figure 13: running Windows Server 2019 in a server farm

Licenses need to be assigned to that physical server, and you could choose to purchase either 16 Datacenter Core licenses, or 64 Standard Core licenses.

One of the reasons for having virtual machines running in a server farm is that you may want those virtual machines to move dynamically to different servers for availability or load balancing purposes, for example. If the virtual machines were to move en masse to the second physical server, what would happen to the licenses – are they allowed to move too? In fact, they're not. Well, strictly speaking they could move every 90 days but that is unlikely to be enough to support the requirements of this server farm. So, you need to assign licenses to the second server so that if the virtual machines are moved to that server, then there are licenses waiting for them. The same is true of the third server of course.

Datacenter edition is a popular edition to use for licensing the servers in a server farm since it means that all of the servers are already licensed for an unlimited number of virtual machines, and they may move freely around the server farm without any potential licensing compliance issues. It also means that if some more virtual machines are introduced into the server farm then there are no additional licensing costs.

There is a Software Assurance benefit called License Mobility across Server Farms which relaxes the 90-day rule and allows licenses to be reassigned to servers in a server farm as often as required. Note that this SA benefit is NOT available for Windows Server Standard and Datacenter Core licenses. However, it IS available for the External Connector license. So, if Software Assurance was purchased with the External Connector license shown in Figure 11 on page 22 then it would mean that the external users could access any ONE of the 3 servers since the license could be assumed to be dynamically allocated to the necessary server as required. Note that if the external users need to access ANY of the 3 servers, then 3 External Connector licenses would be required.

Licensing for Disaster Recovery

Customers with Software Assurance on both their Windows Server 2019 Standard and/or Datacenter Core licenses and CALs are entitled to special rights for Disaster Recovery scenarios. They can install Windows Server on a "cold" – that is, a turned off – backup server for the purposes of Disaster Recovery; if the main server fails, then the organization is licensed to turn on the cold server and run Windows Server from there without being concerned about license reassignment rules.

Downgrade and down-edition rights

Both editions of Windows Server include downgrade rights, so purchasing a Windows Server 2019 Datacenter license allows you to run any previous version of Datacenter edition, and the same goes for Windows Server 2019 Standard. There was once an Enterprise version of Windows Server (discontinued when Windows Server 2012 was launched) and both of today's editions of Windows Server allow you to run a previous version of Enterprise edition if you need to.

Windows Server 2019 Datacenter also has down-edition rights allowing you to choose to install Standard edition if you've acquired Windows Server 2019 Datacenter Core licenses. In addition, both Windows Server Standard and Datacenter editions also include the rights to install the Essentials edition (see page 30) as an alternative.

Step-up licenses

Customers with Software Assurance on their Windows Server licenses are eligible to purchase Step-up licenses. There is a Step-up license available to move from Windows Server Standard to Windows Server Datacenter and you can imagine that this is a useful benefit for a Windows Server 2019 customer as it enables them to move from Standard to Datacenter licenses as their virtualization needs grow.

Servicing Channels

A Servicing Channel controls how often feature updates are applied to software, and there are two Servicing Channels available for Standard and Datacenter editions of Windows Server: the Long-Term Servicing Channel and the Semi-Annual Channel.

If you buy just a license for Windows Server 2019 then the software is supported by the Long-Term Servicing Channel. Security updates are delivered regularly but no new features or functionality is provided until the next LTSC release which is typically every two to three years. In terms of support, customers are entitled to five years of mainstream support and five years of extended support. Organizations choose the Long-Term Servicing Channel when stability and predictability is important to them.

Customers purchasing Windows Server licenses with Software Assurance are entitled to use either the Long-Term Servicing Channel or the Semi-Annual Channel for their Windows Server deployments. Whilst LTSC software is perfect for stability, the Semi-Annual Channel is ideal for organizations that want to innovate by always taking advantage of new features for Windows Server as they become available. The Semi-Annual Channel provides new releases every six months – in the spring and autumn – and each release is supported for 18 months before a customer must install a newer release.

The next LTSC release is Windows Server 2022 and it's expected in the second half of 2021.

Extended Security Updates

Windows Server 2008 and Windows Server 2008 R2 reached the end of their support lifecycle on January 14, 2020, which means that regular security updates are no longer programmatically provided for these products. However, customers who need to continue running these versions of Windows Server can purchase Extended Security Updates (ESU) subscriptions if they have active Software Assurance on their Windows Server licenses.

The Extended Security Updates will be available for three years starting from January 2020 and the licenses are labelled "1st year", "2nd year" and "3rd year". To cover your servers for these security updates for the period between January 2020 and January 2021 you would purchase the "1st year" licenses, and to continue covering your servers for 2021 you would purchase the "2nd year" licenses. Note that if you had decided to live dangerously during 2020 and didn't purchase any ESU licenses, you would need to purchase both the "1st year" and "2nd year" licenses if you decided to protect your servers in the middle of 2021.

The ESU licenses are Standard and Datacenter Core licenses, sold in 2- or 16-packs, and follow the Windows Server 2019 licensing rules. You only need to purchase them for the servers that you want to protect, and the underlying Windows Server licenses assigned to the server must have active Software Assurance, as must all of the CALs or External Connector licenses that will be used to access the services of covered servers.

In terms of cost, they are priced at 75% of the cost of a Windows Server license without Software Assurance, and the price is the same for the 1st, 2nd and 3rd year licenses. They are only available for customers to purchase through an Enterprise or Enterprise Subscription Enrollment, or a Server and

Cloud Enrollment, but the underlying licenses with SA can have been purchased through any Volume Licensing agreement.

Licensing for the cloud

This first section of the book is about how the traditional software products are licensed in an on-premises environment. However, some of these traditional licenses, including Windows Server 2019, also include rights to use those licenses in the cloud.

Azure Hybrid Benefit

Customers with active Software Assurance on their Windows Server 2019 Standard or Datacenter Core licenses (or Windows Server Subscriptions as described below) are eligible for the Azure Hybrid Benefit. This allows them to choose whether they use the licenses in an on-premises data center or in Azure. The Azure Hybrid Benefit is covered in detail in the section on page 343 onwards.

Windows Server (Software) Subscriptions

The various licenses for Windows Server that we've considered in this section are available through the Volume Licensing agreements, with or without Software Assurance, depending on the agreement. Licenses acquired through an Open Value Subscription agreement or an Enterprise Subscription Enrollment are non-perpetual licenses of course.

However, there's another way to acquire Windows Server licenses and that's as a Server Subscription, or a Software Subscription, through CSP. Microsoft use both terms interchangeably – look for the **Software Subscriptions** price list if you're a CSP partner, but search for **Server Subscriptions for Azure** in the Product Terms website. I'll follow the lead of the Product Terms and use the term Server Subscriptions for this section.

You can buy a 1- or 3-year subscription for Windows Server Standard Core licenses which are sold in a pack of 8 Core licenses. This, as you might recall, is different to regular Windows Server Standard Core licenses which are sold in packs of 2 or 16 licenses. This gives a hint as to their original purpose, which was to be used to license the Windows Server portion of a virtual machine in Azure, since a minimum of 8 licenses are required for each virtual machine (see page 343 for more details on the Azure Hybrid Benefit). However, they can actually be used with an Azure virtual machine OR in an on-premises infrastructure where they behave exactly the same as a regular Windows Server license purchased through a Volume Licensing agreement.

This might raise a couple of questions in your mind – are there Windows Server Datacenter edition Server Subscriptions available, and are there CALs available since those would be needed in an on-premises deployment of Windows Server? Well, there AREN'T Windows Server Datacenter edition Server Subscriptions available but both 1- and 3-year User and Device CALs are available.

There is no notion of Software Assurance in CSP and these Server Subscriptions don't come with SA, but they DO come with entitlements to some of the benefits that we would normally refer to as Software Assurance benefits. In particular, they entitle customers to the Azure Hybrid Benefit, Disaster Recovery rights, and to use Semi-Annual Channel releases of Windows Server. In addition, if a new version of Windows Server is released during the term of the Server Subscription, then that may be deployed in the on-premises infrastructure if required. Equally (and this isn't, I know, an SA benefit) customers may take advantage of downgrade rights and deploy an earlier version of Windows Server if required.

Windows Server 2019 Essentials edition

The Windows Server 2019 Essentials edition is aimed at smaller customers since it's restricted to 25 user accounts and 50 devices. It's licensed with a single Server license which gives host virtualization rights and rights to run the software in a single physical or virtual operating system environment. The Essentials edition is only available as a Long-Term Servicing Channel release.

Availability of Windows Server 2019 licenses

Windows Server 2019 Standard/Datacenter Core licenses and CALs are available with or without Software Assurance through the Volume Licensing agreements.

The above licenses are also available without Software Assurance only through the Cloud Solution Provider program. In addition, Server Subscriptions for Windows Server 2019 Standard Core licenses are also available through CSP.

As usual, check out the Product Terms website for specifics.

WINDOWS SERVER 2019 SERVICES

Windows Server 2019 includes two services which a customer may choose to deploy: Remote Desktop Services and Active Directory Rights Management Services.

Remote Desktop Services (RDS)

Remote Desktop Services was previously known as Terminal Services and is often used to enable an organization to install Office on a server and to have users access it from their client devices over the network. All of the application processing is done on the server, and it's been a great way for organizations to continue to use older hardware since the client device does not need to be powerful enough to run Office.

Licensing RDS

There are no additional licensing requirements for the Windows Server itself, but every user or device that accesses the RDS services of the server must be covered with an RDS User or Device CAL.

Licensing external users

There is an External Connector license available to license RDS for external users.

Availability of RDS licenses

RDS User and Device CALs and RDS External Connector licenses are available with or without Software Assurance through the Volume Licensing agreements.

The above licenses are also available without Software Assurance only through the Cloud Solution Provider program. In addition, Server Subscriptions for RDS User and Device CALs are also available through CSP.

As usual, check out the Product Terms website for specifics.

Active Directory Rights Management Services (AD RMS)

AD RMS can be used to protect documents using information rights management (IRM) which allows a user to attach access permissions to a particular document which can prevent it from being opened, forwarded or printed by unauthorized people, for example.

Licensing AD RMS

In common with RDS, there are no additional licensing requirements for the Windows Server itself, but every user or device that accesses the AD RMS services of the server must be covered with an AD RMS User or Device CAL.

Licensing external users

Again, for external users there is an AD RMS External Connector available.

Availability of AD RMS licenses

AD RMS User and Device CALs and AD RMS External Connector licenses are available with or without Software Assurance through the Volume Licensing agreements.

The above licenses are also available without Software Assurance only through the Cloud Solution Provider program. In addition, Server Subscriptions for AD RMS User and Device CALs are also available through CSP.

As usual, check out the Product Terms website for specifics.

SYSTEM CENTER 2019

The Microsoft products that enable organizations to manage their client and server infrastructure are all part of the System Center family.

System Center licensing model

In the diagram below the large server represents the management server where the System Center management software is installed, and this server manages a variety of client and server devices. We'll see that every device that is managed by that server needs to have either Client or Server Management Licenses assigned to it. Note that although software is installed on the management server there is no requirement to purchase a license for it – the rights to install the software here are included in the Management Licenses.

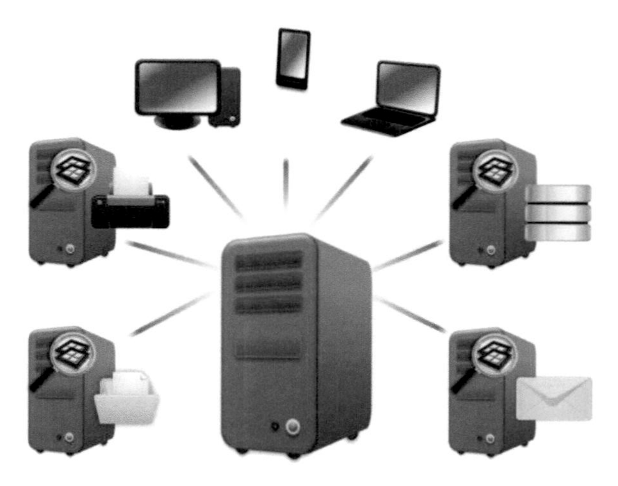

Figure 14: System Center 2019

SYSTEM CENTER 2019: SERVERS

Licensing System Center 2019 for servers

There are two editions of System Center 2019 to license servers: Standard and Datacenter edition. The Server Management Licenses (MLs) are assigned to server devices and both licenses allow installation and use of the following System Center products:

- Microsoft Endpoint Configuration Manager
- System Center Endpoint Protection
- System Center Data Protection Manager
- System Center Operations Manager
- System Center Orchestrator
- System Center Service Manager
- System Center Virtual Machine Manager

System Center 2019 Server MLs follow the same Per Core licensing model as Windows Server 2019 (see page 18). Every physical core in a server needs to be licensed, with a minimum of 8 Core licenses assigned to each processor. Thus, in Figure 14, where all the servers have 2 processors, each of the 4 servers would need to have 16 System Center 2019 Server Management Licenses assigned to them.

In common with Windows Server 2019, System Center 2019 Server Management Licenses are sold in 2-packs or 16-packs which may be assigned as required to physical servers. However, unlike Windows Server licenses, System Center Server Management Licenses may only be acquired with Software Assurance.

Licensing external users

If external users access servers managed by System Center 2019, there are no System Center licensing requirements for those users.

Licensing virtual machines

The rules for licensing servers in a virtualized environment are exactly the same as for Windows Server 2019 but let's have a look at an example specifically for System Center 2019. In the diagram below, there's a physical server running 4 virtual machines with various workloads which need to be licensed so that each of the virtual machines may be managed by System Center 2019. You can see that 32 Server ML Core licenses have been assigned to the physical server and this would make the server compliant for the Datacenter edition since licensing the physical server completely with System Center 2019 Datacenter MLs allows an unlimited number of virtual machines to be managed.

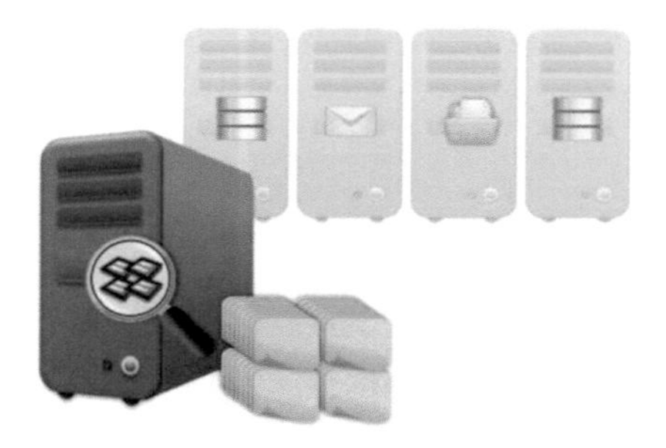

Figure 15: System Center 2019 Datacenter virtualization licensing

However, in common with Windows Server 2019 Standard, licensing the physical server completely with System Center 2019 Standard Server MLs only allows 2 virtual machines to be managed. Thus, to license this scenario you would license the physical server again and assign a total of 64 System Center 2019 Standard Core MLs to the server.

Licensing a server farm

System Center 2019 Standard and Datacenter Server MLs are not eligible for the License Mobility across Server Farms benefit even if a customer has active Software Assurance on their licenses. Thus, in common with Windows Server 2019, every physical server in a server farm must be licensed to receive the maximum number of virtual machines as they move around the server farm. As with Windows Server 2019, System Center 2019 Datacenter edition is a popular choice if there are a large number of virtual machines, or if a customer wants to make it easy to remain compliant as additional virtual machines are added to a server farm.

Licensing for Disaster Recovery

If System Center 2019 Standard and Datacenter Server MLs are covered by active Software Assurance then an organization is eligible for the Disaster Recovery SA benefit.

Downgrade and down-edition rights

The usual downgrade rights to previous versions such as System Center 2016 are available. The only difference between System Center 2019 Standard and Datacenter licenses are the virtualization rights and so down-edition rights aren't available (or needed) for System Center 2019.

System Center Branches

The majority of the System Center 2019 components (Data Protection Manager, Operations Manager, Orchestrator, Service Manager, and Virtual Machine Manager) are supported by the Long-Term Servicing Branch (LTSB) with 5 years of mainstream and 5 years of extended support. In addition, new features are made available every six months through Update Rollup releases during the mainstream support period.

Microsoft Endpoint Configuration Manager is also supported by a Current Branch release cadence which provides feature updates three times a year, for customers with active Software Assurance. There is also an LTSB flavor of Configuration Manager which is intended for customers with perpetual licenses who have let their SA expire who would no longer be entitled to the Current Branch releases.

Licensing for the cloud

This first section of the book is about how the traditional software products are licensed in an on-premises environment. However, some of these traditional licenses, including System Center 2019 Server MLs, also include rights to use those licenses in the cloud.

License Mobility through SA

System Center 2019 Standard and Datacenter Server MLs with active Software Assurance are eligible for the License Mobility through SA benefit. This means that licenses may be used in Azure or in a partner's environment. The License Mobility through SA benefit is covered in detail in the section on page 350 onwards.

Step-up licenses

Customers with active Software Assurance on their System Center 2019 Standard Server MLs may purchase a Step-up license to move to System Center 2019 Datacenter Server MLs if required.

Required infrastructure products

SQL Server is a required infrastructure product for System Center 2019, and rights to install SQL Server Standard edition are included when System Center 2019 Server MLs are purchased. As you might expect, the use of SQL Server acquired in this way may only support the System Center deployment.

Core Infrastructure Server Suites

It's worth covering the Core Infrastructure Server (CIS) Suites at this point. These suites are available in Standard and Datacenter editions and are a way of buying licenses for both Windows Server 2019 and System Center 2019. As you can imagine, the CIS Standard Suite includes the Standard edition of Windows Server and System Center, and the CIS Datacenter Suite includes the Datacenter edition of both products. The CIS Suites follow the same licensing rules as the individual products with the requirement to license all cores in the physical server and to assign a minimum of 8 Core licenses to a processor, and with the same virtualization rules that were covered on page 36.

As you might expect, buying the products together as a Suite attracts a discount when they're purchased through the Volume Licensing agreements, the largest of which is available when they are purchased with an enterprise-wide commitment through the Server and Cloud Enrollment.

Availability of System Center 2019 Server MLs

System Center 2019 Server MLs are only available with Software Assurance through the Volume Licensing agreements. As usual, check out the Product Terms website for specifics.

SYSTEM CENTER 2019: CLIENTS

Licensing System Center 2019 for clients

Client Management Licenses (CMLs) must be purchased for any client devices managed by System Center 2019, but these are split into different offerings rather than the single "System Center 2019" licenses that are available for the servers:

- Microsoft Endpoint Configuration Manager CML
- System Center Endpoint Protection 1606 SL
- System Center 2019 Data Protection Manager CML
- System Center 2019 Operations Manager CML
- System Center 2019 Orchestrator CML
- System Center 2019 Service Manager CML

In fact, all of the Client Management Licenses are available in a per user version or a per OSE (Operating System Environment) version in a similar way to the User and Device CALs available for Windows Server 2019. System

Center Endpoint Protection is available as a User or Device Subscription License (SL). As with the Server MLs, all Client MLs must be initially purchased with SA.

Many customers will acquire their Client Management Licenses through the CAL Suites, and both the Core and Enterprise CAL Suites include the first two licenses. See the section on the CAL Suites on page 79 for the full list of licenses included in these suites.

Licensing external users

Organizations with external users should acquire CMLs/SLs for the relevant users or devices.

Downgrade and down-edition rights

Downgrade rights are available for all components, but down-edition rights don't apply.

Required infrastructure products

SQL Server is a required infrastructure product for System Center 2019, and rights to install SQL Server Standard edition are included when System Center 2019 Client MLs are purchased. Again, the use of SQL Server acquired in this way may only support the System Center deployment.

Availability of System Center 2019 Client MLs

System Center 2019 Client MLs are only available with Software Assurance through the Volume Licensing agreements. As usual, check out the Product Terms website for specifics.

SQL SERVER 2019

SQL Server is Microsoft's enterprise database solution. There are several editions of SQL Server 2019 available to purchase, but organizations generally choose between Standard and Enterprise editions dependent on their specific needs. The main part of this section focuses on the licensing of these editions, and then we look at the licensing of the other editions, Express and Developer, on page 59.

Licensing SQL Server 2019

There are two licensing models that are used to license the Standard and Enterprise editions of SQL Server 2019 – the Server/CAL model and the Per Core model. You can choose either model if you're deploying the Standard edition, whereas the Enterprise edition is always licensed with the Per Core model.

Server/CAL licensing model

In the Server/CAL licensing model a SQL Server 2019 Standard Server license is assigned to the server allowing any number of installations (also called instances) of SQL Server to run in the physical operating system environment. Users or devices are then licensed with SQL Server 2019 User or Device CALs, as shown in the diagram below:

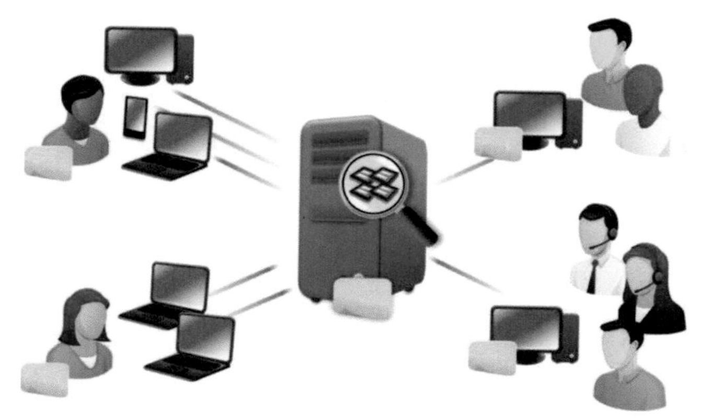

Figure 16: SQL Server 2019 Server/CAL licensing model

Multiplexing

While we're talking about the Server/CAL licensing model it's a good moment to consider the notion of multiplexing. Multiplexing is probably most easily explained with an example. Imagine that you have a server which runs a line of business application that all of an organization's users access. In turn, that line of business application accesses a different physical server running SQL Server. Now, the users themselves aren't directly accessing the server running SQL Server, so do they need to be licensed for it?

The answer, perhaps unsurprisingly, is that they do indeed need to be licensed for SQL Server 2019 and this scenario we've just looked at is an example of multiplexing – where a particular technical solution reduces the number of users/devices directly accessing a server running SQL Server. However, because the users are still indirectly accessing SQL Server they need to be licensed, and the general rule is that multiplexing does not reduce the number of CALs required.

SQL Server components

SQL Server 2019 has a number of different components, such as Reporting Services and Integration Services, which may be run on different physical servers. Note that if you choose to deploy SQL Server 2019 in this way, then each physical server needs to be licensed for SQL Server 2019. This holds true for the Server/CAL licensing model that we've just looked at, and also the Per Core model which we'll look at now.

Per Core licensing model

The second licensing model is the Per Core licensing model. You can choose to license SQL Server 2019 Standard edition with Core licenses if you wish, but for the Enterprise edition it's the only option.

In this model, you count the number of cores in the physical server and assign that number of Core licenses to the server, making sure that you assign at least 4 Core licenses to each processor. You can see in the diagram below that there's a physical server with 2 x 4-core processors and so 8 Core licenses are assigned to the server. There's no need for separate CALs for either internal or external users accessing the server, the Core licenses are all that is required.

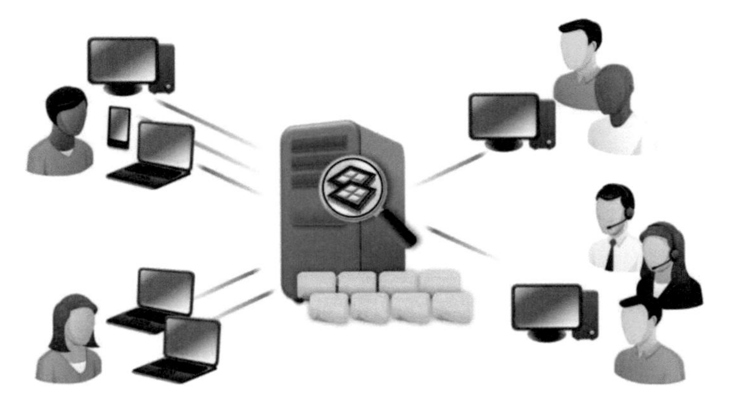

Figure 17: SQL Server 2019 Per Core licensing model

SQL Server 2019 Core licenses are purchased in 2-packs and, as with Windows Server, these licenses are not permanently joined together, it's just a purchasing mechanism.

Licensing external users

There are no External Connector licenses available for SQL Server 2019. If a customer has chosen to license with the Server/CAL model, then they must buy CALs for external users and this does become expensive when there are many external users. It is generally more cost-effective to choose to license with the Per Core model if there is a large number of external users, since this will cover all internal users and any number of external users.

Licensing virtual machines

In this section we'll look at how the different editions of SQL Server 2019 are licensed in a virtual infrastructure. There are different rules dependent on the edition of SQL Server 2019 – you either focus at the individual virtual machine level and calculate the number of licenses required, or assign licenses to the physical server and receive rights to run a specific number of SQL Server virtual machines on that server. As with the rules for the physical infrastructure, SQL Server may be installed multiple times in each virtual machine.

Let's start with the simplest set of rules – when SQL Server 2019 is licensed with the Server/CAL model.

Virtualization licensing: Server/CAL (individual virtual machines)

If SQL Server 2019 Standard is licensed with the Server/CAL model, then you follow the same rules as you would for licensing separate physical servers. Look at the diagram below: it shows a physical server and then 4 virtual machines, 2 of which are running SQL Server 2019 (depicted by the database icon). Looking at the physical server you can see that 2 Server licenses have been assigned to it.

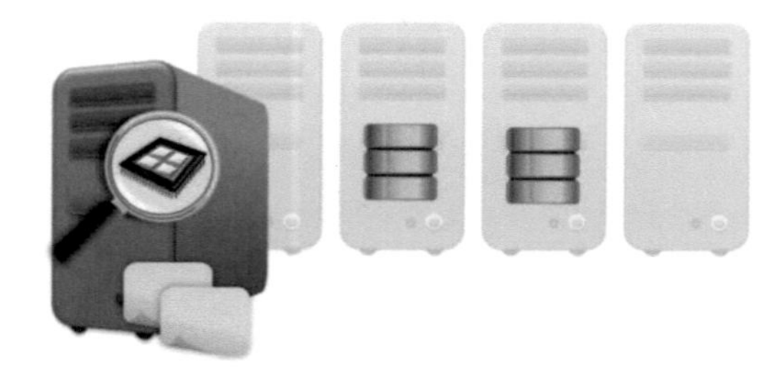

Figure 18: virtualization licensing – SQL Server 2019 Server licenses

So, what's the rule here? You simply count the number of virtual machines running SQL Server and buy that number of SQL Server licenses. Those licenses are assigned to the physical server and you get rights to run a virtual machine with SQL Server for each license. If you want to run more virtual machines with SQL Server, then you would simply assign more licenses to the physical server.

Virtualization licensing: Per Core (individual virtual machines)

Let's take a similar example to the one above to see how the Per Core licensing model works in a virtual environment. The diagram below is again a physical server with 4 virtual machines, 2 of which are running SQL Server 2019. You can see that we need some extra information in this example, and this is the number of virtual cores that are assigned to each virtual machine. You may call these "virtual processors" rather than virtual cores, and that's probably the language that you'd use if you were setting them up technically, but I think it's easier to call them virtual cores as we have a Per Core licensing model. So, you can see that there are 2 virtual cores assigned to each virtual machine and the licensing rules are that you need to assign Core licenses to the virtual machines based on the number of virtual cores, with a minimum of 4 Core licenses per virtual machine. Again, the licenses are assigned to the physical server, and you can see that there are 8 Core licenses assigned to it.

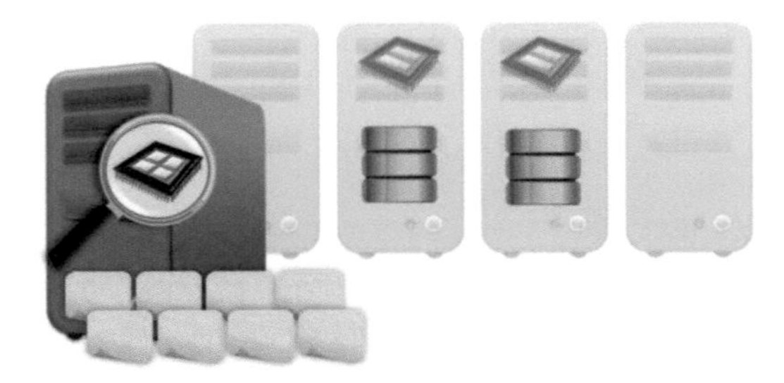

Figure 19: virtualization licensing – SQL Server 2019 Core licenses

Virtualization licensing: Per Core (rights per server)

With SQL Server 2019 Enterprise there is additional flexibility in licensing a virtualized environment. If you license the physical server completely following the usual per Core licensing rules on page 42, then you can run SQL Server 2019 in a virtual machine for each Core license that you have assigned to the server. Consider the diagram below where you see a server with 2 x 4-core processors. To license that server completely you need to assign 8 Core licenses to the physical server and then you can run SQL Server in 8 virtual machines, as shown below:

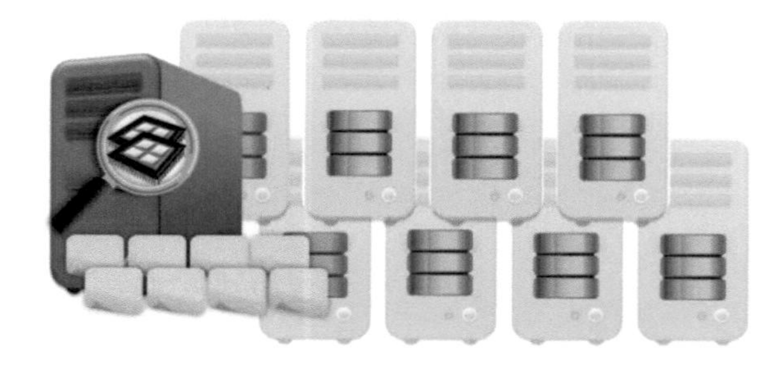

Figure 20: Virtualization licensing – SQL Server 2019 Enterprise Core licenses

If you need to run further virtual machines, you can simply assign further Core licenses to the physical server; assign an additional license for each additional virtual machine. Don't be perturbed that SQL Server 2019 Core licenses are only available in packs of 2; you can buy a 2-pack and then split the licenses across physical servers if, for example, you need to run 9 SQL Server virtual machines in the example above.

Virtualization licensing: Per Core (unlimited virtualization)

And the final part of virtualization licensing to consider is that of licensing for unlimited virtualization. This is only available for the Enterprise edition and is actually a Software Assurance benefit, but I think it makes sense to include it here. The rules are simple: if you license a physical server with Enterprise Core licenses with Software Assurance then you can run an unlimited number of virtual machines with SQL Server on that server.

The server below has, again, 2 x 4-core processors and so 8 Core licenses with SA need to be assigned to the server. You can see 10 virtual machines running SQL Server, but an unlimited number would be allowed:

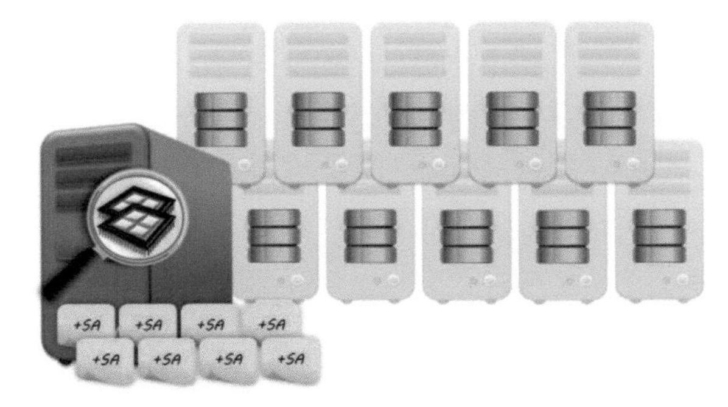

Figure 21: unlimited virtualization – SQL Server 2019 Enterprise Core licenses

Advanced Per Core licensing

So far, when we looked at licensing virtual machines with Core licenses we've assumed that there's a one-to-one relationship between the physical cores and the virtual cores. However, you can configure a virtual machine so that a physical core supports a number of virtual cores, or several physical cores support a single virtual core. In both of these cases the licensing of the virtual machines is affected.

Take a look at the diagram on the next page which shows a virtual machine with 8 cores running SQL Server, where a single physical core is used to support 2 virtual cores. Should you count the number of virtual cores that are used from a licensing point of view, or the number of physical cores? The rules state that the number of licenses you need is the same as the number of virtual cores that are used in the virtual machine and so, in this case, 8 Core licenses must be assigned to the physical server.

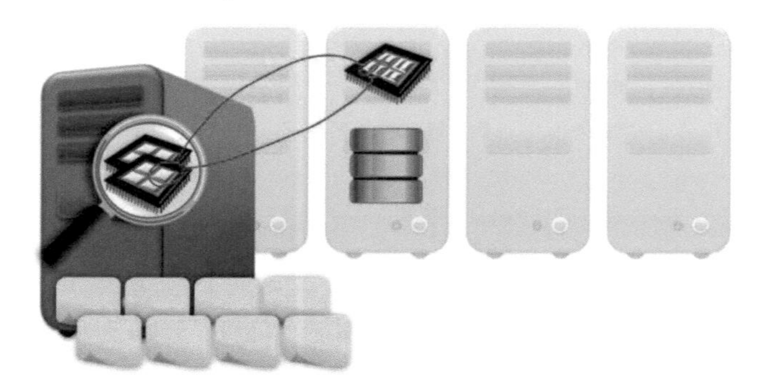

Figure 22: a single core supporting multiple virtual cores

Let's now take the opposite example, when multiple physical cores support a virtual core. Does the same rule apply – that we need to just license the virtual cores? Well, in this case, another rule comes into play, which states that if a virtual core is mapped to more than 1 hardware thread, then you need a license for each hardware thread that is used.

In the diagram below, the 4-core virtual machine has been configured so that 2 physical cores are supporting each virtual core. As we've just seen, in this situation you need to assign a Core license for every physical core that is supporting the virtual machine. So, although the virtual machine has been configured with only 4 virtual cores, because there are 8 physical cores supporting the virtual machine, there must be 8 licenses assigned to it.

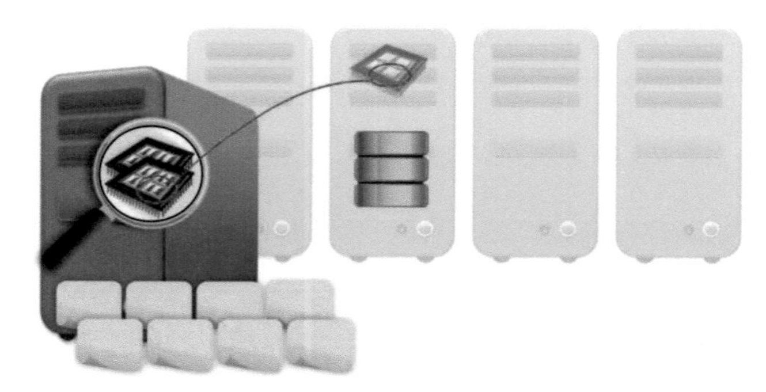

Figure 23: multiple physical cores supporting a single virtual core

Licensing SQL Server with container technology

SQL Server 2019 can be deployed on Linux and Docker platforms. This allows customers to not only choose their platform, but also to deploy SQL Server 2019 in containers using Docker container technology. The rules for licensing SQL Server 2019 in the containers are exactly the same as the rules for licensing virtual machines that we've just considered, including the nuances for multi-threading as described above.

Licensing a server farm

Let's take a look now at the considerations for licensing SQL Server 2019 in a server farm.

Server licenses

The diagram below shows a server farm consisting of 3 physical servers and currently there are 2 virtual machines running SQL Server 2019 on the first physical server. 2 licenses have been assigned to that server to allow the running of those two virtual machines, and this is all correctly licensed.

Figure 24: licensing a server farm

One of the technical benefits of virtualization is that virtual servers can move between physical servers and this is desirable for all sorts of reasons. It might be load balancing – so perhaps the 2 SQL Server virtual machines move to the second physical server because it has more capacity available at a given time than the first server that they're currently running on. Or it could be that the first server fails and the virtual machines fail over to the second server.

The dynamic moving of virtual machines between physical servers is a technical feature that can be managed by the IT team within parameters that they specify, but what happens from a licensing perspective?

Let's assume that the 2 SQL Server virtual machines have moved to the second physical server – perhaps for either of the two reasons that we talked about above. Are the licenses allowed to move too? Well, licenses CAN be moved between servers as long as they obey the "90-day rule". This rule states that licenses can be moved between machines no more frequently than every 90 days. In this scenario, we could move the licenses to the second server once, but would then have to wait 90 days before we moved them again. This isn't really an agile enough solution for most server farms that use virtualization.

So, what options are there? Well, you could assign 2 licenses to each of the physical servers, as shown below, so that this would cover all eventualities of where the virtual servers might move to, be it both virtual machines on a single server, or each virtual machine on a separate server.

Figure 25: licensing a server farm

You can probably imagine that this is potentially a pretty expensive option; if we were licensing these 2 SQL Server machines in a physical environment we would just need 2 licenses, but when we deploy them in a virtual infrastructure we need 6 licenses. Any time we want to add a SQL Server virtual machine we need to purchase another 3 licenses – one for each server in this example.

The alternative is to make sure that you have License Mobility across Server Farms rights. This benefit is available when you buy Software Assurance with a license and it essentially allows you to ignore the 90-day rule. So, in the diagram below, if we buy 2 licenses with Software Assurance then they are temporarily assigned to whichever physical servers are hosting the virtual machines and as the virtual machines move, the licenses can (in effect) move too.

Figure 26: using License Mobility in a server farm

Per Core licenses

The rules for licensing across a server farm with SQL Server 2019 Standard and Enterprise Core licenses are the same. If you choose to license at the virtual machine level, then you can move the licenses between physical servers as long as you have purchased Software Assurance with the licenses to ensure that you have License Mobility across Server Farms rights.

If you choose to license the physical server with Enterprise Core licenses without Software Assurance so that you get rights to run virtual machines on that server equal to the number of licenses, then you just need to be careful of the maximum number of virtual machines that you run across the server farm. Look at the diagram on the next page:

Figure 27: Enterprise Core virtualization rights

Each physical server has been licensed completely, so 8 Enterprise Core licenses have been assigned to each server and this gives rights to run 8 virtual machines on each server. When you choose to license in this way you need to make sure that two extreme scenarios are covered. The first is that there are sufficient licenses if all the virtual machines are on different servers, and we can see that there is currently an even spread of virtual machines and there are plenty of licenses to cover this situation.

The second is ensuring that there are enough licenses if all of the virtual machines are deployed to a single server. In this server farm, if all 6 virtual machines are at any time running on the same physical server then, again, there are sufficient licenses since up to 8 virtual machines may run on each physical server. However, you should consider how near the upper limit this licensing solution is. Adding another 2 virtual machines to the server farm would be fine with the current licenses allocated, but as soon as the ninth is added, another license needs to be assigned to EACH physical server to account for the worst-case scenario of all 9 virtual machines running on any one physical server.

Use this method of licensing servers when you have a relatively light level of virtualization across a server farm and consider unlimited virtualization when you have a heavier level of virtualization and you want to ensure that you're always compliant.

Unlimited virtualization

All of the servers in the server farm below have been licensed for unlimited virtualization – so every physical core has been assigned a SQL Server 2019 Enterprise Core license with Software Assurance. This means that an unlimited number of virtual machines may run on every server, and the virtual machines may move around the server farm as required without the need to keep detailed records to ensure compliance.

Figure 28: unlimited virtualization across a server farm

Licensing for High Availability and Disaster Recovery

SQL Server 2019 can be configured so that if one server fails, its processing will be picked up, recovered, and continued by another server. A failover server runs SQL Server and synchronizes with the primary server to maintain the failover database. A passive failover server is one that, while maintaining the database in question, does not serve SQL Server data to clients or run active SQL Server workloads. A server configured for High Availability is defined as a passive server with continuous replication and automated failover, while a server configured for Disaster Recovery is defined as a passive server with scheduled replication and manual failover.

For each on-premises server licensed with SQL Server 2019 and covered with active Software Assurance, customers can use the following passive servers in anticipation of a failover event:

- One passive failover server for High Availability in a separate OSE
- One passive failover server for Disaster Recovery in a separate OSE
- One passive failover server for Disaster Recovery in a single VM on Azure

Note that if the Core licensing model is being used then the failover server must have the same or fewer cores than the active server. This is so that if the workloads are transferred to the passive server, then there are enough Core licenses to cover it.

If further passive servers are needed for failover, then those servers must have licenses assigned to them. If an active server is used for failover then it must be licensed in the usual way.

Downgrade and down-edition rights

SQL Server 2019 Standard and Enterprise licenses include the usual downgrade rights to previous versions. However, there have been a whole host of different editions of SQL Server over the ages which makes the down-edition rights an interesting read. Essentially, customers with Enterprise Core licenses can deploy Standard, Business Intelligence, Workgroup, Small Business or Datacenter editions, and customers with Standard licenses can deploy Workgroup or Small Business editions.

SQL Server Enterprise Server licenses

For new customers choosing to license SQL Server 2019 Enterprise there is just one licensing model – the Per Core licensing model. However, certain customers can use SQL Server 2019 Enterprise licensed with the Server/CAL model.

Let's take a step back in time to understand where this special edition of SQL Server came from. In the days of SQL Server 2008 R2 the Enterprise edition could be licensed with either the Server/CAL or Per Processor licensing models, similar to the choices available for SQL Server 2019 Standard today. However, when SQL Server 2012 was released, the licensing model changed from Per Processor to Per Core and the Enterprise edition was only available to be licensed Per Core. This, of course, gave a problem for those customers who had licensed SQL Server 2008 R2 Enterprise with the Server/CAL model with Software Assurance who would clearly be expecting an upgrade to SQL Server 2012 and subsequent versions.

The answer was a special flavor of SQL Server 2012 Enterprise which could continue to be licensed with Server licenses. This special edition wasn't available to new customers, only as an SA renewal for existing customers. That continues today, and so customers may renew the SA into the future.

There are a couple of special licensing rules to be aware of. The first is a technical and licensing limitation that restricts the running of this Enterprise edition to a physical server with 20 cores or less. This extends to a virtualized infrastructure as well, with a limit of 20 virtual cores used by the virtual machines running on a physical server. The second thing to be aware of is that each of these Server licenses, when assigned to a physical server, allows the running of SQL Server in up to 4 virtual machines. If you want to run SQL Server in further virtual machines, then you can assign additional licenses to the server to run another 4 virtual machines per license.

Step-up licenses

Customers with Software Assurance on their SQL Server Standard Core licenses are eligible to purchase a Step-up license for SQL Server Enterprise Core licenses. This means that they just pay the difference in price between the two Core licenses rather than having to purchase brand new Enterprise Core licenses.

Extended Security Updates

SQL Server 2008 and SQL Server 2008 R2 reached the end of their support lifecycle on July 9, 2019, which means that regular security updates are no longer programmatically provided for these products. However, customers who need to continue running these versions of SQL Server can purchase Extended Security Updates (ESU) subscriptions if they have active Software Assurance on their SQL Server licenses.

The Extended Security Updates will be available for three years starting from July 2019 and the licenses are labelled "1st year", "2nd year" and "3rd year". To cover your servers for these security updates for the period between July 2019 and July 2020 you would purchase the "1st year" licenses, and to continue covering your servers from July 2020 you would purchase the "2nd year" licenses. Note that if you had decided to live dangerously during 2019/2020 and didn't purchase any ESU licenses, you would need to purchase both the "1st year" and "2nd year" licenses if you decided to protect your servers in, say, March of 2021.

The ESU licenses are Standard and Enterprise Core licenses, sold in 2-packs, as well as Standard and Enterprise Server licenses, and they follow the standard SQL Server 2019 licensing rules. You only need to purchase them for the servers that you want to protect, and the underlying SQL Server licenses assigned to the server must have active Software Assurance, as must all of the CALs that will be used to access the services of covered servers.

In terms of cost, they are priced at 75% of the cost of a SQL Server license without Software Assurance, and the price is the same for the 1st, 2nd and 3rd year licenses. They are only available for customers to purchase through an Enterprise or Enterprise Subscription Enrollment, or a Server and Cloud Enrollment, but the underlying licenses with SA can have been purchased through any Volume Licensing agreement.

Licensing for the cloud

This first section of the book is about how the traditional software products are licensed in an on-premises environment. However, some of these traditional licenses, including SQL Server 2019, also include rights to use those licenses in the cloud.

Azure Hybrid Benefit

Customers with active Software Assurance on their SQL Server 2019 Standard or Enterprise Core licenses (or SQL Server Subscriptions as described below) are eligible for the Azure Hybrid Benefit. This allows them to choose whether they use the licenses in an on-premises data center or in Azure. The Azure Hybrid Benefit is covered in detail in the section on page 343 onwards.

License Mobility through SA

Customers with active Software Assurance on their SQL Server 2019 Standard and Enterprise Core licenses, and SQL Server 2019 Server and CAL licenses, are eligible for the License Mobility through SA benefit. This means that licenses may be used in Azure or in a partner's environment. The License Mobility through SA benefit is covered in detail in the section on page 350 onwards.

Additional Software Assurance benefits

Power BI Report Server

Organizations using Power BI to analyze and report on their business data need to license both the users who publish reports and those who consume them. However, Power BI Report Server is an on-premises server product that enables licensed Power BI Pro users to publish Power BI reports and distribute them across the organization and, more importantly, removes the need to license individual report consumers.

Rights to run Power BI Report Server are available for organizations with active Software Assurance on their SQL Server 2019 Enterprise Core licenses.

Customers may actually deploy Power BI Report Server in an Azure virtual machine as an alternative to using their own dedicated hardware, and they're allowed to deploy it on as many cores as they have qualifying licenses. For example, if they have active SA on 24 SQL Server Enterprise Core licenses, they can deploy Power BI Report Server across 24 cores.

Machine Learning Server

Machine Learning Server is an advanced analytics platform and customers licensed with SQL Server 2019 Enterprise Core or Server licenses with SA are entitled to use Machine Learning Server for Windows or Linux running on their own servers. Additionally, customers with SQL Server 2019 Enterprise Core licenses are also allowed to run Machine Learning Server for Hadoop on up to 5 of their own servers.

SQL Server (Software) Subscriptions

The various licenses for SQL Server that we've considered in this section are available through the Volume Licensing agreements, with or without Software Assurance, depending on the agreement. Licenses acquired through an Open Value Subscription or an Enterprise Subscription Enrollment are non-perpetual licenses of course.

However, there's another way to acquire SQL Server licenses and that's as a Server Subscription or a Software Subscription through CSP. Microsoft use both terms interchangeably – look for the **Software Subscriptions** price list if you're a CSP partner, but search for **Server Subscriptions for Azure** in the Product Terms website. I'll follow the lead of the Product Terms and use the term Server Subscriptions for this section.

You can buy a 1- or 3-year subscription for SQL Server Standard or Enterprise Core licenses which are sold in a pack of 2 Core licenses. There is no notion of Software Assurance in CSP and these Server Subscriptions don't come with SA, but they DO come with entitlements to some of the benefits that we would normally refer to as Software Assurance benefits. In particular, they entitle customers to the Azure Hybrid Benefit, Disaster Recovery and Failover rights, License Mobility across Server Farms, and Unlimited Virtualization.

Customers with SQL Server Enterprise Core Server Subscriptions may also use Machine Learning Server for Windows, Linux, or Hadoop, and Power BI Report Server.

In addition, if a new version of SQL Server is released during the term of the Server Subscription then that may be deployed in the on-premises infrastructure if required. Equally (and this isn't, I know, an SA benefit) customers may take advantage of downgrade rights and deploy an earlier version of SQL Server if required.

Additional editions of SQL Server

SQL Server Express edition

SQL Server 2019 Express is the entry-level edition of SQL Server 2019 with the most limited set of features, and is free to download. It's recommended for people who want to learn about SQL Server or who will be building desktop, web and small server applications.

SQL Server Developer edition

There is a Developer edition of SQL Server 2019 which is functionally equivalent to the Enterprise edition, but its use is limited to deployments for development and testing rather than for production environments, or even for use with production data. There are, however, no restrictions on the number of devices that the software can be installed and run on.

These days (from April 2016) the Developer edition is a free download as long as you're a member of the Dev Essentials program, which is itself free to join. You can find details about this program here: https://bit.ly/BOKVSDevEss.

Availability of SQL Server 2019 licenses

SQL Server 2019 Standard Server licenses and CALs, and SQL Server 2019 Standard/Enterprise Core licenses are available with or without Software Assurance through the Volume Licensing agreements.

The above licenses are also available without Software Assurance only through the Cloud Solution Provider program. In addition, Server Subscriptions for SQL Server 2019 Standard/Enterprise Core licenses are also available through CSP.

As usual, check out the Product Terms website for specifics.

BIZTALK SERVER 2020

BizTalk Server 2020 enables companies to automate business processes using adapters which can communicate with and connect the different software systems used in an enterprise.

Licensing BizTalk Server 2020

There are three editions of BizTalk Server 2020: Branch, Standard, and Enterprise editions. All three editions follow the same Per Core licensing model that SQL Server 2019 uses (see page 42). So, you count the number of cores in the physical server and assign that number of Core licenses to the server, making sure that you assign at least 4 Core licenses to each processor. There are no requirements for any CALs.

Licensing external users

There are no licensing requirements for external users.

Licensing virtual machines

Again, the licensing of BizTalk Server 2020 for virtual machines follows exactly the same rules as SQL Server 2019 which you can find on page 43. However, let's do a quick summary in this section.

Virtualization licensing: individual virtual machines

For BizTalk Server 2020 Branch and Standard editions (like the Per Core licensed SQL Server 2019 Standard edition – see page 45) you license at the virtual machine level. You need to license all of the virtual cores assigned to a virtual machine with a minimum of 4 Core licenses assigned to each virtual machine. As usual, you calculate the number of Core licenses required by looking at the virtual machines but the licenses are, in reality, assigned to the physical server.

Virtualization licensing: rights per server

For BizTalk Server 2020 Enterprise edition there's the same option as there is for SQL Server 2019 Enterprise (see page 46) where you can license the physical server completely and then run BizTalk in 1 virtual machine for every license assigned to that server, with the option of assigning additional licenses if you want to run further virtual machines.

Virtualization licensing: unlimited virtualization

Licensing for unlimited virtualization is only available (as with SQL Server 2019 – see page 46) when BizTalk Server 2020 Enterprise Core licenses have been purchased with Software Assurance. You need to license a physical server completely, and then you're licensed to run BizTalk Server 2020 in an unlimited number of virtual machines.

Licensing a server farm

All editions of BizTalk Server 2020 are eligible for the License Mobility across Server Farms benefit when licenses are purchased with Software Assurance. This means that the 90-day rule is relaxed, and licenses can be dynamically assigned across a server farm as required. See page 49 for more details.

Licensing for Disaster Recovery

All editions of BizTalk Server 2020 are eligible for the Disaster Recovery benefit if customers have active Software Assurance on their Core licenses. This means that they can install BizTalk Server on a "cold" – that is, a turned off – backup server for the purposes of Disaster Recovery; if the main server fails, then the organization is licensed to turn on the cold server and run BizTalk Server from there without being concerned about license reassignment rules.

Downgrade and down-edition rights

Although there are the usual downgrade rights available for BizTalk Server 2020 to downgrade to BizTalk Server 2016, for example, there are no down-edition rights at all between the different editions.

Step-up licenses

There are Step-up licenses available to enable customers with active Software Assurance on their licenses to step-up from BizTalk Server Branch to either BizTalk Server Standard or Enterprise, and from BizTalk Server Standard to BizTalk Server Enterprise.

Licensing for the cloud

This first section of the book is about how the traditional software products are licensed in an on-premises environment. However, some of these traditional licenses, including BizTalk Server 2020, also include rights to use those licenses in the cloud.

License Mobility through SA

Core licenses with active Software Assurance for all editions of BizTalk Server 2020 are eligible for the License Mobility through SA benefit. This means that licenses may be used in Azure or in a partner's environment. The License Mobility through SA benefit is covered in detail in the section on page 350 onwards.

Required infrastructure products

BizTalk Server 2020 requires SQL Server 2019, preferably the Enterprise edition, and so licensing solutions for BizTalk Server 2020 should always include SQL Server 2019 Enterprise Core licenses as well.

BizTalk Server 2020 Developer edition

There's a Developer edition of BizTalk Server 2020 which is used in conjunction with any of the three main editions and is available for download for users with an eligible Visual Studio subscription.

Availability of BizTalk Server 2020 licenses

BizTalk Server 2020 Core licenses for all editions are available with or without Software Assurance through the Volume Licensing agreements, and without Software Assurance only through the Cloud Solution Provider program. As usual, check out the Product Terms website for specifics.

PROJECT SERVER 2019

Project Server 2019 is a project management server solution that allows project managers, key stakeholders, and other team members to collaborate on a project. The project plans themselves are created in Project Professional 2019 by a project manager and then saved to the Project Server. It's quite likely that no one else on the project will then use Project Professional, they'll just use a web browser to connect to the server to either see what tasks they've been assigned (as a team member) or to see whether the project is progressing to time and to budget (as a key stakeholder).

Licensing Project Server 2019

Project Server 2019 is licensed with the basic Server/CAL licensing model. In this model there's a Project Server 2019 license assigned to the server and then users or devices are licensed with Project Server 2019 User or Device CALs, as shown in the diagram below. All users, whether they are accessing Project Server 2019 from a browser or Project Professional, must be licensed with a CAL.

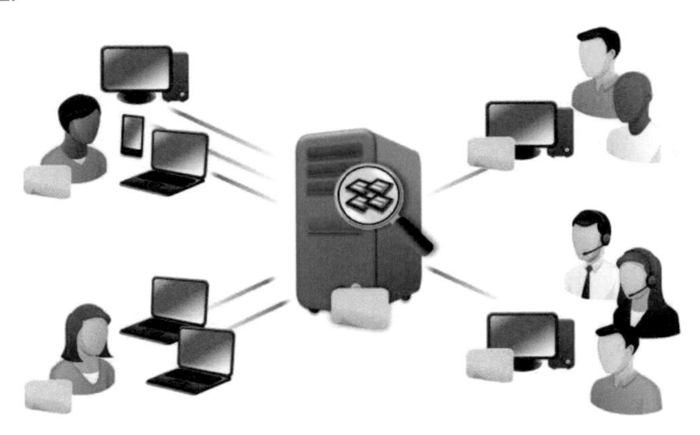

Figure 29: Project Server 2019 licensing

There's a special exception for customers who purchase Project Professional 2019 – they are deemed to have one Project Server 2019 Device CAL.

Licensing external users

There is no External Connector license available for Project Server 2019, so an organization must buy Project Server 2019 User or Device CALs for its external users to access the services of their Project Servers.

Licensing virtual machines

The rules here are exactly the same as with SQL Server when it's licensed with the Server/CAL model (page 41): a Project Server license is assigned to a physical server and this allows the software to be run in a single virtual machine. Extra licenses can be assigned to a physical server to allow Project Server to run in multiple virtual machines.

Licensing a server farm

Again, the rules here are exactly the same as with SQL Server when it's licensed with the Server/CAL model (see page 44): a Project Server license with Software Assurance has the License Mobility across Server Farms benefit and can be reassigned to another server as often as required. If Software Assurance isn't purchased with the licenses, then every physical server must be licensed with a Server license for every virtual machine in the server farm.

Licensing for Disaster Recovery

Project Server 2019 is eligible for the Disaster Recovery benefit if customers have active Software Assurance on both their Server licenses and CALs. This means that they can install Project Server on a "cold" – that is, a turned off – backup server for the purposes of Disaster Recovery; if the main server fails, then the organization is licensed to turn on the cold server and run Project Server from there without being concerned about license reassignment rules.

Downgrade and down-edition rights

Customers with Project Server 2019 licenses may use any previous version of the product. There's only one edition of Project Server 2019 so down-edition rights don't apply.

Licensing for the cloud

This first section of the book is about how the traditional software products are licensed in an on-premises environment. However, some of these traditional licenses, including Project Server 2019, also include rights to use those licenses in the cloud.

License Mobility through SA

Project Server 2019 Server and CAL licenses with active Software Assurance are eligible for the License Mobility through SA benefit. This means that licenses may be used in Azure or in a partner's environment. The License Mobility through SA benefit is covered in detail in the section on page 350 onwards.

Required infrastructure products

There are three products that are required pieces of the technology infrastructure for Project Server: SQL Server, SharePoint Server and, of course, Windows Server. Therefore, any licensing recommendations you make for Project Server should also include licenses for these products. From a SQL Server perspective, this can be covered with either Core licenses or Server licenses and CALs, and for SharePoint, the Server licenses and both Standard and Enterprise CALs are required.

Note that if external users are being licensed, they need to be licensed for these products too, with the Windows Server element likely to be covered by an External Connector license.

Availability of Project Server 2019 licenses

Project Server 2019 Server licenses and CALs are available with or without Software Assurance through the Volume Licensing agreements, and without Software Assurance only through the Cloud Solution Provider program. As usual, check out the Product Terms website for specifics.

EXCHANGE SERVER 2019

Exchange Server 2019 is the Microsoft email server. Users can access their email, as well as calendar and contact information from Outlook, from Outlook on the web, or from a mobile device through a variety of apps.

Licensing Exchange Server 2019

Exchange Server 2019 is licensed with the Server/CAL model but rather than there just being one level of CAL, there are two CALs available for organizations to purchase. These CALs allow access to different levels of functionality, which means that customers can be licensed for whatever functionality their users need to use.

The two CALs are Standard and Enterprise CALs. The Standard CALs are also known as Base CALs and the Enterprise CALs as Additive CALs. An Additive CAL may only ever be purchased in addition to a Base CAL, never solely alone. This means that customers must purchase Standard CALs for all users accessing an Exchange Server and then, additionally, Enterprise CALs for those users who need access to the higher-level functionality.

The diagram below shows some users licensed with just Standard CALs, and others licensed with both Standard and Enterprise CALs. The Standard CAL and the corresponding server functionality is shown in the darker color, and the Enterprise CAL and corresponding functionality is shown in the lighter color:

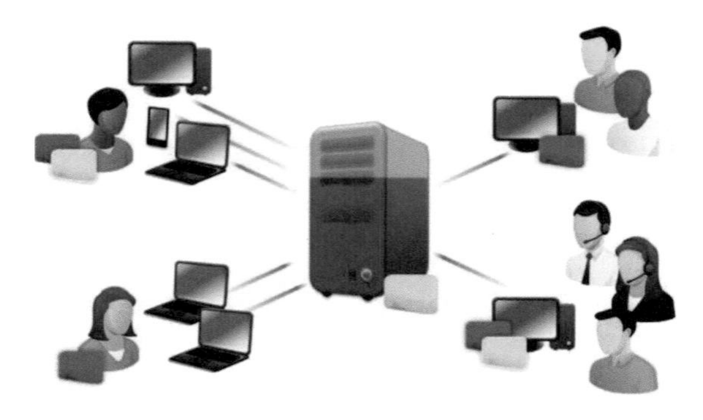

Figure 30: Exchange Server 2019 licensing

Exchange 2019 Standard and Enterprise CALs are available as either User or Device CALs.

Exchange Standard CALs allow users to access the basic functionality of Exchange Server and this includes accessing their email, calendar, contacts and tasks from a variety of clients including Outlook, Outlook on the web, or an app on a mobile device. Note that if users are accessing Exchange from a free app they do still need to be licensed with a CAL. As you would expect, if users have several devices that they access the Exchange Server from, then User CALs are a good recommendation.

An Enterprise CAL adds on access to some more sophisticated features, and it's also available **with Services**, which licenses users with active SA for the following:

- **Data Loss Prevention (DLP)**: this enforces compliance requirements for sensitive data so that important data can't be emailed, or it's checked against a template before emailing, for example
- **Exchange Online Protection**: this provides anti-malware and anti-spam services

Licensing external users

The Server license itself covers an unlimited number of external users for access to the basic functionality of the server. However, if external users require access to the advanced functionality of the server then they must be licensed with both Standard and Enterprise CALs.

Licensing virtual machines

As with all of the other Server/CAL licensed products, an Exchange Server 2019 Server license is assigned to a physical server and licenses Exchange Server 2019 to run in a single virtual machine. Additional Server licenses may be assigned to the server to run Exchange Server 2019 in further virtual machines. See the SQL Server section on page 44 for more details.

Licensing a server farm

Exchange Server 2019 is consistent with the other products licensed with the Server/CAL model – if Server licenses are purchased with Software Assurance the License Mobility across Server Farms benefit is included, and licenses can be reassigned between servers in a server farm as often as required. This topic is covered in detail in the SQL Server section on page 49.

Licensing for Disaster Recovery

Exchange Server 2019 is eligible for the Disaster Recovery benefit if customers have active Software Assurance on both their Server licenses and CALs. This means that they can install Exchange Server on a "cold" – that is, a turned off – backup server for the purposes of Disaster Recovery; if the main server fails, then the organization is licensed to turn on the cold server and run Exchange Server from there without being concerned about license reassignment rules.

Exchange Server 2019 server editions

Exchange Server 2019 is available in Standard and Enterprise editions. The Standard edition is the base level edition with the Enterprise edition offering a greater level of scalability.

Note that the edition of the Server license is a completely separate purchasing decision for the customer from the CALs. They do NOT need Enterprise CALs with an Enterprise Server license for example. When you're selecting licenses, consider the scalability needs first and decide on the server edition, then consider the functionality required by the users and decide on the CALs required.

Downgrade and down-edition rights

The usual downgrade rights apply to both Exchange Server 2019 Standard and Enterprise editions. In addition, if a customer has purchased an Exchange Server 2019 Enterprise license, then they can choose to deploy Standard edition if they need to.

Step-up licenses

There's a Step-up license available to enable customers with active Software Assurance on their licenses to step up from Exchange Server Standard edition to Enterprise edition.

Exchange Online Voice Mail Service

Customers who have active Software Assurance on Exchange Server 2019 Standard or Enterprise licenses are entitled to use the Exchange Online Voice Mail Service of Cloud Voicemail to access voice messages from Outlook.

Licensing for the cloud

This first section of the book is about how the traditional software products are licensed in an on-premises environment. However, some of these traditional licenses, including Exchange Server 2019, also include rights to use those licenses in the cloud.

License Mobility through SA

Exchange Server 2019 Standard and Enterprise Server and CAL licenses with active Software Assurance are eligible for the License Mobility through SA benefit. This means that licenses may be used in Azure or in a partner's environment. The License Mobility through SA benefit is covered in detail in the section on page 350 onwards.

Availability of Exchange Server 2019 licenses

Exchange Server 2019 Server licenses and CALs are available with or without Software Assurance through the Volume Licensing agreements, and without Software Assurance only through the Cloud Solution Provider program. As usual, check out the Product Terms website for specifics.

SHAREPOINT SERVER 2019

SharePoint Server 2019 is a content management, workflow automation, and collaboration portal, which also allows a single infrastructure for Internet, intranet and extranet sites. Users typically connect to the SharePoint sites or portals through a web browser.

Licensing SharePoint Server 2019

SharePoint Server 2019 is licensed with the Server/CAL model and, as with Exchange Server 2019 (see page 68), there are Standard and Enterprise CALs available to license access to different functionality. Again, the Enterprise CALs are Additive CALs and may only be purchased in addition to the Standard CAL, never solely alone. SharePoint Server 2019 Standard and Enterprise CALs are available as either User or Device CALs.

Licensing external users

As with Exchange Server 2019 (page 69), the Server license covers any number of external users. However, there's another nuance with SharePoint Server licensing that you need to know about – how intranet, extranet, and Internet scenarios are licensed.

In an **intranet** scenario, a Server license is assigned to the server and all internal users (or devices) are licensed with CALs. There are no licensing requirements for the external users since they do not have access to the SharePoint content.

In an **extranet** scenario, a Server license is again assigned to the server and all internal users (or devices) are licensed with CALs. This time external users do have access, but there are again no licensing requirements because access to the server is covered by the Server license.

In an **Internet** scenario, a Server license is, as usual, assigned to the server, and in this scenario there are no additional licensing requirements for either the internal or the external users. This relaxing of the licensing requirements is allowed since external users have access to all of the content on the SharePoint server.

Licensing virtual machines

In common with the other products that are licensed with a Server/CAL model, a SharePoint Server 2019 Server license is assigned to a physical server and this allows SharePoint to run in a single virtual machine. Additional Server licenses may be assigned to the server to run SharePoint Server 2019 in further virtual machines. See the SQL Server section on page 44 for more details.

Licensing a server farm

SharePoint Server is consistent with the other products licensed with the Server/CAL model – if Server licenses are purchased with Software Assurance the License Mobility across Server Farms benefit is included, and licenses can be reassigned between servers in a server farm as often as required. This topic is covered in detail in the SQL Server section on page 49.

Licensing for Disaster Recovery

SharePoint Server 2019 is eligible for the Disaster Recovery benefit if customers have active Software Assurance on both their Server licenses and CALs. This means that they can install SharePoint Server on a "cold" – that is, a turned off – backup server for the purposes of Disaster Recovery; if the main server fails, then the organization is licensed to turn on the cold server and run SharePoint Server from there without being concerned about license reassignment rules.

Downgrade and down-edition rights

Customers with SharePoint Server 2019 licenses may use any previous version of the product. There's only one edition of SharePoint Server 2019 so down-edition rights don't apply.

Licensing for the cloud

This first section of the book is about how the traditional software products are licensed in an on-premises environment. However, some of these traditional licenses, including SharePoint Server 2019, also include rights to use those licenses in the cloud.

License Mobility through SA

SharePoint Server 2019 Server and CAL licenses with active Software Assurance are eligible for the License Mobility through SA benefit. This means that licenses may be used in Azure or in a partner's environment. The License Mobility through SA benefit is covered in detail in the section on page 350 onwards.

Required infrastructure products

SQL Server is a required infrastructure product for SharePoint Server, and so any licensing recommendations you make for SharePoint Server should also include licenses for SQL Server which can be covered with either Core licenses or Server licenses and CALs (see page 41).

Availability of SharePoint Server 2019 licenses

SharePoint Server 2019 Server licenses and CALs are available with or without Software Assurance through the Volume Licensing agreements, and without Software Assurance only through the Cloud Solution Provider program. As usual, check out the Product Terms website for specifics.

SKYPE FOR BUSINESS SERVER 2019

Skype for Business Server 2019 is the server solution for instant messaging, presence information, web conferencing, and enterprise telephony. There are a variety of clients that users can use to access the services of Skype for Business Server 2019, ranging from the full Skype for Business client to free apps.

Licensing Skype for Business Server 2019

Skype for Business Server 2019 has three CALs available for customers to purchase. There's the Base CAL which is the Standard CAL, and then two Additive CALs called the Enterprise and Plus CALs. All Skype for Business Server users need to be licensed with the Standard CAL and then the organization can choose to purchase them Enterprise and/or Plus CALs dependent on what functionality those users need to use.

The diagram below shows users licensed with a variety of CALs dependent on what they will be doing with Skype for Business Server, with the Standard CAL and corresponding server functionality shown in the darkest color, the Plus CAL and functionality shown in the lightest color, and the Enterprise CAL and functionality in the color in between.

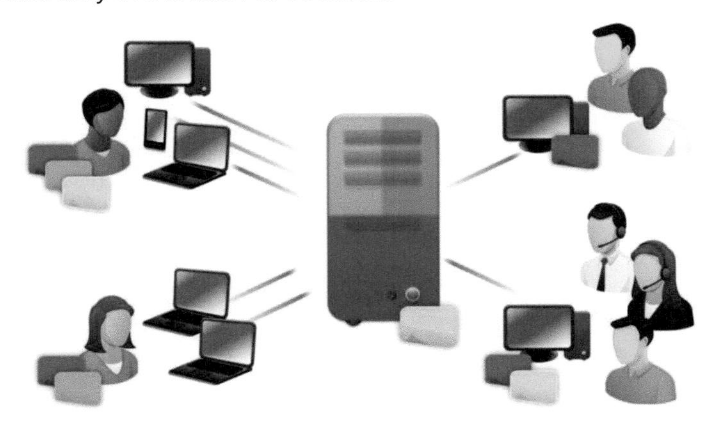

Figure 31: Skype for Business Server 2019 licensing

Organizations purchase Skype for Business Server 2019 Standard CALs when they want to license their users for the instant messaging and integrated presence functionality of Skype for Business Server 2019. If they want their users to be able to set up web conferences, they optionally purchase the Skype for Business Server 2019 Enterprise CAL. And finally, the Plus CAL licenses users for enterprise telephony functionality.

All CALs are available as User and Device CALs.

Licensing external users

The Skype for Business Server 2019 Server license is assigned to a physical server and allows an unlimited number of external users to access the services of the server.

Licensing virtual machines

As with all of the other Server/CAL licensed products, a Skype for Business Server 2019 Server license is assigned to a physical server and licenses Skype for Business Server 2019 to run in a single virtual machine. Additional Server licenses may be assigned to the server to run Skype for Business Server 2019 in further virtual machines. See the SQL Server section on page 44 for more details.

Licensing a server farm

Skype for Business Server 2019 is consistent with the other products licensed with the Server/CAL model – if Server licenses are purchased with Software Assurance the License Mobility across Server Farms benefit is included, and licenses can be reassigned between servers in a server farm as often as required. This topic is covered in detail in the SQL Server section on page 49.

Licensing for Disaster Recovery

Skype for Business Server 2019 is eligible for the Disaster Recovery benefit if customers have active Software Assurance on both their Server licenses and CALs. This means that they can install Skype for Business Server on a "cold" – that is, a turned off – backup server for the purposes of Disaster Recovery; if the main server fails, then the organization is licensed to turn on the cold server and run Skype for Business Server from there without being concerned about license reassignment rules.

Downgrade and down-edition rights

Customers with Skype for Business Server 2019 licenses may use any previous version of the product. There's only one edition of Skype for Business Server 2019 so down-edition rights don't apply.

Licensing for the cloud

This first section of the book is about how the traditional software products are licensed in an on-premises environment. However, some of these traditional licenses, including Skype for Business Server 2019, also include rights to use those licenses in the cloud.

License Mobility through SA

Skype for Business Server 2019 Server and CAL licenses with active Software Assurance are eligible for the License Mobility through SA benefit. This means that licenses may be used in Azure or in a partner's environment. The License Mobility through SA benefit is covered in detail in the section on page 350 onwards.

Required infrastructure products

SQL Server is a required infrastructure product for Skype for Business Server 2019, and so any licensing recommendations you make for Skype for Business Server 2019 should also include licenses for SQL Server which can be covered with either Core licenses or Server licenses and CALs (see page 41).

Availability of Skype for Business Server 2019 licenses

Skype for Business Server licenses and CALs are available with or without Software Assurance through the Volume Licensing agreements, and without Software Assurance only through the Cloud Solution Provider program. As usual, check out the Product Terms website for specifics.

THE CAL SUITES

Many customers buy one of two suites of CALs for convenience and cost-effectiveness – the Core CAL Suite or the Enterprise CAL Suite. These CAL Suites can be purchased for Users or Devices, and initial purchases always include Software Assurance. The license itself is designated as a **Suite** license which means that its components cannot be split across several users or devices.

The components of the Core and Enterprise CAL Suites are shown below:

	Core infrastructure	Productivity servers
Core CAL Suite	• Windows Server 2019 CAL • Microsoft Endpoint Configuration Manager Client Management License (CML) • System Center Endpoint Protection 1606 Subscription License (SL)	• Exchange Server 2019 Standard CAL • SharePoint Server 2019 Standard CAL • Skype for Business Server 2019 Standard CAL
Enterprise CAL Suite	• Windows Server 2019 Active Directory Rights Management Services CAL • Advanced Threat Analytics 2016 CML	• Exchange Server 2019 Enterprise CAL with Services • SharePoint Server 2019 Enterprise CAL • Skype for Business Server 2019 Enterprise CAL • Exchange Online Archiving for Exchange Server SL

Figure 32: the Core and Enterprise CAL Suites

There are a couple of components in the table above that are not covered in other sections of the book: the Advanced Threat Analytics 2016 CML, and the Exchange Online Archiving for Exchange Server SL.

Advanced Threat Analytics is security technology which uses machine learning to learn what's normal behavior for users and devices so that it can identify suspicious behavior which may indicate a malicious attack.

Exchange Online Archiving for Exchange Server is a cloud-based solution for organizations that have deployed Exchange Server 2019 on-premises and helps with archiving, compliance, regulatory and eDiscovery requirements.

Exchange Online Archiving for Exchange Server, and the services included with the Exchange Server 2019 Enterprise CAL with Services (Data Loss Prevention and Exchange Online Protection) are dependent on a customer having active Software Assurance.

Step-up licenses

There's a Step-up license available to enable customers with Software Assurance on their licenses to step-up from the Core CAL Suite to the Enterprise CAL Suite.

Availability of the CAL Suite licenses

Licenses for the Core and Enterprise CAL Suites are available with Software Assurance through the Volume Licensing agreements. As usual, check out the Product Terms website for specifics.

DYNAMICS 365 SERVER

Dynamics 365 Server provides Customer Relationship Management (CRM) functionality, enabling organizations to get a holistic view about what's happening across their customers.

Licensing Dynamics 365 Server

Dynamics 365 Server is licensed with the familiar Server/CAL model – with one difference you may perhaps spot in the diagram below:

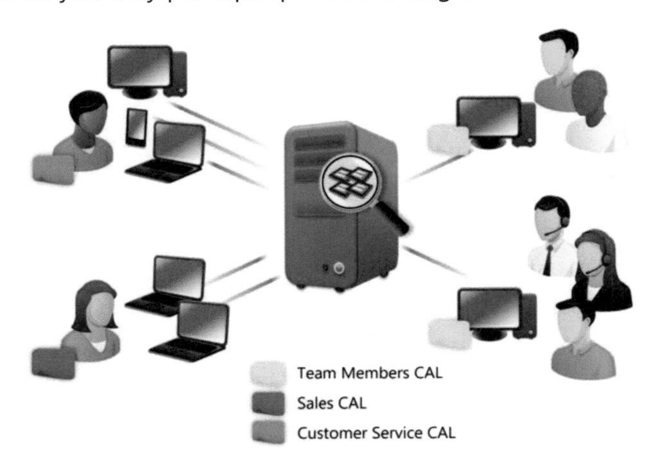

Figure 33: Dynamics 365 Server licensing

And the difference? Although this product is officially licensed with a Server/CAL model there is no Server license available to purchase; the rights to install the server product are included when you buy one of the three CALs shown. It's important to be able to choose the right CAL for a particular user so let's look at the CALs in a bit more detail now.

The Sales and Customer Service CALs are aimed at professionals who work in those fields. So, if you're a Customer Service agent and your organization has invested in Dynamics 365 Server then it's likely you'll be licensed with a Customer Service CAL. If you have more of a supporting role – you could be asked to look something up for a salesperson for example, then the (much cheaper) Team Members CAL is likely to be an appropriate license. The Team Members CAL licenses a user for light access to both Sales and Customer Service functionality.

The Sales and Customer Service CALs themselves include Team Members rights to the other area of functionality, so someone licensed with a Sales CAL will be able to perform light tasks in the area of Customer Service. All of the CALs are available as User or Device CALs and must initially be purchased with Software Assurance.

Licensing external users

External user access is included with an organization's internal Sales and Customer Service CALs, and thus external users don't require CALs to access Dynamics 365 Server.

Licensing virtual machines

There's no Server license for Dynamics 365 Server so how do you license for the software running in virtual machines? The answer is interesting: customers who have Dynamics 365 Server CALs may install and use any number of copies of the server software on a physical server dedicated to their use, owned by them or by an Authorized Outsourcer partner. So, as long as CALs are purchased, the software may run in as many physical and virtual machines as required.

Licensing a server farm

Following on from the previous point, if you can install the server software as many times as you like then it's very easy to license a server farm! So, just to confirm, as long as you have CALs there are no extra licensing requirements to license the server software throughout a server farm.

Licensing for Disaster Recovery

Again, due to the unlimited installation rights there's no need to have a special benefit to license for Disaster Recovery.

Downgrade and down-edition rights

Customers with Dynamics 365 Server CALs can downgrade and use the previous versions of the product which was formerly known as CRM Server. This can get a little bit tricky in terms of working out what you're actually licensed for since the licensing model changed when CRM Server 2016 became Dynamics 365 Server. For instance, you are automatically given a grant to a server license (since there was one required for CRM Server 2016) and then a Team Members CAL licenses you for a CRM Server 2016 Essential CAL, and the Sales/Customer Service CALs can be used as CRM Server 2016 Basic or Professional CALs.

There's only one edition of the Dynamics 365 Server software so down-edition rights don't apply here.

Step-up licenses

There are Step-up licenses available to enable customers with Software Assurance on their licenses to step-up from a Team Members CAL to either a Sales or Customer Service CAL.

Licensing for the cloud

This first section of the book is about how the traditional software products are licensed in an on-premises environment. However, some of these traditional licenses, including Dynamics 365 Server, also include rights to use those licenses in the cloud.

Strictly speaking, Dynamics 365 Server does not have the License Mobility through SA right, but customers with Dynamics 365 CALs and active Software Assurance may install and use any number of copies of the corresponding Dynamics 365 Server software on a shared server.

Additional Software Assurance benefits

CustomerSource

CustomerSource is a password-protected site which enables Dynamics users to find answers to their product questions using self-help resources such as troubleshooters, searching the Knowledge Base, and using how-to articles and videos. They also get unlimited access to online training courses and resources such as fact sheets and presentations, as well as access to user groups in the Dynamics Community. This is also where deployment teams would go to download software and updates.

Organizations with active Software Assurance on their Dynamics 365 CALs have access to CustomerSource.

Unified Service Desk

Unified Service Desk enables organizations to quickly build applications for call centers so that agents can get a unified view of customer data. Customers with Dynamics 365 Sales or Customer Service CALs with active SA may install and use Unified Service Desk. The right to use the product is limited to the user or device to whom the qualifying CAL is assigned.

Required infrastructure products

SQL Server is a required infrastructure product for Dynamics 365 Server.

Availability of Dynamics 365 Server licenses

Dynamics 365 Server CALs are available with Software Assurance through the Volume Licensing agreements. As usual, check out the Product Terms website for specifics.

DYNAMICS 365 FOR OPERATIONS SERVER

Dynamics 365 for Operations Server provides Enterprise Resource Planning (ERP) functionality enabling an organization to manage processes and departments within and across the entire organization.

Licensing Dynamics 365 for Operations Server

Dynamics 365 for Operations Server is licensed with the Server/CAL model, and it's exactly as you would expect with Server and CAL licenses as shown in the diagram below.

Figure 34: Dynamics 365 for Operations Server licensing

Again, it's important to be able to recommend the right license for a particular user. Let's start with the Team Members CAL since this is exactly the same sort of user as with Dynamics 365 Server – someone in a support role who needs light access to all functionality across the solution.

The full Operations CAL is for someone whose main role is in the finance and operations part of a business, and the Activity CAL is (at a simple level) for the user who needs to do more than would be allowed via a Team Members CAL but doesn't need a full Operations CAL. And, finally, the Device CAL is primarily for licensing devices in a retail environment where several people will use the same device where it's being used as a point-of-sale device, shop floor device, warehouse device or store manager device.

Note that Dynamics 365 for Operations Server licenses are only available with Software Assurance, and the product itself may only be used by customers that have active Software Assurance. If SA lapses, then a customer must uninstall the server software and if they have perpetual rights to the software then may install Dynamics AX 2012 R3 Server.

Licensing external users

In common with products like Exchange Server 2019 and SharePoint Server 2019, the Dynamics 365 for Operations Server license covers an unlimited number of external users for access to the server functionality.

Licensing virtual machines

As with (just about) all of the other Server/CAL licensed products, a Dynamics 365 for Operations Server license is assigned to a physical server and can be used to license Dynamics 365 for Operations Server running in a single virtual machine, and further licenses may be assigned to cover additional virtual machines. See the SQL Server section on page 44 for more details.

Licensing a server farm

Dynamics 365 for Operations Server licenses are always purchased with Software Assurance and customers are entitled to the License Mobility across Server Farms benefit which means that licenses can be reassigned between servers in a server farm as often as required. This topic is covered in detail in the SQL Server section on page 49.

Licensing for Disaster Recovery

As mentioned above, Dynamics 365 for Operations Server licenses are always purchased with Software Assurance and customers are entitled to the Disaster Recovery benefit. This means that they can install Dynamics 365 for

Operations Server on a "cold" – that is, a turned off – backup server for the purposes of Disaster Recovery; if the main server fails, then the organization is licensed to turn on the cold server and run Dynamics 365 for Operations Server from there without being concerned about license reassignment rules.

Licensing for failover

Another Software Assurance benefit that customers are entitled to is failover rights. This means that Dynamics 365 for Operations Server can be configured to provide redundancy so that if one server fails, its processing will be picked up, recovered, and continued by another server without the need for additional licenses. Note that the failover server must be a passive server, which means that it can't be running active workloads or serving data to clients.

Downgrade and down-edition rights

There's only one edition of the Dynamics 365 for Operations Server software so down-edition rights don't apply here. Customers with Dynamics 365 for Operations Server CALs can downgrade and use the previous versions of the product which was formerly known as Dynamics AX. This can get a little bit tricky in terms of working out what you're actually licensed for since the licensing model changed when Dynamics AX 2012 R3 Server became Dynamics 365 for Operations Server. For instance, a Team Members CAL licenses you for an AX Self Serve User or Device CAL, and the full Dynamics 365 for Operations CAL can be used as an AX Enterprise User or Device CAL.

Step-up licenses

There are Step-up licenses available to enable customers with Software Assurance on their licenses to step-up from a Team Members CAL to a Dynamics 365 for Operations Activity CAL, or from a Dynamics 365 for Operations Activity CAL to a full Dynamics 365 for Operations CAL.

Licensing for the cloud

This first section of the book is about how the traditional software products are licensed in an on-premises environment. However, some of these traditional licenses, including Dynamics 365 for Operations Server, also include rights to use those licenses in the cloud.

License Mobility through SA

Dynamics 365 for Operations Server and CAL licenses with active Software Assurance are eligible for the License Mobility through SA benefit. This means that licenses may be used in Azure or in a partner's environment. The License Mobility through SA benefit is covered in detail in the section on page 350 onwards.

CustomerSource

CustomerSource is a password-protected site which enables Dynamics users to find answers to their product questions using self-help resources such as troubleshooters, searching the Knowledge Base, and using how-to articles and videos. They also get unlimited access to online training courses and resources such as fact sheets and presentations, as well as access to user groups in the Dynamics Community. This is also where deployment teams would go to download software and updates.

Organizations with active Software Assurance on their CALs for Dynamics 365 for Operations Server have access to CustomerSource.

Required infrastructure products

SQL Server is a required infrastructure product for Dynamics 365 for Operations Server.

Availability of Dynamics 365 for Operations Server licenses

Dynamics 365 for Operations Server and CAL licenses are available with Software Assurance through the Enterprise Agreement, Enterprise Subscription Agreement, Server and Cloud Enrollment, and via a partner through the Dynamics Price List.

DYNAMICS 365 BUSINESS CENTRAL ON-PREMISES

Licenses for the Dynamics 365 Business Central on-premises solution are only available through the Dynamics Price List (DPL) and thus are not covered in this book.

LICENSING THE DEVELOPER TOOLS

You can think of the Microsoft developer tools as being in two categories: Visual Studio subscriptions, and the Azure DevOps tools.

Visual Studio subscriptions are assigned to an individual user who is typically a developer and needs tools to create and test applications. A Visual Studio subscription gives these users access to the Visual Studio software and a whole host of benefits. There are two ways of buying these Visual Studio subscriptions. Firstly, they can be purchased as a license with Software Assurance through a Volume Licensing agreement, and these are known as Standard subscriptions. Secondly, they're available as Cloud subscriptions which are monthly subscriptions and are purchased against an Azure Subscription. Standard subscriptions are covered in this section, and the Cloud subscriptions in the Azure section of this book at page 374.

The Azure DevOps tools form an Application Lifecycle Management solution which provides an environment where software developers, testers, project managers, and other members of a software development team can communicate and collaborate throughout the process of designing, building, testing, and deploying software. These tools are available either as an on-premises solution called Azure DevOps Server 2020 which is covered in this section of the book on page 96, or as a cloud-based solution called Azure DevOps which is covered in the Azure section on page 376.

VISUAL STUDIO

Visual Studio Standard subscriptions

There are four Visual Studio Standard subscriptions available, aimed at the different users who will participate in software development projects:

Subscription	User
Visual Studio Professional	Developer
Visual Studio Enterprise	Developer
Visual Studio Test Professional	Tester
MSDN Platforms	IT and Operations staff

Figure 35: Visual Studio Standard subscriptions

There are three main parts to a Visual Studio subscription in terms of what's available to the licensed user:

- The Visual Studio Integrated Development Environment (IDE) where developers create their apps
- Access to Azure DevOps on-premises and/or cloud solutions
- Subscriber benefits such as Azure credit, access to software for Dev/Test use, training and education tools, support tools, and partner offers

The Visual Studio Professional and Enterprise subscriptions are aimed at developers and are thus the only subscriptions which include the Visual Studio IDE. However, all subscriptions also include an Azure DevOps Server CAL for the licensed user and the rights to install Azure DevOps Server 2020, as well as licenses for Azure DevOps in the cloud: a Basic plan license for Visual Studio Professional users, and a Basic + Test plan license for Visual Studio Enterprise/Test Professional and MSDN Platform users.

Subscriber benefits

The included subscriber benefits vary widely between the four different Visual Studio Standard subscriptions and Microsoft sites such as this one: https://bit.ly/BOKVSSubscriberBenefits are useful to see what the differences are. However, here's an overview of the six areas of subscriber benefits and what's available in which subscription:

Cloud services

- Azure credit: $50 per month for Visual Studio Professional/Test Professional, $100 for MSDN Platforms, $150 for Visual Studio Enterprise
- Access to Azure Dev/Test pricing and Windows Virtual Desktop for all subscriptions

Software for Dev/Test

- Windows, Windows Server, and SQL Server available for all Subscriptions
- Other server software available for Visual Studio Enterprise and MSDN Platforms, and Office available for Visual Studio Enterprise

Software for production use

- Microsoft 365 Apps for enterprise and Office Professional Plus 2019 available for Visual Studio Enterprise

Training and education

- LinkedIn Learning and Pluralsight training included in Visual Studio Professional/Enterprise
- DataCamp subscription for all subscriptions

Support

- Access to technical support incidents, concierge chat, communities and forums for all subscriptions

Visual Studio partner offers

- All available for Visual Studio Enterprise, some available for Visual Studio Professional, and none available for the other subscriptions

Using subscriber software

One of the most popular subscriber benefits is the ability to install and use a wide range of Microsoft software for dev and test purposes. The licensed individual can install the software on any device that they want, including personally owned devices. Other users licensed with Visual Studio subscriptions may also access the software, but they must make sure that their subscription does include rights to the specific product being accessed. For example, a Visual Studio Enterprise licensed user could install BizTalk Server, but this is not included in a Visual Studio Professional subscription.

If a developer is, for example, an independent contractor, working with a number of different organizations, he could purchase himself a Visual Studio subscription and he would have access to software installed for Dev/Test purposes at any customer that he worked for – as long as the particular product was included in his subscription of course.

Licensed users can also use most of the subscriber software in Azure virtual machines. The exceptions are Windows Server, which isn't allowed at all – the developer must pay the charges for a Windows Server VM, and Windows client VMs for which there are restrictions in exactly which Azure Subscriptions they may run.

Everyone who accesses the software must be licensed with a Visual Studio subscription, and that includes IT staff who might assist in setting up the software. The software may only be used for dev and test purposes and that includes products like System Center. If System Center is being used to actively manage a Dev/Test environment, then it's actually being used in a production manner and must be licensed with regular licenses. Be careful too of physical servers that run both production and Dev/Test workloads – the physical server would need to be licensed with production Windows Server licenses.

The one exception when users can access software licensed via Visual Studio subscriptions without having a subscription of their own, is when they are a regular end user carrying out User Acceptance Testing (UAT). This is the process of assessing an application to determine whether it meets the necessary criteria for release, and there are no licensing requirements for these users.

Buying Visual Studio Standard subscriptions

The four Visual Studio Standard subscriptions are available through all of the Volume Licensing agreements. Although they are called "subscriptions" this is a little bit misleading since they're transacted as a license with Software Assurance and in an agreement where licenses for on-premises products are perpetual – like the Open Value agreement for example – then rights to the Visual Studio IDE are perpetual, even if the Software Assurance isn't renewed.

Step-up licenses

Customers with active Software Assurance can purchase a Step-up license to move from Visual Studio Professional or Visual Studio Test Professional to Visual Studio Enterprise.

Renewing down

At the renewal of the Volume Licensing agreement a customer can choose to "renew down" from a higher-level Visual Studio subscription to a lower-level one. As you might expect, they immediately lose the benefits of the higher-level subscription and would need to discontinue using and deinstall any products associated with the original subscription.

Other editions

Visual Studio with GitHub Enterprise

In an Enterprise Agreement a customer may purchase the following licenses to license users for both the Visual Studio subscription and for access to a private version of GitHub.com:

- Visual Studio Professional with GitHub Enterprise
- Visual Studio Enterprise with GitHub Enterprise

Alternatively, these licenses may be purchased for any users already licensed for Visual Studio Enterprise or Professional to additionally license users for GitHub Enterprise:

- GitHub Enterprise for Visual Studio Professional
- GitHub Enterprise for Visual Studio Enterprise

And finally, as you might expect, there's a Step-up license to move from Visual Studio Professional with GitHub Enterprise to Visual Studio Enterprise with GitHub Enterprise.

Visual Studio Professional 2019

Visual Studio Professional 2019 is the standalone perpetual license for Visual Studio aimed at users who just need the Visual Studio Professional IDE. Users have rights to previous versions of Visual Studio Professional but don't get any of the subscriber benefits or access to either on-premises or online Azure DevOps solutions. These licenses are only available through the Volume Licensing agreements where Software Assurance isn't mandatory – so Open License, Select Plus and MPSA agreements.

Visual Studio Community 2019

Visual Studio Community 2019 is a free IDE aimed at individual developers building free or paid-for apps. There are restrictions on using it in organizations with more than 250 PCs where use is limited to classroom learning environments, for academic research, or for contributing to open-source projects.

Availability of Visual Studio licenses

The four Visual Studio Standard subscriptions are available through all of the Volume Licensing agreements, with the Visual Studio Professional 2019 standalone license available through the Open License, Select Plus and MPSA agreements.

AZURE DEVOPS SERVER 2020

Azure DevOps Server 2020 is the Application Lifecycle Management solution part of the developer tools.

Licensing Azure DevOps Server 2020

Azure DevOps Server 2020 is licensed with the Server/CAL model and there is just one type of CAL, available as a User or a Device CAL which, as usual, may be mixed if required. Both server licenses and CALs must be purchased with Software Assurance. If you're new to Server/CAL licensing, check out the Windows Server section on page 20 to learn about CALs, and the SQL Server section on page 41 for a Server/CAL licensing diagram.

It's worth noting that there are certain activities that users carry out that do not need to be licensed with a CAL. These activities include entering, editing and viewing work items, accessing Azure DevOps Server reports, and providing approvals to stages as part of the Release Management pipeline. It's worth checking out the Product Terms site or the Visual Studio Licensing Guide for more details if this may apply to your deployment of the product.

Licensing users with Visual Studio subscriptions

All Visual Studio Standard subscriptions (see page 91) and Visual Studio Cloud subscriptions (see page 374) include a CAL for the licensed user, and the rights to install Azure DevOps Server 2020. Note, however, that if a licensed user is a developer carrying out work as an independent contractor he can't bring his own CAL to another organization – if he needs to access Azure DevOps Server in a customer environment, then the customer themselves must purchase and assign a CAL to the developer.

Licensing external users

CALs are required to license external users and similarly to the situation above, one organization's CALs cannot be used to access another organization's server.

Licensing virtual machines

As with (just about) all of the other Server/CAL licensed products, an Azure DevOps Server 2020 license is assigned to a physical server and can be used to license the product running in a single virtual machine, and further licenses may be assigned to cover additional virtual machines. See the SQL Server section on page 44 for more details.

Licensing a server farm

Azure DevOps Server 2020 licenses are always purchased with Software Assurance and customers are entitled to the License Mobility across Server Farms benefit which means that licenses can be reassigned between servers in a server farm as often as required. This topic is covered in detail in the SQL Server section on page 49.

Licensing for Disaster Recovery

As mentioned above, Azure DevOps Server 2020 licenses are always purchased with Software Assurance and customers are entitled to the Disaster Recovery benefit. This means that they can install Azure DevOps Server 2020 on a "cold" – that is, a turned off – backup server for the purposes of Disaster Recovery; if the main server fails, then the organization is licensed to turn on the cold server and run Azure DevOps Server from there without being concerned about license reassignment rules.

Downgrade and down-edition rights

There's only one edition of the Azure DevOps Server 2020 product so down-edition rights don't apply here. Customers may downgrade to a previous version of the product which, it's worth noting, before Azure DevOps Server 2019 was called Visual Studio Team Foundation Server.

Licensing for the cloud

This first section of the book is about how the traditional software products are licensed in an on-premises environment. However, some of these traditional licenses, including Azure DevOps Server 2020, also include rights to use those licenses in the cloud.

License Mobility through SA

Azure DevOps Server 2020 Server and CAL licenses with active Software Assurance are eligible for the License Mobility through SA benefit. This means that licenses may be used in Azure or in a partner's environment. The License Mobility through SA benefit is covered in detail in the section on page 350 onwards.

Required infrastructure products

SQL Server is a required infrastructure product for Azure DevOps Server 2020. Rights to install SQL Server Standard edition are included when an Azure DevOps Server 2020 license is purchased, and it's downloadable as part of the Azure DevOps Server installation. As you might expect, the use of SQL Server acquired in this way may only support the Azure DevOps Server deployment.

Availability of Azure DevOps Server 2020 licenses

Azure DevOps Server 2020 Server licenses and CALs are available with Software Assurance through the Volume Licensing agreements. As usual, check out the Product Terms website for specifics.

WINDOWS 10 (DEVICE)

Windows 10 is the Microsoft client operating system. There are two editions aimed at businesses – Windows 10 Pro and Windows 10 Enterprise with, as you might expect, more features available in the Enterprise edition.

Licensing Windows 10

Historically, Windows has always been a device licensing model, but now user licenses are also available for some editions. In this section we will focus on the traditional device licenses, and you can find information on the Windows 10 User SLs on page 174.

Customers may acquire Windows 10 Pro through the OEM channel pre-installed on a new computer. This is a non-transferrable license which means that the software lives and dies on that machine – when the device is retired, the software may not be transferred to another machine.

Windows 10 Pro and Windows 10 Enterprise licenses are available through Volume Licensing agreements where the licenses are both upgrade licenses, requiring a Qualifying Operating System on a device before a license may be assigned to it. These are the most recent Qualifying Operating Systems that organizations will make use of:

- Windows 10 Enterprise or Pro
- Windows 8/8.1 Enterprise or Pro
- Windows 7 Enterprise, Professional or Ultimate

Downgrade and down-edition rights

One of the benefits of acquiring licenses through a Volume Licensing agreement is the availability of downgrade rights. However, OEM licenses do give some downgrade rights as the table below shows, and typically, this right is to the last two versions of the product.

Windows 10 Enterprise also gives down-edition rights – not only can you install an earlier version of the same edition (Windows 7 Enterprise, for example) but you can also install different editions – Windows 8.1 Pro or Windows Vista Business, for example.

	Windows 10 Pro (OEM)	Windows 10 Pro (VL)	Windows 10 Enterprise
Windows 8/8.1 Enterprise			✔
Windows 8.1 Pro	✔	✔	✔
Windows 7 Enterprise			✔
Windows 7 Professional	✔	✔	✔
Windows Vista Enterprise			✔
Windows Vista Business		✔	✔
Windows XP Professional		✔	✔
Windows 2000 Professional		✔	✔
Windows 95/98/NT		✔	✔

Figure 36: Windows 10 downgrade and down-edition rights

Servicing Channels

The Windows 10 Servicing Channels control how often feature updates are available for Windows 10 devices, with security updates delivered each month on the second Tuesday.

The **Semi-Annual Channel** makes feature update releases available twice a year, around March and September, and applies to both Windows 10 Pro and Windows 10 Enterprise editions. Historically, a Semi-Annual Channel release has been supported for 18 months, but the fall (September) releases of the

Enterprise edition have an additional 12 months of servicing for a total of 30 months from the initial release.

The **Long-Term Servicing Channel** provides less frequent feature update releases, every 2-3 years, and they are supported for 10 years. This channel is designed for special-purpose PCs such as those used in point-of-sale systems or controlling factory or medical equipment where it's not possible, or desirable, to have features updated regularly.

There is a special flavor of Windows 10 Enterprise which is serviced via the Long-Term Servicing Channel called Windows 10 Enterprise LTSC 2019. This is available to customers through Volume Licensing agreements and CSP. Customers with licenses for the regular Windows 10 Enterprise edition may choose to deploy the Windows 10 Enterprise LTSC 2019 edition if they want to. The previous version was Windows 10 Enterprise LTSC 2016.

The **Windows Insider Program** is another option for businesses running Windows 10 Pro or Enterprise edition. Enrolling devices into the Windows Insider Program provides the IT department with pre-release Windows builds so that they can test features before they become available in the Semi-Annual Channel.

License reassignment rights

Typically, there are some restrictions on how often a device license may be moved between different devices. However, Windows 10 Pro licenses acquired through either the OEM channel or through Volume Licensing agreements may not be moved at all, and the same is true for Windows 10 Enterprise LTSC 2019 licenses purchased through a Volume Licensing agreement or CSP.

Windows 10 Enterprise device licenses may be assigned to another device as long as the customer has active Software Assurance.

Licensing a Virtual Desktop Infrastructure

Organizations may choose to install Windows 10 locally on a device or to set up virtual desktops on their servers and to have their users access them from their devices – a setup known as a Virtual Desktop Infrastructure (VDI).

A Windows 10 Enterprise device license purchased through a Volume Licensing agreement includes Software Assurance which gives this added deployment flexibility of being allowed to create, store, run and access virtual desktops on a server. This right is known as Virtual Desktop Access.

Let's take an example: here's the setup that Spring Grocers want to license:

Figure 37: Virtual Desktop Infrastructure

They've got a server on their premises that is running the virtual desktops and delivering them to the users' desktops. This server could be either one that they own and manage, or one owned and managed by an Authorized Outsourcer – see page 16.

What licenses do Spring Green Grocers need? Well, even though Windows isn't installed on the users' devices, each device does need to be licensed for Windows 10 Enterprise. If the users are all using a device that has a Qualifying Operating System, then a Windows 10 Enterprise device license can be assigned to the device. However, if a user wants to access their virtual desktop from a thin client or some other device that doesn't have a Qualifying Operating System, then a Windows 10 Enterprise license can't be assigned to that device. In this situation, you'd choose an alternative license. A VDA device license is sold as a subscription license and it can be assigned to a device without a Qualifying Operating System. This license includes (as you might expect) VDA rights. So the devices at Spring Green Grocers could be licensed with a mix of Windows 10 Enterprise and VDA licenses.

We need to consider what CALs are required to access the VDI desktops on the server. Let's assume that the VDI server is a Microsoft one and, in that case, it's Windows Server 2019 and Remote Desktop Services that need to be licensed. Each user or device needs a Windows Server 2019 CAL and an RDS 2019 CAL. It's likely that Spring Green Grocers will choose Device CALs since the other components of the solution are licensed by device.

Additional Software Assurance benefits

Windows 10 Pro and Windows 10 Enterprise LTSC 2019 licenses do not include Software Assurance. Windows 10 Enterprise and VDA device licenses do include Software Assurance which gives access to a VDI infrastructure, as described in the previous section, and to the additional benefits described below:

Microsoft Desktop Optimization Pack (MDOP)

There have been several changes over recent years as to how you acquire the tools within the Microsoft Desktop Optimization Pack. Historically, it was something that organizations could buy if they had Software Assurance on their Windows desktop operating system licenses. Today, however, Windows 10 Enterprise and VDA device licenses include the rights to use MDOP.

Windows local virtualization rights

The Windows local virtualization rights benefit is useful in specific scenarios – perhaps developers and testers who need to have several different environments set up to work on different projects. This SA benefit is available when Windows 10 Enterprise licenses are purchased and allows the user to have up to four virtual machines running Windows 10 Enterprise locally on their device. It's also available when VDA licenses are assigned to a device with a Qualifying Operating System.

Windows To Go

With a Windows To Go deployment, an employee is given a USB drive which contains their corporate desktop and when they insert it into a machine their personal desktop is available to them. This is a way of rolling out standard desktops to users without having to set up a Virtual Desktop Infrastructure and it's possibly been attractive because of that. Technically, a Windows To Go USB drive can only be used in a device certified for Windows 7 or later whereas a VDI desktop can be delivered to a device that can't run Windows, like an iPad.

From a licensing perspective, an organization can create up to two USB drives per license, and then those USB drives can be used by any user on any licensed device.

Note that Windows To Go is removed in Windows 10, version 2004 (first available on May 27, 2020) and later operating systems. Microsoft state that this is because Windows To Go doesn't support feature updates and therefore doesn't enable you to stay current. It also requires a specific type of USB that is no longer supported by many OEMs.

Step-up licenses

There are no Step-up licenses available to move between the various Windows 10 licenses that we've covered in this section.

Non-renewal of Software Assurance

If the SA is not renewed on a Windows 10 Enterprise license, then the Windows 10 Enterprise Semi-Annual Channel release must be uninstalled on the licensed device. If the original license was a perpetual license, then a customer can choose to install the version of the Windows 10 Enterprise Long-Term Servicing Channel that was available at the time the SA lapsed.

Extended Security Updates

Windows 7 reached the end of its support lifecycle on January 14, 2020, which means that regular security updates are no longer programmatically provided. However, customers who need to continue running Windows 7

Professional or Windows 7 Enterprise can purchase Extended Security Updates (ESU) subscriptions.

The Extended Security Updates will be available for three years starting from January 2020 and the licenses are labelled "1st year", "2nd year" and "3rd year". To cover your desktops for these security updates for the period between January 2020 and January 2021 you would purchase the "1st year" licenses, and to continue covering your desktops this year you would purchase the "2nd year" licenses. Note that if you had decided to live dangerously during 2020 and didn't purchase any ESU licenses, you would need to purchase both the "1st year" and "2nd year" licenses if you decided to protect your desktops in the middle of 2021.

There are no minimum purchasing requirements for the ESUs, and they can be purchased for devices regardless of how the Windows 7 operating system was (legally) acquired – through a Volume Licensing agreement or through OEM, for example. Customers can acquire these Windows 7 ESUs through an Enterprise Agreement or through CSP.

There is, however, another flavor of the ESU subscription available exclusively for Enterprise Agreement customers. It's called the Windows 7 ESU for Microsoft 365 and may only be assigned to devices meeting one of the following requirements:

- Active Software Assurance for Windows, or
- Used exclusively by users licensed with Windows 10 Enterprise E3/E5, VDA E3/E5 or Microsoft 365 E3/E5/F3 User SLs

In the same way as for the regular ESUs, these Windows 7 ESU for Microsoft 365 subscription licenses may only be assigned to devices also licensed with ESUs for prior years.

Note that if organizations choose to run Windows 7 desktops using the Windows Virtual Desktop service, then Extended Security Updates are included free of charge.

Availability of Windows 10 licenses

Much as I have hesitated in this book to reproduce the tables available at the Product Terms site, the availability of Windows device licenses is pretty tricky to fathom with all the User SLs mixed in, and so here's a summary. The gray tick indicates that the VDA license is not available through the Open License program:

	OEM	Open License MPSA Select Plus	Open Value EA	CSP
Windows 10 Pro	✔	✔		
Windows 10 Enterprise LTSC 2019		✔		✔
Windows 10 Enterprise		✔	✔	
VDA		✔ (gray)	✔	

Figure 38: Windows 10 device license availability

OFFICE 2019

Office 2019 is the Microsoft suite of desktop productivity tools and is a cost-effective way for organizations to license all of these products.

Licensing Office 2019

Office 2019 is licensed by device: a license is assigned to a device and the software is licensed to be used on that device. Office licenses are a special type of license called a **Suite** license. This means that a license is assigned to a device and then all of the Office products must be installed on that single device rather than being split across a number of devices.

Office 2019 is available in several different editions for the PC. Office Standard 2019 and Office Professional Plus 2019 are available to customers through the Volume Licensing agreements and CSP, with the main difference product-wise between these editions being the inclusion of the end-user database solution, Access, in the Professional Plus edition. Office Professional 2019 is the version of Office which is available pre-installed on a new PC via the OEM channel.

There's a single edition of Office for the Mac called Office 2019 for Mac Standard, available through the Volume Licensing agreements with the exception of the EA, and CSP.

Multiple installation rights

It's probably not a requirement that many customers have, but when you assign an Office license to a device then you are allowed to install the Office software as many times as you want to on that licensed device.

Portable use rights

When Office is acquired through some Volume Licensing agreements or CSP then portable use rights for Office are available; if a customer has purchased an Office license for a device, then he is also allowed to install Office on a second portable device for the exclusive use of the main user of the originally licensed device. Note that this is not a way to reduce the licenses required in all situations; customers wouldn't be compliant, for example, if they used portable use rights to license the use of Office on a portable device for a second user. Note also that where there is a requirement within a Volume Licensing agreement to license Office on an organization-wide basis, these rights are not available.

Licensing Office in RDS and VDI scenarios

Another right that is granted when an Office license is acquired through a Volume Licensing agreement or CSP is the right to install Office on a server and use it from there. This means that both RDS scenarios, where Office runs on the server, and VDI scenarios, where Office runs in a virtual desktop on the server, are supported.

Although Office is not installed on the device, an Office license does need to be assigned to each device that will access Office in either type of scenario.

The server where Office is running could be either one that the customer itself owns and manages, or one owned and managed by an Authorized Outsourcer – see page 16. Assuming that the VDI server is a Microsoft one, then both scenarios use Windows Server 2019 and Remote Desktop Services, and thus each user or device also needs a Windows Server 2019 CAL and an RDS 2019 CAL. Windows 10 Enterprise licenses are also required for the VDI scenario – see page 102.

Roaming Rights are available when a customer buys Software Assurance with Office Standard or Professional Plus 2019 licenses through a Volume Licensing agreement. They are useful when Office 2019 is installed on and run from a server in a Remote Desktop Services deployment and users need to access it from third-party owned devices when they're outside the corporate premises. Theoretically, every machine that accesses Office via RDS needs to be licensed with an individual Office license and if users use multiple devices this clearly has the potential to be extremely expensive and/or impossible to license. Roaming Rights relax this condition and give the primary user of the device licensed with Office Standard or Professional Plus

2019 and SA the rights to access Office 2019 through RDS on any third party-owned device outside of the corporate premises.

Work at Home licenses

Work at Home licenses are available for all three editions of Office 2019, and these licenses allow the primary user of a licensed device to install and use the Work at Home software on one device outside of the customer's premises – for example at the user's home. It's probably obvious, but a user of a device licensed for Office Standard 2019 may only use the Work at Home for Office Standard 2019 software, and likewise for the other editions.

The Work at Home licenses are only available through some of the Volume Licensing agreements – as usual, check out the Product Terms site for specifics.

Home Use Program

The Home Use Program has been a popular SA benefit over the years allowing users to purchase Office 2019 at a heavily discounted rate for use at home. Back in 2018/2019 (depending on geography) the rules were changed, and now if a customer has purchased Software Assurance on all their Volume Licensing licenses that qualify for the Applications pool (Office, Project, Visio etc.) then any employee in the organization is eligible to purchase a discounted subscription for Microsoft 365 Family or Microsoft 365 Personal through the Home Use Program website. Even if the employee purchasing the subscription leaves the organization, they may continue to renew it at the discounted rate for as long as they wish to.

Office for the web and Office Online Server

Office for the web is the name for the Microsoft-hosted browser-based versions of Word, PowerPoint, Excel and OneNote. The experience is very similar to the familiar desktop products although there is less functionality available. Office Online Server allows organizations to deliver these browser-based versions of the Office products from their on-premises servers.

If a device is licensed with Office Standard 2019 or Office Professional Plus 2019 licenses with Software Assurance, then that device can be used by any user to access both Office for the web and Office Online Server to edit documents. The primary user of the licensed device, however, can edit documents in Office for the web or Office Online Server from any device.

Downgrade and down-edition rights

Downgrade rights for Office are available if licenses are purchased through a Volume Licensing agreement or CSP. So, if a customer buys a license for Office Professional Plus 2019 then they can install Office Professional Plus 2016 if that suits their business needs better. Note however that there are NO down-edition rights for Office; this means that a license for Office Professional Plus 2019 does NOT permit you to install Office Standard 2019 in its place.

Software Assurance

Software Assurance may be added to Office 2019 licenses acquired through a Volume Licensing agreement or OEM. If the licenses have been acquired through a Volume Licensing agreement then Software Assurance must be added at the time of purchase, and if Office has been purchased pre-installed then it must be added within 90 days of the purchase of the device. Note that Software Assurance can only be purchased through a Volume Licensing agreement so an organization would need to have an active agreement to make SA purchases through.

There's one other quirk to know about SA; when you add SA to an OEM Office Professional 2019 license you actually add Office Standard 2019 SA within the Volume Licensing agreement.

Step-up licenses

There is a Step-up license available for customers with active Software Assurance on their Office Standard licenses to move to Office Professional Plus.

Availability of Office 2019 licenses

The purpose of this book is not to reproduce anything you could easily find at the Product Terms site, but Office 2019 availability is tricky to get straight in your head, so here's the summary. Note that "OW" means Organization-Wide, and the orange tick indicates that the product is an Enterprise Product and must be licensed for every device. See page 127 to find out about Enterprise Products in an EA, and page 156 for how they work in Open Value.

	Open License MPSA Select Plus	Open Value non OW	Open Value OW OVS	EA	CSP
Office Standard 2019 license only	✔				✔
Office Standard 2019 license with SA	✔	✔	✔		
Office Professional Plus 2019 license only	✔				✔
Office Professional Plus 2019 license with SA	✔	✔	✔	✔	
Office 2019 for Mac Standard license only	✔				✔
Office 2019 for Mac Standard license with SA	✔	✔	✔		

Figure 39: Office 2019 license availability

VISIO 2019

Licensing Visio 2019

There are two editions of Visio 2019: Standard and Professional, where the primary difference between the editions is the kind of drawings you can create. With Standard edition you can create business diagrams, flowcharts and organization charts, and with Professional edition you can additionally create advanced diagrams such as engineering schematics, floor plans, network layouts, and process diagrams. Both editions are licensed by device.

Multiple installation rights

When you assign a Visio license to a device then you are allowed to install the Visio software as many times as you want to on that licensed device.

Portable use rights

Portable use rights for Visio Standard/Professional are available; if a customer has purchased a Visio license for a device, then they are also allowed to install Visio on a second portable device for the exclusive use of the main user of the originally licensed device. Note that this is not a way to reduce the licenses required in all situations; customers wouldn't be compliant, for example, if they used portable use rights to license the use of Visio on a portable device for a second user.

Downgrade and down-edition rights

Customers with Visio 2019 Standard licenses may use any previous version of Visio Standard, and customers with Visio 2019 Professional licenses may use any previous version of Visio Professional. There are no down-edition rights, so Visio Professional customers may not install Visio Standard.

Home Use Program

Organizations that purchase Visio Standard or Professional licenses with Software Assurance are eligible for the Home Use Program. This entitles the user of the licensed device to purchase Visio 2019 Professional HUP, at a very cost-effective rate, for use on one device for their use at home. If the user leaves the organization or they are no longer a user of the licensed device, or the underlying Software Assurance expires, then the HUP license expires.

Licensing Visio in RDS and VDI scenarios

When customers purchase a license for Visio Standard or Professional they are entitled to install Visio on a server and use it from there. This means that both RDS scenarios, where Visio runs on the server, and VDI scenarios, where Visio runs in a virtual desktop on the server, are supported.

Roaming Rights are also available when a customer buys Software Assurance with Visio 2019 Standard or Professional licenses. Licensing Visio in RDS and VDI scenarios works in exactly the same way as for Office 2019 which is described on page 108.

Step-up licenses

There is a Step-up license available for customers with active Software Assurance on their Visio Standard licenses to move to Visio Professional.

Availability of Visio 2019 licenses

Visio 2019 Standard and Professional licenses are available with or without Software Assurance through the Volume Licensing agreements, and without Software Assurance only through the Cloud Solution Provider program. As usual, check out the Product Terms website for specifics.

PROJECT 2019

Licensing Project 2019

There are two editions of Project 2019: Standard edition is aimed at individual project managers, and the Professional edition is part of a more comprehensive project management solution integrating with Project Server 2019. Both editions are licensed by device.

Multiple installation rights

When you assign a Project license to a device then you are allowed to install the Project software as many times as you want to on that licensed device.

Portable use rights

Portable use rights for Project Standard/Professional are available; if a customer has purchased a Project license for a device, then he is also allowed to install Project on a second portable device for the exclusive use of the main user of the originally licensed device. Note that this is not a way to reduce the licenses required in all situations; customers wouldn't be compliant, for example, if they used portable use rights to license the use of Project on a portable device for a second user.

Downgrade and down-edition rights

Customers with Project 2019 Standard licenses may use any previous version of Project Standard, and customers with Project 2019 Professional licenses may use any previous version of Project Professional. There are no down-edition rights, so Project Professional customers may not install Project Standard.

Home Use Program

Organizations that purchase Project Standard or Professional licenses with Software Assurance are eligible for the Home Use Program. This entitles the user of the licensed device to purchase Project 2019 Professional HUP, at a very cost-effective rate, for use on one device for their use at home. If the user leaves the organization or they are no longer a user of the licensed device, or the underlying Software Assurance expires, then the HUP license expires.

Licensing Project in RDS and VDI scenarios

When customers purchase a license for Project Standard or Professional they are entitled to install Project on a server and use it from there. This means that both RDS scenarios, where Project runs on the server, and VDI scenarios, where Project runs in a virtual desktop on the server, are supported.

Roaming Rights are available when a customer buys Software Assurance with Project 2019 Standard or Professional licenses. Licensing Project in RDS and VDI scenarios works in exactly the same way as for Office 2019 which is described on page 108.

Step-up licenses

There is a Step-up license available for customers with active Software Assurance on their Project Standard licenses to move to Project Professional.

Availability of Project 2019 licenses

Project 2019 Standard and Professional licenses are available with or without Software Assurance through the Volume Licensing agreements, and without Software Assurance only through the Cloud Solution Provider program. As usual, check out the Product Terms website for specifics.

SOFTWARE ASSURANCE

Customers who buy Software Assurance with their licenses are entitled to a whole host of benefits giving them more flexibility in deploying their software. Different products have different benefits associated with them and I think it's easiest to explain the Software Assurance benefits in the context of the product, and that's what I've done in all the individual product sections that precede this Software Assurance section. However, it's also useful to have a summary of all the most useful benefits and that's what this section does; you'll find the benefits listed on the following pages with references showing where you can find more information if you need it.

Managing Software Assurance Benefits

Software Assurance benefits are allocated automatically to organizations as they buy licenses through their Volume Licensing agreements. Customers then manage these benefits through one of the Volume Licensing portals by choosing individuals in their organization to be Benefits Administrators. The portal shows how many of each benefit an organization has been allocated, and it's also where the benefits are activated (where required) and assigned.

The Volume Licensing Service Center (VLSC) is used for all of the agreements except the MPSA which uses a different portal, the Microsoft Business Center (MBC).

Software Assurance and CSP

Software Assurance is not available in CSP. However, some of the benefits that we think of as Software Assurance benefits are available to customers who buy Server Subscriptions for Windows Server and SQL Server through CSP. Server Subscriptions for Windows Server and SQL Server are covered on pages 29 and 58 respectively.

General SA benefits

These are the benefits that generally apply to all products purchased through all programs.

Benefit name	Description
New version rights *See page 15*	Rights to use a newer version of a product released during the term of an agreement **Applies to:** All products
Step-up licenses *See page 16*	Rights to move from a lower edition of a product to a higher edition by just paying the difference in the license with SA price **Applies to:** Windows Server 2019 Standard, System Center 2019 Standard, SQL Server 2019 Standard, BizTalk Server 2020 Branch/Standard, Exchange Server 2019 Standard, Core CAL Suite, Office Standard 2019, Visio Standard 2019 and Project Standard 2019
Spread payments *See pages 129, 146, 154 and 157*	Rights to make annual payments rather than one upfront payment for license with SA purchases **Applies to:** All products in all agreements except the Open License program

SA benefits for Windows

These benefits are available to customers when they purchase licenses for Windows 10 or VDA. Note that Windows 10 E3/E5 and VDA E3 User SLs purchased through CSP do not include these benefits.

Benefit name	Description
Windows 10 Servicing Channels *See page 100*	Rights to choose either the Semi-Annual Channel or the Long-Term Servicing Channel to receive feature updates **Applies to:** Windows 10 Enterprise and VDA device licenses and Windows 10 Enterprise E3/E5 and VDA E3/E5 User SLs
Microsoft Desktop Optimization Pack (MDOP) *See page 103*	A collection of tools to help organizations deploy and manage their desktops **Applies to:** Windows 10 Enterprise and VDA device licenses and Windows 10 Enterprise E3/E5 and VDA E3/E5 User SLs
Windows To Go *See page 104*	Rights to deploy corporate desktops via a USB drive **Applies to:** Windows 10 Enterprise and VDA device licenses and Windows 10 Enterprise E3/E5 and VDA E3/E5 User SLs

SA benefits for the Office applications

These benefits are available to customers when they purchase licenses with Software Assurance for the applications products. Note that customers buying 2,000 or more licenses for Microsoft 365 E3/E5 are entitled to the Home Use Program benefit outside of Software Assurance – see page 194.

Benefit name	Description
Home Use Program *See pages 109, 113 and 115*	Allows end users to purchase discounted Microsoft 365 Family/Personal subscriptions and/or Visio/Professional 2019 HUP software **Applies to:** Office Standard/Professional Plus 2019, Visio Standard/Professional 2019 and Project Standard/Professional 2019
Roaming Rights *See page 108*	Allows the primary user of a device licensed with application licenses and SA to access the application delivered via RDS on any third party-owned device outside the corporate premises **Applies to:** Office Standard/Professional Plus 2019, Visio Standard/Professional 2019 and Project Standard/Professional 2019
Office for the web and Office Online Server *See page 109*	Office for the web gives access to Microsoft-hosted browser-based versions of the Office applications. Office Online Server allows organizations to deliver the experience from their own on-premises servers **Applies to:** Office Standard/Professional Plus 2019

SA benefits for server deployment

These benefits are available to customers when they buy licenses with Software Assurance for the server products. Some of these benefits are available to customers buying Server Subscriptions for Windows Server and SQL Server outside of Software Assurance – see pages 29 and 58 respectively.

Benefit name	Description
Failover server rights *See page 53*	Rights to configure a product to provide redundancy so that if one server fails, its processing will be picked up, recovered, and continued by another server **Applies to:** SQL Server 2019 and Dynamics 365 for Operations Server
Disaster Recovery rights *See page 26*	Rights to deploy the software on a cold backup server for the purposes of Disaster Recovery **Applies to:** All server products
Windows Server Semi-Annual Channel releases *See page 27*	Rights to install and use the Semi-Annual Channel release of Windows Server **Applies to:** Windows Server 2019
System Center Current Branch *See page 37*	Rights to install and use the Current Branch option of System Center products **Applies to:** System Center 2019
Extended Security Updates *See pages 28 and 56*	Rights to purchase Extended Security Updates for on-premises deployments of Windows/SQL Server 2008/2008 R2 **Applies to:** Windows Server 2019 and SQL Server 2019

SA benefits for additional products and services

These benefits are available to customers when they buy licenses with Software Assurance for the server products. Some of these benefits are available to customers buying Server Subscriptions for Windows Server and SQL Server outside of Software Assurance – see pages 29 and 58 respectively.

Benefit name	Description
Power BI Report Server *See page 57*	Rights to run Power BI Report Server to publish Power BI reports in an on-premises environment with no further licenses required for users to view the reports **Applies to:** SQL Server 2019 Enterprise Core licenses
Machine Learning Server *See page 58*	Rights to run Machine Learning Server for Windows, Linux or Hadoop **Applies to:** SQL Server 2019 Enterprise Core licenses
Exchange Online Voice Mail Service *See page 71*	Rights to use the Exchange Online Voice Mail Service to access voice messages from Outlook **Applies to:** Exchange Server 2019
Unified Service Desk *See page 84*	Rights to install Unified Service Desk to give call center agents a unified view of customer data **Applies to:** Dynamics 365 Server

SA benefits for virtualization

These SA benefits allow additional virtualization rights for organizations deploying server products and Windows 10. Note that Windows 10 E3/E5 and VDA E3 User SLs purchased through CSP do not include these benefits.

Benefit name	Description
Unlimited virtualization rights *See page 46*	Available when a physical server is completely licensed with Enterprise Core licenses with Software Assurance **Applies to:** SQL Server 2019 and BizTalk Server 2020 Enterprise Core licenses
License Mobility across Server Farms *See page 49*	Relaxes the 90-day license reassignment rule so that virtual machines may move freely around a server farm and the server licenses may be reassigned as required **Applies to:** SQL Server 2019, BizTalk Server 2020, Project Server 2019, Exchange Server 2019, SharePoint Server 2019, Skype for Business Server 2019, Dynamics 365 for Operations Server and Azure DevOps Server 2020 **Notable exceptions:** Windows Server 2019 and System Center 2019
Virtual Desktop Access *See page 102*	Rights to create, store and run virtual desktops on a server in a Virtual Desktop Infrastructure **Applies to:** Windows 10 Enterprise and VDA device licenses and Windows 10 Enterprise E3/E5 and VDA E3/E5 User SLs
Windows Local Virtualization rights *See page 103*	Allows a user to install and use up to four virtual machines running Windows 10 Enterprise on his local device **Applies to:** Windows 10 Enterprise and VDA device licenses and Windows 10 Enterprise E3/E5 and VDA E3/E5 User SLs

SA benefits for the cloud

These SA benefits allow an organization flexibility to use their licenses in Azure and sometimes in a partner's infrastructure. Some of these benefits are available to customers buying Server Subscriptions for Windows Server and SQL Server outside of Software Assurance – see pages 29 and 58 respectively.

Benefit name	Description
Azure Hybrid Benefit *See page 343*	Rights to assign server licenses to Azure to license the software components of Azure virtual machines **Applies to:** Windows Server 2019 and SQL Server 2019
License Mobility through SA *See page 350*	Rights to assign server licenses to a partner's infrastructure, or to Azure, to license the software components of virtual machines **Applies to:** System Center 2019, SQL Server 2019, BizTalk Server 2020, Project Server 2019, Exchange Server 2019, SharePoint Server 2019, Skype for Business Server 2019, Dynamics 365 for Operations Server, and Azure DevOps Server 2020 **Notable exceptions:** Windows Server 2019
Disaster Recovery rights in Azure *See page 53*	Rights to run a passive secondary server for Disaster Recovery in Azure **Applies to:** SQL Server 2019

SA benefits for training and support

The benefits in this category have decreased in recent years due to the availability of public resources like Microsoft Learn, for eLearning, and the Microsoft docs documentation for a wealth of technical information. Training Vouchers and Planning Services are nearing their full retirement in December 2021, and the way support is provided will undergo some changes in 2023.

Benefit name	Description
CustomerSource *See page 84*	Rights to a secure site that gives access to resources such as unlimited training courses and support via the Knowledge Base **Applies to:** Dynamics 365 Server and Dynamics 365 for Operations Server
24x7 Problem Resolution Support	Provides web-based or phone support to solve problems relating to Microsoft products **Applies to:** All server products
Training Vouchers	Training Vouchers are exchanged with Microsoft Learning Partners for technical training courses From February 1, 2021, customers cannot accrue further Training Vouchers but may redeem existing vouchers through December 2021
Planning Services	Planning Services are delivered by certified partners to help organizations to plan for the deployment of Microsoft products From February 1, 2021, customers cannot accrue further Planning Services days but may redeem existing vouchers through December 2021

BUYING ON-PREMISES PRODUCTS: EA

The Enterprise Agreement is aimed at larger customers who are prepared to make a commitment when buying the on-premises products under one of three enrollments that sit under the EA.

One of the good things about an Enterprise Agreement, from a customer perspective, is that Microsoft have a number of standard amendments that allow a change in the terms and conditions for greater flexibility. These amendments, and other concessions, are completely at Microsoft's discretion and may not be offered to every customer so I haven't made any reference to them in this section. However, if you've heard about an EA that appears to override the rules I've laid out in this section, then that's probably the reason for it.

Enterprise Enrollment

An Enterprise Enrollment is aimed at customers with more than 500 devices who are prepared to make a commitment to the desktop products.

Product availability

Licenses for the vast majority of on-premises products are available through an Enterprise Enrollment. Exceptions include:

- Products aimed at smaller customers such as Windows Server 2019 Essentials
- License-only offers such as Visual Studio Professional 2019
- Individual components of the Core CAL Suite
- Office Standard 2019; customers wanting to purchase Office must commit to Office Professional Plus 2019 enterprise wide

On the following page there's a summary of the broad categories of products that are available through an Enterprise Enrollment. As usual, check out the Product Terms site for specifics.

Products			
Windows 10	✔	SQL Server	✔
Office 2019	✔	BizTalk Server	✔
Windows Server	✔	Dynamics 365 Server	✔
System Center	✔	Dynamics 365 for Operations Server	✔
Office servers	✔	Azure DevOps Server	✔

Figure 40: availability of software products in an Enterprise Enrollment

License type availability

Licenses for on-premises products purchased through the Enterprise Enrollment are perpetual licenses, and Software Assurance is a mandatory purchase, and so these are the license types available:

License types	
Perpetual license only	
Perpetual license with SA	✔
SA renewal	✔
L&SA subscription	
Monthly Subscription	
Server Subscription	

Figure 41: availability of license types in an Enterprise Enrollment

Enterprise-wide commitment

An Enterprise Enrollment for the on-premises products requires a customer to commit to the desktop products – they must count all the **Qualified Devices** or **Qualified Users** in their organization, and then choose an **Enterprise Product** that they are prepared to license for all of these Qualified Devices/Users. They must also meet a minimum of having 500 Qualified Devices or Users.

A Qualified Device is any device that can run Windows Pro locally in a physical or virtual operating system environment or one that's used to access a Virtual Desktop Infrastructure. A customer must count all devices as part of their Qualified Device total unless they qualify for one of the following exceptions:

- A PC that is used as a server
- An Industry Device – one that only runs hotel booking software, for example
- A device that is not managed by the organization

A Qualified User is anyone who uses a Qualified Device.

All of the products that can be purchased through an Enterprise Agreement are grouped together into three product pools: Systems, Applications and Servers. The Enterprise Products also fit into these pools and a customer may choose one Enterprise Product from a single product pool, or one from each pool, which together are known as a platform. Typically, there are pricing benefits associated with committing to the full platform, resulting in lower prices for each component. The Enterprise Products and their associated pools are listed below:

Systems	Applications	Servers
Windows 10 Enterprise device license VDA device license	Office Professional Plus 2019 device license	Core CAL Suite or Enterprise CAL Suite user or device licenses

Figure 42: Enterprise Products and product pools

If you choose the Systems pool you can buy a combination of Windows 10 Enterprise and VDA device licenses making sure, of course, that the total matches the Qualified Device count. Note that Office Standard 2019 isn't an option to choose in the Applications pool – if an organization wants to purchase licenses for this product, then they must use an alternative agreement – the MPSA perhaps.

In the Servers pool customers choose user or device licenses and either the Core CAL Suite or Enterprise CAL Suite to match the declared number of Qualified Users or Qualified Devices.

For any chosen pool, the customer must purchase the same number of licenses as they have Qualified Devices/Users.

Pricing

There are four different price levels available for an Enterprise Enrollment customer, with discounts increasing between the levels. A customer's price level depends on the number of Qualified Devices or Users that they have, as shown below, and is set for the duration of the 3-year term of their Enterprise Enrollment:

Qualified Devices/Users	Price level
500	A
2,400	B
6,000	C
15,000	D

Figure 43: Enterprise Enrollment price levels

Additional Products

Once the Enterprise Products requirement has been met for an Enterprise Enrollment, customers can also choose to purchase licenses for all of the other available on-premises products through their enrollment. These products (Windows Server 2019 Core licenses, Visio 2019 Standard licenses, SQL Server 2019 CALs etc.) are known as Additional Products. Organizations may buy as many, or as few, of these products as they want to.

Price levels for the Additional Products are set by Enterprise Products in the corresponding product pools. For instance, if a customer has chosen the Core CAL Suite as their Enterprise Product and they have 5,000 devices, they are entitled to Level B pricing both for the Core CAL Suite and for any Additional Products that are in the Servers pool. If they haven't purchased any Enterprise Products in the other two pools, then Additional Products in those pools will be at Level A pricing.

Payment

Enterprise Products and Additional Products that are on the initial order for an Enterprise Enrollment are paid for annually. If it's a brand-new Enterprise Enrollment then, for each product, a customer pays a third of the license cost and a year's Software Assurance at the start of each year of the enrollment. If it's a renewal Enterprise Enrollment, then it's just a year's Software Assurance that is paid each year.

True Up orders

If additional Qualified Devices are added during a year, a customer may use the Enterprise Products on those devices and then pay for the licenses at the end of the year through a process known as True Up. A single payment is made for the additional licenses, rather than the spread annual payments which apply to the original number of licenses. The payment consists of the full amount of the license cost and a pro-rated amount for Software Assurance dependent on when in the enrollment term the purchase was made. For example, if an extra license (L) is added during the first year, the customer pays L + (2.5 x SA), if it's added in the second year they pay L + (1.5 x SA), and if it's added in the third year they pay L + (0.5 x SA).

If customers have added licenses for any Additional Products that were on the initial order, then these are trued up in the same way, using the same calculations.

Price protection

Any licenses for Enterprise Products and Additional Products that are on a customer's initial order when they sign the Enterprise Enrollment have fixed pricing for the three years of the enrollment both for the spread annual payments and the True Up payments. This means that a customer knows exactly how much they will pay for the products each year, and how much they will pay if they need to add additional licenses. These prices are recorded in a document known as the Customer Price Sheet, or CPS. If further products are added that were not on the original CPS then the price is taken from the current price list and is paid in full during the month of installation for the 3-year term, using the same calculations as for the True Up prices.

Software Assurance benefits

All Software Assurance benefits are available through an Enterprise Enrollment.

Managing licenses

The Volume Licensing Service Center (VLSC) is used by Enterprise Enrollment customers to manage their licenses, download software, access Volume License Keys, and to manage SA benefits.

At the end of an Enterprise Enrollment

An Enterprise Enrollment has a term of 3 years, at the end of which a customer can decide to renew the enrollment. If they have previously been paying for licenses with SA, they renew the enrollment just paying for the Software Assurance since they now own the licenses and don't need to pay for them again.

They can decide not to renew the Enterprise Enrollment, of course, since they do own the licenses, but note that if they decide to sign another Enterprise Enrollment in the future they wouldn't be able to just pay for the SA, they would need to repurchase licenses and pay for the SA as well.

Enterprise Subscription Enrollment

The Enterprise Subscription Enrollment works in a very similar way to the Enterprise Enrollment and so I've used a similar structure to the Enterprise Enrollment section and indicated where there are differences.

Product availability

The same products are available as for the Enterprise Enrollment as detailed on page 125.

License type availability

Licenses for on-premises products purchased through the Enterprise Subscription Enrollment are non-perpetual licenses, and Software Assurance is always included. Thus, it's only a subscription for a combined License & Software Assurance offer that's available through an Enterprise Subscription Enrollment:

License types	
Perpetual license only	
Perpetual license with SA	
SA renewal	
L&SA subscription	✔
Monthly Subscription	
Server Subscription	

Figure 44: availability of license types in an Enterprise Subscription Enrollment

Enterprise-wide commitment

This works in the same way as for the Enterprise Enrollment, which you can read about on page 127.

Pricing and price protection

The price levels for an Enterprise Subscription Enrollment are the same as for the Enterprise Enrollment, but the price level is not set for the whole of the 3-year enrollment term; it's set at the beginning of each year, dependent on the number of Qualified Devices/Users for that year, which may be more or less than the previous year, since customers have the flexibility of increasing or decreasing the number of their Qualified Devices/Users as circumstances dictate.

This means that on the Customer Price Sheet there are prices set for the Enterprise Products and Additional Products for each of the price levels.

Additional Products

Additional Products for an Enterprise Subscription Enrollment are available in the same way as for the Enterprise Enrollment, and Additional Products on the initial order are paid for annually. However, if more licenses for those Additional Products are added then they are paid for in the month of installation, using the agreed annual prices from the CPS. If licenses for Additional Products that were not on the initial order are required, they are also paid for in the month of installation using prices from the current price list.

Annual Orders

Enterprise Subscription Enrollment customers pay an agreed annual fee at the start of each year for those Enterprise Products and Additional Products which were on their initial order. However, there's no commitment to keep the numbers the same as the initial order, or the previous year, as long as the program minimum of 500 Qualified Devices/Users is maintained.

Software Assurance benefits

All Software Assurance benefits are available through an Enterprise Subscription Enrollment.

Managing licenses

The Volume Licensing Service Center (VLSC) is used by Enterprise Subscription Enrollment customers to manage their licenses, download software, access Volume License Keys, and to manage SA benefits.

At the end of an Enterprise Subscription Enrollment

Customers with an Enterprise Subscription Enrollment don't own any licenses at the end of their 3-year term and thus, if they don't renew the enrollment, they must deinstall the software that they have been using.

Alternatively, they can choose to buy out their licenses which turns them into perpetual licenses for the latest versions of the products. Buy-out prices for their products are generally included on the CPS. A customer must buy out all Enterprise Products, and if there were any Qualified Devices/Users added in the third year of the enrollment then the annual fee must be paid prior to buy out. Any quantity of Additional Products may be bought out. If customers choose the buy-out option, then they can start an Enterprise Enrollment for Software Assurance only.

Server and Cloud Enrollment

In the Server and Cloud Enrollment a customer can make a commitment to either the server products or to Azure. This section covers the server products, and the commitment to Azure is covered on page 387.

Product availability

The same products are available as for the Enterprise Enrollment as detailed on page 125.

License type availability

Licenses for on-premises products purchased through the Server and Cloud Enrollment are perpetual licenses, and Software Assurance is a mandatory purchase. However, there is also a special Monthly Subscription for certain products as well. So, the license types available through a Server and Cloud Enrollment are shown in the table on the next page.

License types	
Perpetual license only	
Perpetual license with SA	✔
SA renewal	✔
L&SA subscription	
Monthly Subscription	✔
Server Subscription	

Figure 45: availability of license types in a Server and Cloud Enrollment

Enterprise-wide commitment

When a customer buys on-premises products through the Enterprise Enrollments they need to make a commitment to the Enterprise Products for a minimum number of desktops and then they can add Additional Products. The Server and Cloud Enrollment is similar: a customer makes a commitment to one of three server components for a minimum number of licenses, and then can buy Additional Products as needed.

The table on the next page shows the three components, the products that fall under them, and the required minimums for those products. An organization looks at all of the licenses they have in use across their installed base (acquired through any licensing program) and then commits to purchase Software Assurance for all of those licenses for any one (or more) of the components.

Components	Application Platform	Core Infrastructure	Developer tools
Products	SQL Server + optionally BizTalk and/or SharePoint	Windows Server and System Center	Visual Studio
Minimums	**SQL:** 5 Server licenses and 250 CALs, or 50 Core licenses **SharePoint:** 5 Server licenses **BizTalk:** 24 Core licenses	Core Infrastructure Server Suite: 400 Core licenses	Visual Studio Enterprise with MSDN, Visual Studio Enterprise with GitHub Enterprise, and/or MSDN Platforms: 20 user licenses

Figure 46: SCE server components

Application Platform component

As you can see in the table above, the Application Platform component centers around SQL Server. If a customer wants to commit to SQL Server with Software Assurance across their estate, then the SCE is a great mechanism for them to purchase it through. If they are prepared to commit to SQL Server then they can optionally add on SharePoint and/or BizTalk Server too, but do note that they wouldn't be able to sign an SCE with just SharePoint or BizTalk Server.

I think the best way of learning about the SCE is to take a sample customer scenario so let's first consider Cyan Ida's Pharmacy who have SQL Server 2012 and 2016 and are interested in upgrading their whole estate to SQL Server 2019. This makes them an ideal candidate for the SCE, so how would they go about signing an SCE? The first stage is to document the installed base of

SQL Server, and Cyan Ida's Pharmacy's current SQL Server estate is shown below:

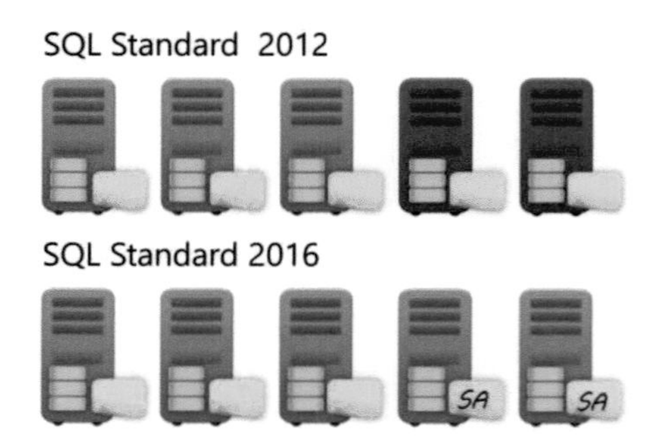

Figure 47: Cyan Ida's Pharmacy – SQL Server estate

You can see that they have a mixed estate of SQL Server Standard 2012 and 2016 and it's licensed with the Server/CAL model. All of the servers have licenses assigned to them, but only two of the SQL 2016 servers have licenses with active Software Assurance. Two of the SQL 2012 servers (shown in red) are currently running SQL Server but will be retired within the next 18 months.

Once the installed base is calculated, Cyan Ida's Pharmacy must sign their SCE with an initial order which covers these baseline licenses with Software Assurance. They have a choice of three types of licenses in order to cover each server with SA: either SA renewal, a new license with Software Assurance (L&SA), or a special Monthly Subscription license.

They should renew the SA for the two servers with active SA, and then purchase L&SA or Monthly Subscription licenses for the other servers. The Monthly Subscription licenses are unique to the Server and Cloud Enrollment so let's find out a bit more about these now.

There are subscription licenses available for all of the different SQL Server licenses – so Server licenses, CALs, and Core licenses – and for all of the editions, and purchasing subscription licenses fulfils the requirement for having active SA on licenses. The subscription licenses are MSUs – Monthly

Subscription Units – which means that they show as a monthly price on the price list which makes for easy pro-rating if a customer adds them part way through an enrollment year. As you would expect from the name, a customer never owns a subscription license. Customers may mix and match MSUs with L&SA or SA to cover their entire estate.

Cyan Ida's Pharmacy have a choice of MSUs or L&SA to cover the servers currently without active SA. Which should they choose? Well, price may be a deciding factor for them; if they don't need or want to own perpetual licenses, they may decide to move to the subscription model since these licenses are priced at about 35% of the license price. They have 8 servers that they need to cover with SA, and buying L&SA for all of them could be too high a cost.

Another reason for buying MSUs is that the number of licenses may be reduced during the term of the enrollment. The red shading in the diagram above indicated that the servers were due to be retired in the next 18 months or so. Because they are currently running SQL Server, they must be included in the enrollment and covered with SA, but Cyan Ida's Pharmacy don't need these servers in the long term and so buying L&SA for these servers doesn't make sense if there is a subscription alternative. As long as they buy 12 months' worth of an MSU they can reduce the number of licenses at the next anniversary.

Cyan Ida's Pharmacy do want to own licenses long-term and so they decide to purchase L&SA for most of the servers and MSUs for the 2 servers that will be retired. This means that their initial order will consist of 2 x SQL Standard Server SA, 6 x SQL Standard Server L&SA, and 2 x SQL Standard Server MSU. At the first anniversary they decide whether they want to continue with the MSUs – they can decrease the number to zero if they no longer need the servers, or pay for another 12 months for one or both of the servers depending on their needs.

Note that there's complete flexibility with the SCE – if Cyan Ida's Pharmacy's plans change, they could add more servers and cover them with MSUs part the way through a year. At anniversary they pay for the complete months that the servers were used in the previous year and for 12 months for the following year. Once 12 months have been paid for, the MSUs can be reduced again if required. Equally, since Cyan Ida's Pharmacy actually prefer to own licenses, they could add a server and then true up the L&SA cost at the next anniversary.

Core Infrastructure component

The Core Infrastructure component is all about Windows Server and System Center which must be purchased together as the Core Infrastructure Server (CIS) Suites. The rules are very similar to the Application Platform component that we've just considered, so let's do what we did before and take another company example.

This time it's the Olive Oil Drum Company who have Windows Server and System Center installed on servers throughout their estate. They are prepared to license all their servers with the CIS Suites and so, again, are an ideal candidate for the SCE. You can see their current installed base below, where each single license represents the full 32 Core licenses required to license the server:

Figure 48: The Olive Oil Drum Company – Windows/System Center estate

You can see that all servers have licenses assigned to them – some of which have active Software Assurance, and some of which do not. The Olive Oil Drum Company must do exactly what Cyan Ida's Pharmacy did – make an initial order which covers all Windows Servers with the CIS Suites with active

SA. Again, they have the option to renew SA where there is active SA, and buy L&SA or MSUs where there is not.

Let's take each group of servers separately and see what they should purchase in each case. The top group of servers are currently licensed with the CIS Suite Standard with active SA. Since the SA is active, the Olive Oil Drum Company would simply purchase CIS Suite Standard SA for these servers in their SCE. Note that the servers could be licensed via separate Windows Server and System Center licenses, and they would still be able to purchase the CIS Suite Standard SA.

The second group of servers has 4 servers which have active SA on Windows Server only, and 4 servers which have no active SA and which are due to be retired in the short term – shown again by the red servers. Let's start with those red servers; they need to be licensed with CIS Suite Standard Core licenses – one license for each server – and because they're due to be retired shortly it's probably a good idea to license them with CIS Standard Suite MSUs. The Olive Oil Drum Company could alternatively choose L&SA for these servers of course if that suited their business needs better.

The other 4 servers in this group need to be licensed with CIS Suite Standard licenses too – but are they L&SA or SA licenses? There is active SA on the Windows Server component, but not the System Center one. They can't therefore renew the SA for CIS, but it seems unfair to make them re-purchase the Windows license by forcing them to buy CIS Suite Standard L&SA. The solution to this is a special flavor of the CIS Suites called **CIS Suite Standard without Windows Server License** L&SA. This, in effect, renews the SA on Windows Server and provides L&SA for the System Center component. There's a Datacenter version of this SKU too, and a **CIS Suite Standard without System Center License** version for the exact opposite – when the customer has active SA on System Center but not on Windows Server.

So, the initial order for the Olive Oil Drum Company is as follows: 5 x 32 x CIS Suite Standard SA, 4 x 32 x CIS Suite Standard without Windows Server License L&SA and 4 x 32 x CIS Suite Standard MSU.

Developer Tools component

The Developer Tools component is the last of the three SCE components that all behave in a very similar way. It is, of course, the mechanism for customers to acquire Visual Studio licenses and all of the rules that we've looked at apply to this component too – the installed base must meet the minimum requirements and then all licenses must be covered with SA.

Pricing

The price level of a Server and Cloud Enrollment is set by a qualifying agreement – so if a customer has a Select Plus, MPSA or Enterprise Enrollment in the relevant pool then that price level is applied to the SCE. For example, if a customer has an MPSA at Level B in the Servers pool then they would be eligible for Level B pricing when they signed an Application Platform SCE. If there is no qualifying agreement, then the SCE is set at price level A.

Price protection, payment, Additional Products

When on-premises products are purchased through the SCE, price protection, payment and the way Additional Products are transacted work in exactly the same way as in the Enterprise Enrollment section above.

Software Assurance benefits

All Software Assurance benefits are available through a Server and Cloud Enrollment.

Managing licenses

The Volume Licensing Service Center (VLSC) is used by Server and Cloud Enrollment customers to manage their licenses, download software, access Volume License Keys, and to manage SA benefits.

At the end of a Server and Cloud Enrollment

A Server and Cloud Enrollment has a term of 3 years. If a customer decides not to renew the SCE then they'll need to deinstall any software licensed by MSUs. Otherwise, their options are the same as those for an Enterprise Enrollment customer.

BUYING ON-PREMISES PRODUCTS: MPSA

The MPSA is aimed at customers with more than 250 users or devices and is classed as a transactional agreement since it doesn't require any sort of enterprise-wide commitment. Customers may use an Enterprise Enrollment to buy some of their products on a committed basis, and also have an MPSA to buy licenses on an ad hoc basis.

Product availability

Licenses for the majority of the on-premises products are available through the MPSA. Exceptions include:

- Products aimed at smaller customers such as Windows Server 2019 Essentials
- Dynamics 365 for Operations Server

Here's a summary of the broad categories of products that are available through the MPSA. As usual, check out the Product Terms site for specifics:

Products			
Windows 10	✔	SQL Server	✔
Office 2019	✔	BizTalk Server	✔
Windows Server	✔	Dynamics 365 Server	✔
System Center	✔	Dynamics 365 for Operations Server	
Office servers	✔	Azure DevOps Server	✔

Figure 49: availability of software products in an MPSA

License type availability

Licenses for on-premises products purchased through the MPSA are perpetual licenses. Although Software Assurance is an optional purchase in the MPSA, where SA is always included with the product purchase – System Center, for example – then those licenses must be purchased with SA in the MPSA too. Thus, these are the license types available through an MPSA:

License types	
Perpetual license only	✔
Perpetual license with SA	✔
SA renewal	✔
L&SA subscription	
Monthly Subscription	
Server Subscription	

Figure 50: availability of license types in an MPSA

Purchasing Accounts

The MPSA enables the signing organization and its affiliates to buy under a single agreement. An affiliate may be a business unit, division, or subsidiary as well as a more-than-50%-owned legal entity. Purchasing Accounts allow an organization to structure themselves exactly as they want with regards to purchasing their licenses. Here are some examples:

- Coff E-Learning Solutions operate a centralized purchasing strategy and have a single Purchasing Account through which all licenses are purchased for all departments of the organization to use
- Cerise Estate Management have a head office and lots of branch offices that they want to allow to purchase their own licenses. They

would set up a Purchasing Account for the head office and one for each of the branch offices

- Fandango Fitness have a whole host of subsidiaries that they'd like to allow to purchase under a single agreement to get a better price level. They'll set up a Purchasing Account for the head office and one for each of the subsidiaries

Each Purchasing Account has its own anniversary which is important for alignment of purchases for Software Assurance and Online Services. Price levels dependent on volume are calculated across all Purchasing Accounts.

Points and pools

Every product that Microsoft offers is categorized into one of three product pools, and these pools are key to the MPSA:

- Systems pool (Windows 10 and VDA, for example)
- Applications pool (Office and the Office family products, for example)
- Servers pool (all Server and CAL licenses)

Each product within these pools is assigned a points count and if you go to the Product Terms site and filter by the MPSA then you'll find a Point Value Chart for each product. Here's the one for the Office applications, for example, where you can see the values assigned to the license, the license with SA, and just SA. You can go directly to this page with this link: https://bit.ly/BOKMPSAPoints.

Point Value Chart

The value assigned to a Product used to calculate the volume pricing level applicable to Customer's volume licensing agreement.

Products	License	License and Software Assurance	Software Assurance
Access 2019	1	2	1
Excel 2019	1	2	1
Office Standard 2019	2	3	1
Office Professional Plus 2019	2	4	2

Figure 51: Office applications Point Value Chart

When a customer is working out what licenses they need they should split their "shopping list" of products into these three pools since the program minimums and price levels are dependent on each pool, rather than being aggregated across all pools. This means that a customer could be eligible for the best price level in one pool and a not so advantageous one in another.

Price levels

Points within an MPSA are important since they determine a customer's price level. A customer needs to buy licenses totaling at least 500 points across all Purchasing Accounts in a particular pool each year to be eligible for an MPSA, although they don't have to purchase licenses totaling these points all on their initial order. This entitles them to Level A – the basic level – pricing. The table below shows the different numbers of points that customers have to reach each year to be eligible for that pricing, with Level D offering the best prices to customers.

Points	Price level
500	A
4,000	B
10,000	C
25,000	D

Figure 52: MPSA price levels

The MPSA is targeted at customers with 250 PCs or more and although the program minimums don't refer to a specific number of PCs, if a customer with 250 PCs bought Office for all of those machines at 2 points per license, this would total 500 points – the program minimum.

The price level within an MPSA can change, dependent on orders that are placed within a year. Let's take Coff E-Learning Solutions as our example organization, and see how the price levels work across a number of years for them.

The first order that Coff E-Learning Solutions place is for 1,200 points and this is at Level A pricing. Within the next few months they place further orders, also at Level A pricing, and have now made purchases totaling 3,250 points. Their next order is for 1,000 points and because this means that their total number of points will be over 4,000, they receive Level B pricing for the whole of this order.

At the end of the first year of their agreement they have 4,250 points and there's a price level review which sets their price level for the following year. Because their total number of points fits into the Level B price band they start the second year eligible for Level B pricing. They actually purchased 250 points over the minimum required for Level B and so they carry these points forward to the following year.

What happens next? Well, here are the different things that could happen for Coff E-Learning Solutions during the next year:

- They spend just 500 points in a single order. This order is at Level B pricing. Since their total spend is not eligible for Level B pricing for the following year they are re-levelled down one price level to Level A pricing
- They spend 5,000 points in multiple orders through the year. All orders are at Level B pricing. At the end of the year they have 5,250 points which entitles them to Level B pricing for the next year, with 1,250 points carried over
- They spend 12,000 points in multiple orders through the year. Most of the orders will be at Level B pricing, but the order that takes them over 10,000 points is at Level C pricing. They are eligible for Level C pricing for next year, and carry over 2,250 points

Payment

Payment options for MPSA customers are dependent on whether Software Assurance is purchased with licenses: if you buy licenses without SA then the payment is due in full at the time of software installation, and if you buy licenses with SA then there is the option to spread payments. The MPSA offers a couple of different payment options, but whichever one a customer chooses they always make three payments where the cost of the license and (up to) three years of SA are split between those payments.

Let's take an example to see how the payments work. Cerise Estate Management want to purchase a license with SA for a product where the license cost is $1,000 and the SA is $250 per year. They need to pay the full price of the license, and Software Assurance up to the third Purchasing Account anniversary. So, if it's March and the Purchasing Account anniversary is June, then there are 3 months to the anniversary this year, and then 24 months to the third anniversary. Thus, Cerise Estate Management need to pay for the license and 27 months of Software Assurance, which is $1,000 + (27 x (250/12)) = $1,562.50.

They can choose to make the three payments aligned either to their Purchasing Account anniversary or to the order anniversary. If they choose the Purchasing Account anniversary, then the total figure they must pay is divided by 27, to give $57.87 and they pay 3 lots of this as their first payment, and then 12 lots of this on each of the next 2 Purchasing Account anniversaries.

If they choose to align to the order anniversary, they pay 12 lots of the amount now, and 12 lots 1 year later, and then the remaining 3 lots a year after that.

Price protection

There is no price protection for on-premises products in an MPSA since customers pay for an order at that moment in time at the current pricelist price. The amounts used in the payment schedules described above are taken from the pricelist at the time of order and then remain consistent across the three payments.

Software Assurance benefits

MPSA customers can choose to commit to buying Software Assurance on all licenses in a particular pool (Applications, Systems or Servers) which is known as Software Assurance Membership or SAM. When Training Vouchers and Planning Services were key SA benefits, an MPSA customer had to commit to SAM before they were eligible for these benefits. Today, to be eligible for the Online Services part of the Home Use Program a customer needs to either purchase a minimum number of qualifying licenses or have SAM coverage for the Applications pool.

Managing licenses

The Microsoft Business Center (MBC) is used by MPSA customers to manage their licenses, download software, access Volume License Keys, and to manage SA benefits.

At SA renewal

There's no notion of an MPSA expiring since it's an evergreen agreement, but if customers have purchased licenses with SA, then the SA will be due for renewal at some point (see the **Payment** section above). In common with all of the Volume Licensing agreements, customers can simply renew the 3 years of SA rather than buying the licenses with SA again.

BUYING ON-PREMISES PRODUCTS: SELECT PLUS

In July 2014 the retirement of Select Plus was announced and although this process has not yet been completed there has been no new innovation in this licensing program since then, and new customers cannot sign a Select Plus agreement. This is an older agreement where customers with more than 250 PCs can only purchase perpetual licenses for on-premises products with optional Software Assurance on those licenses.

As a program it works in a very similar way to the MPSA with the same products and license types available, the same notion of points and pools, with the same price levels and SA benefits available.

There are a couple of slight differences: there's nothing called a Purchasing Account although Affiliates work in pretty much the same way, you manage licenses through VLSC rather than the MBC, and there are slightly different calculations used to work out the prorated L&SA payments which, like the MPSA, can be aligned to Affiliate anniversary or order anniversary.

BUYING ON-PREMISES PRODUCTS: OPEN PROGRAMS

Microsoft use the term **Open Programs** to mean a collection of three licensing agreements aimed at smaller organizations: the Open License program (often just called "Open"), Open Value, and Open Value Subscription agreements.

Open License program

The Open License program will retire at the end of December 2021. Licenses for on-premises software purchased through the Open License program are perpetual licenses and thus a customer owns them forever, they just won't be able to purchase more licenses through this agreement. After this date, if they want to purchase licenses without Software Assurance they will purchase them through CSP, and if they do want SA they will use one of the Open Value agreements.

Product availability

Licenses for the vast majority of the on-premises products are available through the Open License program including license-only offers such as Windows 10 Pro and Visual Studio Professional 2019. Dynamics 365 for Operations Server licenses are not available.

There's a summary of the broad categories of products that are available through the Open License program on the next page. As usual, check out the Product Terms site for specifics.

Products			
Windows 10	✔	SQL Server	✔
Office 2019	✔	BizTalk Server	✔
Windows Server	✔	Dynamics 365 Server	✔
System Center	✔	Dynamics 365 for Operations Server	
Office servers	✔	Azure DevOps Server	✔

Figure 53: availability of software products in the Open License program

License type availability

Licenses for on-premises products purchased through the Open License program are perpetual licenses, and Software Assurance is (usually) an optional purchase; products that always include Software Assurance, such as System Center, are only available with SA. So, these are the license types available through the Open License program:

License types	
Perpetual license only	✔
Perpetual license with SA	✔
SA renewal	✔
L&SA subscription	
Monthly Subscription	
Server Subscription	

Figure 54: availability of license types in the Open License program

Minimums

There is a requirement for a minimum of 5 licenses of, for example, Office Professional Plus 2019 to start an Open License agreement although some single licenses are eligible to start the 2-year agreement too. If you go to the Product Terms site and filter by the Open License program you can see **Open Minimum** next to some products which indicates that they qualify to start the agreement on their own. Here's the page for Windows Server which you can go to directly with this link: https://bit.ly/BOKOpenMinimums.

Product	OL	Date Available	Program Attribute
Windows Server 2019 Active Directory Rights Management Services CAL	✔	10/18	
Windows Server 2019 Active Directory Rights Management Services External Connector	✔	10/18	Open Minimum
Windows Server 2019 CAL	✔	10/18	
Windows Server 2019 Datacenter (16-packs of Core Licenses)	✔	10/18	Open Minimum
Windows Server 2019 Datacenter (2-packs of Core Licenses)	✔	10/18	Open Minimum

Figure 55: Windows Server Open Minimums

Payment

Customers pay for licenses in full upfront and there is no option to spread payments across the term of the agreement, even if the customer has purchased the license with Software Assurance.

Price protection

There is no notion of price protection in the Open License program since all licenses are paid for upfront with prices taken from the current price list.

Price levels

There is only one price level in the Open License program.

Managing licenses

The Volume Licensing Service Center (VLSC) is used by Open License agreement customers to manage their licenses, download software, access Volume License Keys, and to manage SA benefits.

At the end of an Open License agreement

If a customer has purchased licenses without Software Assurance through their Open License agreement, then there is no particular action for them at the end of the 2-year agreement since they own these licenses. If, a few months later, they need more licenses without Software Assurance, they can simply start a new Open License agreement and purchase those licenses.

If they have purchased licenses with Software Assurance, then there's the option to renew the Software Assurance by signing a new agreement and since they own the licenses, they will just pay the price for 2 years of SA. If they don't renew the SA then they can use the licenses forever, but if they want to add SA in the future, they can't, and would need to repurchase licenses with SA.

Open Value non Organization-Wide

The 3-year Open Value agreement enables a customer to choose at the time of signing if they want to commit to purchasing licenses organization wide or not. We'll start with looking at how the non Organization-Wide agreement works.

Product availability

Licenses for the vast majority of the on-premises products are available through an Open Value non Organization-Wide agreement.

There's a summary of the broad categories of products that are available on the next page; as usual, check out the Product Terms site for specifics.

Products			
Windows 10	✔	SQL Server	✔
Office 2019	✔	BizTalk Server	✔
Windows Server	✔	Dynamics 365 Server	✔
System Center	✔	Dynamics 365 for Operations Server	
Office servers	✔	Azure DevOps Server	✔

Figure 56: availability of software in an Open Value non Organization-Wide agreement

License type availability

Licenses for on-premises products purchased through the Open Value non Organization-Wide agreement are perpetual licenses, and Software Assurance is always included. This, then, is the summary of the license types available:

License types	
Perpetual license only	
Perpetual license with SA	✔
SA renewal	✔
L&SA subscription	
Monthly Subscription	
Server Subscription	

Figure 57: availability of license types in an Open Value non Organization-Wide agreement

Minimums

There is a requirement for a minimum of 5 licenses of, for example, Office Professional Plus 2019 to start an Open Value non Organization-Wide agreement although some single licenses, are eligible to start the agreement too. If you go to the Product Terms site and filter by the Open Value program you can see **Open Minimum** next to some products which indicates that they qualify to start the agreement on their own. It also shows which products may be purchased without an organization-wide commitment indicated by the **Non-Organization Wide in Open Value** marker. Here's the page for Windows Server which you can go to directly with this link: https://bit.ly/BOKOVMinimums.

Product	OV/OVS	Date Available	Program Attribute
Windows Server 2019 Active Directory Rights Management Services CAL	✓	10/18	Non-Organization Wide in Open Value
Windows Server 2019 Active Directory Rights Management Services External Connector	✓	10/18	Open Minimum,Non-Organization Wide in Open Value
Windows Server 2019 CAL	✓	10/18	Non-Organization Wide in Open Value
Windows Server 2019 Datacenter (16-packs of Core Licenses)	✓	10/18	Open Minimum,Non-Organization Wide in Open Value
Windows Server 2019 Datacenter (2-packs of Core Licenses)	✓	10/18	Open Minimum,Non-Organization Wide in Open Value

Figure 58: Windows Server Open Minimums/organization-wide commitment

Payment

For products on the initial order, customers have the choice to pay for licenses upfront, or to make three annual payments where they pay for 1/3 of the license cost and a year of SA each year.

Additional licenses may be purchased at any time during the 3-year agreement and customers pay for the license (L) and Software Assurance for the current and remaining years of the agreement. That means that in the first year, they pay L + (3 x SA), in the second year L + (2 x SA) and in the third year L + (1 x SA). They can choose whether to pay the total cost upfront or spread the payments by making the first payment immediately and subsequent payments on the anniversary of the agreement.

Price protection

There is no price protection available in an Open Value non Organization-Wide agreement – the price for every order is taken from the current price list. However, if the customer opts for spread annual payments these are always for the same amount each year.

Price levels

There is only one price level in the Open Value non Organization-Wide agreement.

Software Assurance benefits

All of the SA benefits are available to customers purchasing through an Open Value non Organization-Wide agreement apart from the ability to purchase From SA licenses which require an organization-wide commitment.

Managing licenses

The Volume Licensing Service Center (VLSC) is used by Open Value non Organization-Wide agreement customers to manage their licenses, download software, access Volume License Keys, and to manage SA benefits.

At the end of an Open Value non Organization-Wide agreement

Open Value non Organization-Wide agreement customers can renew their Software Assurance by signing a new agreement and, since they own the licenses, they will just pay the price for 3 years of SA. If they don't renew the SA then they can use the licenses forever, but if they want to add SA in the future, they can't, and would need to repurchase licenses with SA.

Open Value Organization-Wide

The products and license types available in the Open Value Organization-Wide agreement are exactly the same as for the Open Value non Organization-Wide agreement (see pages 152 and 153), but almost everything else is different, as we shall see.

Organization-wide commitment

An Open Value Organization-Wide agreement requires a customer to commit to the desktop products – they must count all the **Qualified Devices** in their organization, and then choose an **Enterprise Product** that they are prepared to license for all of these Qualified Devices. They must also meet a minimum of having 5 Qualified Devices.

A Qualified Device is any device that can run Windows Pro locally in a physical or virtual operating system environment or one that's used to access a Virtual Desktop Infrastructure. A customer must count all devices as part of their Qualified Device total unless they qualify for one of the following exceptions:

- A PC that is used as a server
- An Industry Device – one that only runs hotel booking software, for example
- A device that is not managed by the organization

These are the Enterprise Products for the Open Value Organization-Wide agreement:

- Windows 10 Enterprise device license
- Office Professional Plus 2019 device license
- Core CAL Suite user or device license, or Enterprise CAL Suite user or device license

Additional Products

Once the Enterprise Products requirements have been met for an Open Value Organization-Wide agreement, customers can also choose to license all of the other available on-premises products as Additional Products.

Organizations may buy as many, or as few, of these products as they want to.

Payment

As with the Open Value non Organization-Wide agreement, for products on the initial order, customers have the choice to pay for licenses upfront, or to make three annual payments where they pay for 1/3 of the license cost and a year of SA each year. If additional licenses are added during the agreement then the payment is exactly the same as for the Open Value non Organization-Wide agreement as detailed on page 154.

Price protection

There is price protection for the Enterprise Products in an Open Value Organization-Wide agreement. If additional licenses for existing Enterprise Products are ordered they must be paid for during the month of first installation and the price will be the same as the initial order.

There is no price protection for Additional Products but, if the customer opts for spread annual payments these are always for the same amount each year.

Price levels

There is only one price level in an Open Value Organization-Wide agreement.

Software Assurance benefits

All of the SA benefits are available to customers purchasing through an Open Value Organization-Wide agreement.

Managing licenses

The Volume Licensing Service Center (VLSC) is used by Open Value Organization-Wide agreement customers to manage their licenses, download software, access Volume License Keys, and to manage SA benefits.

At the end of an Open Value Organization-Wide agreement

An Open Value Organization-Wide agreement customer can renew their agreement by renewing the SA on their Enterprise Products for all of their Qualified Devices. They own these licenses so will just pay for 3 years of SA in the new agreement. If they had Additional Products in the original agreement they can renew the SA on those products too.

If they choose not to renew the agreement then they can use the licenses forever, but if they want to add SA in the future, they can't, and would need to repurchase licenses with SA.

Open Value Subscription

Product availability

Licenses for the vast majority of the on-premises products are available through the Open Value Subscription agreement.

Here's a summary of the broad categories of products that are available through the Open Value Subscription agreement; as usual, check out the Product Terms site for specifics.

Products			
Windows 10	✔	SQL Server	✔
Office 2019	✔	BizTalk Server	✔
Windows Server	✔	Dynamics 365 Server	✔
System Center	✔	Dynamics 365 for Operations Server	
Office servers	✔	Azure DevOps Server	✔

Figure 59: availability of software products in Open Value Subscription

License type availability

Licenses for on-premises products purchased through the Open Value Subscription agreement are non-perpetual licenses, and Software Assurance is always included. Thus, it's only a subscription for a combined License & Software Assurance offer that's available through this agreement:

License types	
Perpetual license only	
Perpetual license with SA	
SA renewal	
L&SA subscription	✔
Monthly Subscription	
Server Subscription	

Figure 60: availability of license types in Open Value Subscription

Organization-wide commitment

An Open Value Subscription agreement requires an organization-wide commitment, and this works in exactly the same way as for the Open Value Organization-Wide agreement detailed on page 156. Again, the minimum number of Qualified Devices to start the agreement is 5.

Up-To-Date discount (UTD)

If a customer is already licensed with a perpetual license for one of the Enterprise Products for the current or previous version, then they are entitled to an Up-To-Date discount. This is just available for the first year and is a 50% discount off the regular price of the Enterprise Product.

Additional Products

Once the Enterprise Products requirements have been met, OVS customers can choose to license as many, or as few, of the other available on-premises products as Additional Products.

Payment

An annual fee is paid for the Enterprise Products on each anniversary and, if the number of Qualified Devices has decreased, then a customer just pays for the current number of devices for the following year, as long as the program minimum of 5 Qualified Devices is maintained. If a customer has added Qualified Devices during a year, then additional licenses for the Enterprise Products are paid for at the end of the year at anniversary.

Additional Products on the initial order are also paid for at anniversary and may be completely removed at anniversary, if required. If further licenses for Additional Products are ordered during the year, they must be paid for during the month of first installation.

Price protection

There is price protection for both the Enterprise Products and the Additional Products in an Open Value Subscription agreement. If additional licenses for existing products are ordered they will be at the same price as the initial order. If new Enterprise Products or Additional Products are ordered, they are at the current price list price but will be price protected for additional purchases from then on.

Price levels

There is only one price level in an Open Value Subscription agreement.

Software Assurance benefits

All of the SA benefits are available to customers purchasing through an Open Value Subscription agreement.

Managing licenses

The Volume Licensing Service Center (VLSC) is used by Open Value Subscription customers to manage their licenses, download software, access Volume License Keys, and to manage SA benefits.

At the end of an Open Value Subscription agreement

Customers with an OVS agreement don't own any licenses at the end of their 3-year term and thus, if they don't renew the agreement, they must deinstall the software that they have been using.

Alternatively, they can choose to buy out their licenses which turns them into the latest versions of perpetual licenses. If there were any Qualified Devices added in the third year of the agreement, then the annual fee must be paid prior to buy-out. Enterprise Products must be bought out in equal quantities: if a customer has 100 Qualified Devices licensed for Windows and Office, they may buy out 75 Windows and 75 Office licenses but couldn't just buy out the Office licenses. Any quantity of Additional Products may be bought out. If customers choose the buy-out option, then they could sign an alternative agreement for Software Assurance only.

BUYING ON-PREMISES PRODUCTS: CSP

There are two sorts of licenses for the on-premises products that customers can buy through CSP: licenses without Software Assurance for most of the products (see below), and Server Subscriptions for Windows Server and SQL Server.

Product availability

There are a couple of the traditional software products that are not available to be purchased through CSP and those are the ones where the purchase must include Software Assurance. SA is not available in CSP and so customers can't acquire perpetual licenses for System Center, the Dynamics 365 on-premises servers or Azure DevOps Server through this program. Only Windows 10 Enterprise LTSC 2019 is available, hence the gray tick in the Windows section below:

Products			
Windows 10	✔ (gray)	SQL Server	✔
Office 2019	✔	BizTalk Server	✔
Windows Server	✔	Dynamics 365 Server	
System Center		Dynamics 365 for Operations Server	
Office servers	✔	Azure DevOps Server	

Figure 61: availability of software products in the Open License program

License type availability

Licenses for on-premises products purchased through the CSP program are perpetual licenses, and Software Assurance is not available at all. Server Subscriptions are only available for Windows Server and SQL Server. This, then, is the summary of the license types available through CSP:

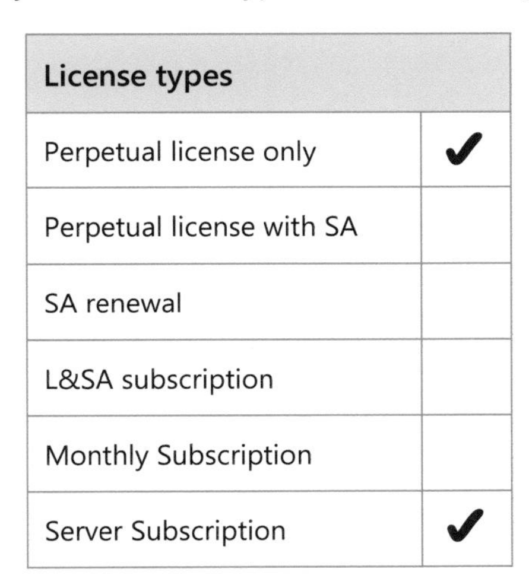

License types	
Perpetual license only	✔
Perpetual license with SA	
SA renewal	
L&SA subscription	
Monthly Subscription	
Server Subscription	✔

Figure 62: availability of license types in the CSP program

Minimums

There are no minimum purchase requirements in CSP – a customer may purchase one or many licenses whenever he chooses.

Purchasing perpetual licenses

Perpetual licenses for software in CSP are paid for in full upfront.

Purchasing Server Subscriptions

Server Subscriptions are available for Windows Server or SQL Server. These licenses, as you might imagine, are subscription licenses and are available for terms of 1 year or 3 years. They are paid for in full upfront.

The following licenses are available as Server Subscriptions:

- Windows Server Standard Core licenses (8-pack)
- Windows Server Device and User CALs
- Windows Server RMS Device and User CALs
- Windows Server RDS User CALs
- SQL Server Standard/Enterprise Core licenses (2-pack)

Price protection

There is no notion of price protection when buying licenses for software in CSP since all licenses are paid for upfront with prices taken from the current price list.

Pricing

There is just a single price level in CSP, and to-customer pricing is entirely decided by the partner.

Deployment benefits

There is no notion of Software Assurance in CSP, but Server Subscriptions include many of the benefits available to SA customers buying Windows Server or SQL Server licenses through the Volume Licensing agreements.

The following benefits are available with Windows Server Subscriptions:

- Azure Hybrid Benefit
- Disaster Recovery rights
- Rights to Semi-Annual Channel releases
- Rights to new versions

The following benefits are available with SQL Server Subscriptions, where the asterisk indicates that the benefit is only available for Enterprise edition:

- Azure Hybrid Benefit
- Unlimited virtualization rights *
- License Mobility across Server Farms rights
- Disaster Recovery rights
- Failover rights
- Rights to Power BI Report Server *
- Rights to Machine Learning Server *
- Rights to new versions

Managing licenses

The Microsoft 365 Admin Center is used by CSP customers to manage their licenses, download software, and to access Volume License Keys. Partners can assist customers with these tasks with some limited access through the Partner Center portal.

Buying through the Microsoft Customer Agreement

Customers buying licenses through CSP accept the terms of the Microsoft Customer Agreement which doesn't expire. A customer owns a perpetual license forever and may continue to deploy the version of the software that they purchased, or take advantage of unlimited downgrade rights if they want to. Server Subscriptions have a term of 1- or 3-years and since there is no auto-renew option, customers simply purchase another Server Subscription at the end of the term.

BUYING ON-PREMISES PRODUCTS: ENTERPRISE MCA

Licenses for on-premises products are not available to be purchased through the Enterprise MCA at this time.

LICENSING ONLINE SERVICES

Use this section to get some general information on how the Online Services products are licensed and then get more detail in the individual product sections that follow.

Licenses for Online Services products

Online Services are generally licensed with User Subscription Licenses (User SLs) with just a few products licensed with Device Subscription Licenses (Device SLs). The licenses are always non-perpetual, just allowing access to the service for as long as the subscription is active.

License reassignment rights

User Subscription Licenses are assigned to individual, named users, and although licenses may be reassigned between users, in common with the on-premises software licenses, this is typically no more than every 90 days.

Versions and editions

With traditional, on-premises software there's the notion of versions and editions: Windows Server 2019 Standard, for example. The version tells us how new the technology is, and the edition tells us how much functionality there is. There's no notion of versions with the Online Services since the technology is constantly updated, but there are still editions with, for example, an Office 365 E3 license allowing access to more functionality than an Office 365 E1 one.

Downgrade and down-edition rights

Downgrade and down-edition rights don't apply to the Online Services.

Online Services plans

These days there are a lot of different Online Services and for some of them you can buy individual licenses – Exchange Online, for example. Often there are different plans which license different amounts of the functionality – Exchange Online Plan 1 and Plan 2, for example. Note that when this is the case you would never buy both Plans 1 and 2 since an Online Services Plan 2 includes all the technology licensed by Plan 1, rather than adding on to it.

So, some licenses for individual Online Services are available, but the majority of customers buy plans which are a collection of Online Services, which may, or may not, be available separately. For example, Office 365 E3 includes Exchange Online Plan 2, which is available separately, as well as Delve and Planner, which are not. There is complete flexibility in mixing the standalone licenses, as well as any of the plans, across an organization.

This section of the book is focused on the licensing of the Online Services rather than specifically which of the dozens of services are included in each plan. However, it is of course something which is useful to know about and, at the time of writing this book (May 2021), Microsoft publish a useful Office 365/Microsoft 365 plan comparison document at this link each month: https://bit.ly/BOKPlanComparisons.

User types

The different Online Services plans licensed by user are each aimed at one of three different user types. Firstly, there are users who work for small and medium businesses. There's always a debate about how big a small and medium business actually is, but it's easy here from a licensing perspective since the plans aimed at SMB users are technically limited to 300 licenses. So, an SMB user is one who works for an organization of less than 300 users and who carries out ordinary tasks for a business of that size.

The second type of user is an enterprise user, and enterprise user plans don't have technical restrictions on the number of licenses. An organization with more than 300 users may have different technology requirements to a small and medium business – it could have more sophisticated security and management needs, or it could need more deployment flexibility, and so the enterprise user plans reflect this.

Now, is it this compartmentalized in reality? Of course not. The SMB and enterprise plans are a good starting point for organizations as they choose the best licenses for their business, but that SMB which needs advanced compliance functionality should consider the enterprise plans, and that organization of 500 users could look at the SMB plans since it's actually each plan type that is limited to 300 users – so they could purchase 250 of two different plans if that suited them.

The final type of user may work for an SMB or a larger organization and is known as a Frontline Worker. A Frontline Worker is someone who does need technology in their role but doesn't spend all day sitting in front of a PC creating PowerPoint presentations or Excel spreadsheets. Examples include doctors, people working in hospitality and retail, or in manufacturing, and you can imagine that these people may need to review documents, check email, or access health and safety information on an intranet, for example. Thus, there are Frontline Worker plans which license these users to access the relevant amount of technology needed for their roles. Note that Frontline Workers were previously known as Firstline Workers.

And, again, organizations can combine all of these plans as they need to.

Types of Online Services User SLs

As I said at the start of this section, the majority of the Online Services are licensed with User Subscription Licenses. However, there are a number of different types, so let's take a look.

Full User SLs

The regular User Subscription License is a Full license which means that there are no prerequisites for purchasing it. If you have users who need to benefit from the services licensed by Office 365 E3 then you just buy Office 365 E3

User Subscription Licenses and assign them to the users. Customers can buy Full User SLs through all Volume Licensing agreements and through CSP.

Add-on User SLs

An Add-on User SL is one for which there IS a prerequisite, when you need a qualifying license to be eligible to purchase the Add-on User SL. You need to make sure that you retain the underlying license to be compliant with having bought the Add-on. There are two types of Add-on User SLs and Microsoft don't differentiate between these in what they call them, but I think it's convenient to give them some names to avoid any confusion.

One type of Add-on is used when a customer has on-premises licenses with active Software Assurance and wants to add on access to corresponding Online Services. For example, a user with a Core CAL Suite license with SA has access to on-premises productivity servers such as Exchange Server and SharePoint Server. If an Office 365 E1 Add-on User SL is also assigned to them then it additionally licenses that user for access to Exchange Online, SharePoint Online and Teams. Let's call this a "**To-cloud Add-on**" since its purpose is to get a user to the cloud. There are just a few of these To-cloud Add-ons available in the Open programs, more in the MPSA, and the complete list of To-cloud Add-on User SLs in an EA. They are not available through CSP. It's worth knowing that Microsoft have these To-cloud Add-on User SLs available to move to the cloud, but always check the Product Terms website and the relevant price lists to check that a particular move in a specific program is supported by an available SKU.

The other type of Add-on we'll call an "**In-cloud Add-on**" since this adds on additional services for users already licensed with an Online Services User SL. One example of this type of Add-on is the Microsoft 365 E5 Security User SL which can only be assigned to a user already licensed with, for example, a Microsoft 365 E3 User SL. These In-cloud Add-ons are typically available through both the Volume Licensing agreements and CSP.

Step-up User SLs

A Step-up User SL is used when a customer has purchased a lower edition of an Online Service but then wants to make use of a higher edition. Let's take Lilac Landscaping Services who purchased Microsoft 365 E3 User SLs for their users through an Enterprise Agreement. They paid for the licenses upfront at the start of the year, but midway through the year some of the users need to use Microsoft 365 E5. The cost of a Step-up User SL is the difference in price between the lower and higher editions, and Lilac Landscaping Services would purchase Microsoft 365 E3 to E5 Step-up User SLs and assign them to the relevant users enabling them to use Microsoft 365 E5.

Step-up licenses are generally available in the EA, with some transition licenses which do the same sort of thing in the MPSA. They're not available in CSP – and not needed – since, to achieve the same thing, a partner would reduce the number of Microsoft 365 E3 licenses and transact some new Microsoft 365 E5 licenses to assign to the users who need to use the additional services.

From SA User SLs

From SA User SLs are special-priced licenses that customers with active Software Assurance can purchase as they move to the cloud. For example, let's take Vermilion Jewellers who have an Enterprise Agreement and have made their enterprise-wide commitment to Windows, Office and CAL Suite licenses. They now want to move to Microsoft 365 E3, and rather than buying the Full User SL, they would be entitled to stop paying for their on-premises licenses with SA and buy a From SA license. This license gives access to the same set of Online Services but is attractively priced to acknowledge that Vermilion Jewellers have made an investment in Software Assurance over the years.

Again, the full range of From SA User SLs is available through the Enterprise Agreement, and these are covered in more detail on page 301. From SA User SLs for the Dynamics products are also available through CSP.

Tenant-level services

A tenant-level service is an Online Service that when it's purchased for any user in the tenant is activated in part or in full for all users in the tenant. Sometimes it's not possible to restrict access to the service for a particular user and so unlicensed users are still technically able to access the service. What happens with the licensing in this situation? Well, you should purchase licenses for those users that you DO intend to benefit from the service. Microsoft has some useful licensing guidance for remaining compliant when using these tenant-level services which you can find here: https://bit.ly/BOKTenantLevelServices.

On-premises use rights

Many of the Online Services User SLs also include rights to access a licensed on-premises server. For example, an Office 365 E3 User SL includes the same rights as an Exchange Standard and Enterprise CAL, a SharePoint Standard and Enterprise CAL and a Skype for Business Standard and Enterprise CAL. The snippet below is from the CAL and ML Equivalency Licenses page on the Product Terms site: here: https://bit.ly/BOKCALEquivalency.

	Office 365 Enterprise		
Servers	**E1**	**E3**	**E5**
Exchange Server 2019 Standard			
Base	X	X	X
Additive		X	X
Exchange Server 2019 Enterprise			
Base	X	X	X
Additive		X	X
SharePoint Server 2019			
Base	X	X	X
Additive		X	X
Microsoft Audit and Control Management Server 2013			
Base		X	X
Skype for Business Server 2019			
Base	X	X	X
Additive (Enterprise)	X	X	X
Additive (Plus)			X

Figure 63: CAL Equivalency Licenses for Office 365

These "CAL Equivalency" rights are for the latest versions of the CALs and can thus be used with any on-premises software version. Customers are entitled to these rights however they purchase their licenses – through an Enterprise Agreement or through CSP, for example.

Some Online Services User SLs also include rights to install on-premises software, and the rights that are included are detailed in the individual product sections that follow. You can use the index to find the on-premises use rights for the particular product you're interested in.

Other types of Online Services licenses

With the Dynamics 365 products there are a couple of further types of Online Services licenses.

Tenant licenses

A tenant license is a single license that is purchased for a tenant and enables the required functionality for the whole of the tenant. Dynamics 365 Marketing is licensed in this way, for example.

Capacity licenses

Most Dynamics 365 licenses include a default entitlement to Dataverse storage, and when additional storage is required, a Capacity Add-on license is purchased. Some Dynamics 365 products are licensed by the number of transactions and, again, Capacity Add-on licenses are available when more transactions are required.

Commitment

The typical commitment to any Online Services license is for 12 months, even though all pricing is monthly. The exception to this is the Enterprise Agreement where the commitment can be up to the next anniversary.

This commitment applies to all of the license types including the Capacity Add-on licenses. For example, imagine a Capacity Add-on which enables 100 transactions per month. If you won't have transactions in some months, do you still need to buy a Capacity Add-on? Indeed you do – you would need to commit to 12 months of the Capacity Add-on and thus would have 100 transactions available each month. Be careful to check on a product-by-product basis whether unused transactions roll over to the next month or not – some do, and some don't.

Buying Online Services

The rules for buying licenses for Online Services are different in each of the Volume Licensing agreements and in CSP, so do check out the section which covers this, starting on page 293.

WINDOWS 10 (USER)

In the on-premises licensing section of this book we cover the licensing of the Windows 10 client when it's licensed by device, and you can find the rules for that on page 99. In this section of the book we look at the rules when Windows is licensed by user, alongside other products licensed with User SLs.

Licensing Windows 10

It's only the Enterprise version of Windows 10 that's available to be licensed with User SLs. There are two editions available: E3 and E5, and the main difference between them is that Windows 10 Enterprise E5 includes Microsoft Defender for Endpoint.

Even when Windows is licensed with User SLs there is still a requirement for a Qualifying Operating System. The licensed user must be the primary user of at least one device with a Qualifying Operating System, and this one device must also be the user's primary work device.

Many users these days may well have a Windows 10 Pro device and that's a Qualifying Operating System through all of the ways to buy Windows 10 Enterprise E3 and E5 User SLs. If a user has a device running an older operating system, perhaps Windows 8 Pro, then the Windows 10 Enterprise E3/E5 User SLs include the rights to upgrade Windows 7, 8 or 8.1 Pro to Windows 10 Pro.

Azure AD-based activation

There's a touch of magic when a user logs in with their Azure Active Directory credentials using a Windows 10 Pro device. If they've been assigned a Windows 10 Enterprise E3/E5 User SL, then the operating system turns from Windows 10 Pro to Windows 10 Enterprise, and all the Windows 10 Enterprise E3/E5 features are unlocked. If the Windows 10 Enterprise E3/E5 User SL is not renewed or is transferred to another user, then the operating system will return to Windows 10 Pro automatically after 90 days. The user may activate and use Windows 10 Enterprise on up to five devices.

Servicing Channels

Windows 10 Enterprise E3 and E5 receive security updates on the second Tuesday of each month. Feature updates are delivered via the **Semi-Annual Channel** twice a year, around March and September. Historically, a Semi-Annual Channel release has been supported for 18 months, but the fall (September) releases have an additional 12 months of servicing for a total of 30 months from the initial release.

The **Windows Insider Program** is another option for businesses running Windows 10 Enterprise E3 or E5. Enrolling devices into the Windows Insider Program provides the IT department with pre-release Windows builds so that they can test features before they become available in the Semi-Annual Channel.

Licensing virtual desktops

As an alternative to installing Windows 10 Enterprise locally, an organization could choose to deploy virtual desktops so that the desktops themselves are running on a server and delivered to a user's device. The licensing for these scenarios depends on how the licenses are acquired (through CSP or a Volume Licensing agreement) and where the virtual desktops are hosted (either on hardware dedicated to the customer, or shared hardware).

There's also another license type that we need to get acquainted with, which is the VDA User SL. It's available in E3 and E5 flavors in the EA and MPSA and as an E3 license in CSP. VDA stands for Virtual Desktop Access and this license is specifically aimed at scenarios where access to a virtual desktop is required, but there's no Qualifying Operating System on the device used by a user. This could be some sort of thin client or an iPad, for example.

There's a useful table in the section starting on page 369 which summarizes the options that a customer has for delivering Windows 10 Enterprise in virtual desktops to their users.

Software Assurance benefits

Windows 10 Enterprise E3 and E5 and VDA E3 and E5 User SLs acquired through a Volume Licensing agreement include the same Software Assurance benefits as the Windows 10 Enterprise and VDA device licenses. These SA benefits are detailed on page 103.

Licenses purchased through CSP never include Software Assurance.

Extended Security Updates

Windows 7 reached the end of its support lifecycle on January 14, 2020, which means that regular security updates are no longer programmatically provided. However, customers who need to continue running Windows 7 Professional or Windows 7 Enterprise can purchase Extended Security Updates (ESU) subscriptions. These are covered in detail on page 104.

Windows 10 in Microsoft 365

Microsoft 365 E3/E5

Customers who acquire Microsoft 365 E3 User SLs have rights to Windows 10 Enterprise E3, and customers with Microsoft 365 E5 have rights to Windows 10 Enterprise E5. The rules for license assignment and Windows use rights are detailed in the Microsoft 365 E3/E5 section on page 190.

Microsoft 365 F3

A Microsoft 365 F3 licensed user also has rights to Windows 10 Enterprise E3 and the rules for license assignment and Windows use rights are detailed in the **Plans for Frontline Workers** section on page 201.

Microsoft 365 Business Premium

Microsoft 365 Business Premium licenses include the rights to Windows 10 Business which is a set of cloud services and device management capabilities that build on Windows 10 Pro. Windows 10 Business is covered in full on page 198.

Step-up licenses

There are a couple of Step-up licenses available for customers who need to move to a higher edition of the software. As usual, check the Product Terms website and the relevant price list for exact availability:

Original license	Step-up User SLs
Windows 10 Enterprise E3	Windows 10 Enterprise E5
VDA E3	VDA E5

Figure 64: Windows 10 Enterprise and VDA Step-up licenses

Add-on licenses (To-cloud)

Customers who have bought a Windows 10 Enterprise device license and have active Software Assurance can purchase Windows 10 Enterprise E3 or E5 Add-on User SLs to "userfy" their Windows 10 licensing. This means in an Enterprise Agreement, for example, that if an Add-on licensed user starts to use an additional device, it would not need to be counted and licensed as a Qualified Device for Windows.

From SA licenses

Customers who have bought a Windows 10 Enterprise device license and have active Software Assurance can purchase Windows 10 Enterprise E3 or E5 From SA User SLs to move to Windows 10 Enterprise E3 or E5. As usual, use the Product Terms site and price lists to check program availability.

Availability of Windows 10 Enterprise licenses

Windows 10 Enterprise E3/E5 and VDA E3 User SLs are available through CSP and the MPSA and EA. Additionally, VDA E5 User SLs are available through the MPSA and EA.

As usual, check out the Product Terms website for specifics.

MICROSOFT 365 APPS

In April 2020, Microsoft renamed Office 365 ProPlus and Office 365 Business to Microsoft 365 Apps for enterprise and Microsoft 365 Apps for business, respectively.

Microsoft 365 Apps User SLs

Both Microsoft 365 Apps for enterprise and Microsoft 365 Apps for business suites are available as User SLs and allow licensed users to install the familiar Office apps of Word, Excel, PowerPoint, OneNote, Outlook, Access and Publisher on up to 5 PCs or Macs. Users may also use the Office Mobile apps on up to 5 tablets and 5 smartphones, and the Office for the web apps through a browser on any device.

The Microsoft 365 Apps are installed locally and users don't need to be connected to the internet to use them. However, licensed users must connect to the internet at least once every 30 days so that the status of their license can be checked. If a license has been removed from a user, or the Microsoft 365 Apps subscription hasn't been renewed, then the apps go into Reduced Functionality Mode. In this mode users can open and view existing files but all features for editing or creating new documents are disabled.

In common with other Online Services labelled with the word "Business", Microsoft 365 Apps for business is limited to 300 users on one tenant.

Update Channels

One of the benefits of the Microsoft 365 Apps compared to a traditional Office Professional Plus 2019 license is that new and updated features are provided on a regular basis. Organizations can control how often users get these new features by choosing an Update Channel.

The **Current Channel** provides feature and non-security updates as soon as they are ready, usually once a month, but on no set schedule. Security updates are provided once a month, on the second Tuesday of the month, and a Current Channel version is supported until the next Current Channel version is released.

The **Monthly Enterprise Channel** provides feature, security, and non-security updates on the second Tuesday of the month, and a Monthly Enterprise Channel release is supported for two months.

The **Semi-Annual Enterprise Channel** is aimed at organizations who want to do extensive testing before they roll out new features. Thus, feature updates are provided twice a year, in January and July, on the second Tuesday of those months. Security and non-security updates happen every month on the second Tuesday, and a Semi-Annual Enterprise Channel release is supported for 14 months.

Licensing shared devices

There are two options for licensing scenarios where users will share devices.

Shared Computer Activation

Shared Computer Activation is used when a user is licensed for Microsoft 365 Apps for enterprise, for example, and needs to log in with their usual credentials and use the apps on a shared device. When Shared Computer Activation is enabled for a device, licensed users can activate the apps on that device without it counting against their limit of installing the apps on up to 5 PCs.

When a licensed user logs on to that shared device and starts one of the Office applications, Microsoft 365 Apps for enterprise contacts the Office Licensing Service to obtain a licensing token. This licensing token is stored on the computer and Microsoft 365 Apps for enterprise is activated for that user. Because the shared computer has to contact the Office Licensing Service, a reliable internet connection is necessary.

Microsoft allow a single user to activate Microsoft 365 Apps for enterprise on a reasonable number of shared computers in a given time period. They don't publish specific limits since they may be subject to change, but expect it to be unlikely that a user will exceed the limits.

Microsoft 365 Apps for enterprise licenses include rights to use Shared Computer Activation, Microsoft 365 Apps for business licenses do not. However, if a customer has acquired Microsoft 365 Business Premium licenses, which include Microsoft 365 Apps for business, then Shared Computer Activation rights ARE included.

Microsoft 365 Apps for enterprise Device SLs

Enterprise Agreement customers also have the option to acquire Microsoft 365 Apps for enterprise Device SLs. In this scenario, a license is assigned to the device that will be used by many users who are not individually licensed for Microsoft 365 Apps for enterprise. These users do not even need an Azure Active Directory account, and anyone with access to the device is able to use the Microsoft 365 Apps on that device without any user-level activation taking place.

Licensing for server-based deployment

Organizations can choose to deploy the Microsoft 365 Apps to a server and to deliver them to a user's desktop from there. They could choose to install Windows locally and just deliver the apps from the server, or to deliver the whole desktop, including Windows and the Microsoft 365 Apps, from the server.

The licensing of the Microsoft Apps in both scenarios is the same and is an option for Microsoft 365 Apps licenses that include Shared Computer Activation rights, as below:

- Microsoft 365 Apps for enterprise
- Office 365 E3/E5
- Microsoft 365 E3/E5
- Microsoft 365 Business Premium

The licensing rules are the same, regardless of how the licenses are acquired, and organizations may deploy the Microsoft 365 Apps via Shared Computer Activation using the following server solutions:

- A customer-owned server, dedicated to them
- A server managed by an Authorized Outsourcer, dedicated to the customer
- Using Azure Dedicated Host
- Using Azure multi-tenant hardware
- Using a QMTH partner's multi-tenant hardware
- Using the Windows Virtual Desktop service

You might notice that the Listed Providers are missing from this list – or rather, the three Listed Providers that are not Microsoft – Alibaba, Amazon, and Google, And, to confirm, the Microsoft 365 Apps licenses can't be used with the infrastructure of these organizations.

Microsoft Teams

The Teams app is installed by default with the Microsoft 365 Apps. Note though, that if you've acquired the Microsoft 365 Apps as a standalone license, you're not licensed for the Teams service, as you are if you acquire a plan like Microsoft 365 E3 which includes both the Teams app and access to the Teams service. You need a license for the Teams service to arrange a meeting, for example. Teams licensing is covered in detail on page 209.

Step-up licenses

There are no Step-up licenses available for either Microsoft 365 Apps for enterprise or Microsoft 365 Apps for business.

Add-on licenses (To-cloud)

There are no To-cloud Add-on licenses available for either Microsoft 365 Apps for enterprise or Microsoft 365 Apps for business.

From SA licenses

Customers with active Software Assurance on their Office Professional Plus 2019 licenses may purchase a Microsoft 365 Apps for enterprise From SA User SL. As usual, use the Product Terms website and price lists to check program availability.

Availability of Microsoft 365 Apps licenses

Microsoft 365 Apps for business is aimed at smaller organizations and licenses are thus only available through CSP and the Open programs, while Microsoft 365 Apps for Enterprise User SLs are available through the Volume Licensing agreements and CSP. The Microsoft 365 Apps for enterprise Device SL is only available through the Enterprise Agreement. As usual, check out the Product Terms website for specifics.

OFFICE 365 PLANS

The Office 365 family consists of hosted versions of the productivity servers (Exchange, SharePoint and Skype for Business – now delivered via Teams) and other related Online Services such as Delve and Planner. It also includes the Microsoft 365 Apps (the familiar Office applications) where these products are installed locally and then managed from the cloud. Organizations can either purchase licenses for the separate services, or a plan which gives access to a variety of services. Licenses for both the individual services and the plans are User SLs.

The table below isn't meant to be an exhaustive list of the differences between the Office 365 plans, but rather to show in overview how they compare to each other.

	Office 365 F3	**Office 365 E1**	**Office 365 E3**	**Office 365 E5**
Install Office apps locally			✔	✔
Use Office mobile apps and Office for the web	✔	✔	✔	✔
Exchange Online	✓	✔	✔	✔
SharePoint Online	✓	✔	✔	✔
Teams	✔	✔	✔	✔
Further Online Services			✓	✔
Advanced security				✔
Advanced Online Services				✔

Figure 65: Office 365 plans comparison

For instance, the Frontline Worker plan (F3) doesn't allow users to install the Office apps but does allow users to use the mobile apps or Office for the web. It gives access to the Teams service (see page 209) and light access to Exchange and SharePoint Online (indicated by the gray tick). Office 365 E1 gives regular access to Exchange and SharePoint Online, and Office 365 E3 allows users to install the Office apps locally. It also gives access to a few more Online Services, although not as many as Office 365 E5 which adds advanced security, and advanced Online Services such as Power BI Pro, Phone System and Audio Conferencing.

Use of the Office apps

Microsoft 365 Apps for enterprise is included in the Office 365 E3/E5 licenses, and all the use rights for the users are exactly the same as described in the **Microsoft 365 Apps** section on page 178.

Step-up licenses

There are a whole host of Step-up licenses available in the EA and/or MPSA allowing customers to step-up from Exchange Online Plan 1 to Office 365 E1 for example. I have only included the Office 365 plan Step-up User SLs below, but if you need to know more about the dozens of other options then you should consult the Product Terms website and the relevant price lists:

Original license	Step-up User SL
Office 365 F3	Office 365 E1 or Office 365 E3
Office 365 E1	Office 365 E3 or Office 365 E5
Office 365 E3	Office 365 E5

Figure 66: Office 365 Step-up licenses

Add-on licenses (To-cloud)

The Office 365 To-cloud Add-on User SLs are mainly available through the Enterprise Agreement but the last row, marked by a * is a special Add-on license only available through Open Value and Open Value Subscription agreements where an organization-wide commitment has been made:

Qualifying license	Add-on User SL
Core CAL Suite User or Device	Office 365 E1
Core CAL Suite User or Device + Office Professional Plus	Office 365 E3 or Office 365 E5
Enterprise CAL Suite User or Device + Office Professional Plus	Office 365 E3 or Office 365 E5
Office Professional Plus	Office 365 E3*

Figure 67: Office 365 To-cloud Add-on licenses

From SA licenses

These are some From SA licenses available to move customers with active Software Assurance from on-premises licenses to Office 365. For example:

Qualifying license	From SA User SL
Core CAL Suite	Office 365 E1
Core CAL Suite / Enterprise CAL Suite + Office Professional Plus	Office 365 E3 or Office 365 E5

Figure 68: Office 365 From SA licenses

On-premises use rights

The Office 365 E1, E3 and E5 plans include rights to access licensed on-premises Exchange, SharePoint and Skype for Business Servers as shown below. These rights are available however a customer has purchased their licenses. There are no on-premises use rights included in Office 365 F3 licenses:

	Office 365 E1	Office 365 E3	Office 365 E5
Exchange Server Standard CAL	✔	✔	✔
Exchange Server Enterprise CAL		✔	✔
SharePoint Server Standard CAL	✔	✔	✔
SharePoint Server Enterprise CAL		✔	✔
Skype for Business Server Standard CAL	✔	✔	✔
Skype for Business Server Enterprise CAL	✔	✔	✔
Skype for Business Server Plus CAL			✔

Figure 69: Office 365 on-premises use rights

Availability of Office 365 plans

The four Office 365 plans are available through the Volume Licensing agreements and CSP, with the exception of Office 365 E5 and F3 which are not available through the Open programs. As usual, check out the Product Terms website for specifics.

EMS PLANS

User licensing for Windows and Office means that a user isn't tied to using a single device, and this is usually considered to be great for their productivity. However, if a user is using more than one device then there's likely to be an increased burden on the IT department that needs to keep the devices and the information that they access secure. The Enterprise Mobility + Security suite ensures users and the devices they use are covered for a range of security and management technologies.

There are two EMS suites – EMS E3 and E5 – which consist of the components shown in the table below. The suites are sold as a single User SL which allows the management of up to 5 devices for a user. All of the components apart from Azure Information Protection Premium Plan 2 are available as standalone User SLs.

	EMS E3	**EMS E5**
Azure Active Directory Premium Plan 1	✔	
Azure Active Directory Premium Plan 2		✔
Azure Information Protection Premium Plan 1	✔	
Azure Information Protection Premium Plan 2		✔
Microsoft Intune	✔	✔
Microsoft Cloud App Security		✔
Microsoft Defender for Identity		✔

Figure 70: EMS plans comparison

Step-up licenses

Customers can step-up from EMS E3 to EMS E5 in the EA and MPSA. As usual, check the Product Terms website and the relevant price lists for exact availability.

Add-on licenses (To-cloud)

Customers with Software Assurance on licenses for the Core or Enterprise CAL Suites can purchase EMS E3/E5 Add-on User SLs to move to the cloud:

Qualifying license	Add-on User SL
Core CAL Suite User or Device	EMS E3 or EMS E5
Enterprise CAL Suite User or Device	EMS E3 or EMS E5

Figure 71: EMS To-cloud Add-on licenses

From SA licenses

Customers with active Software Assurance on one of the CAL Suites are eligible to purchase EMS E3 or EMS E5 From SA User SLs.

On-premises use rights

The EMS E3 and E5 plans include rights to the CALs and CMLs as shown in the table below:

	EMS E3	EMS E5
Windows Server Standard CAL	✔	✔
Windows Server RMS CAL	✔	✔
Microsoft Identity Manager CAL	✔	✔
Advanced Threat Analytics CML	✔	✔
Microsoft Endpoint Configuration Manager CML	✔	✔
System Center Service Manager CML	✔	✔
System Center Endpoint Protection SL	✔	✔

Figure 72: EMS on-premises use rights

Availability of EMS plans

The two EMS plans are available through the Volume Licensing agreements and CSP. As usual, check out the Product Terms website for specifics.

MICROSOFT 365 PLANS FOR ENTERPRISE USERS

Microsoft 365 Enterprise was launched in July 2017 as the new name for a collection of products previously called Secure Productive Enterprise, and before that called the Enterprise Cloud Suite.

Today we have Microsoft 365 E3 and E5 for enterprise users, and these are probably the easiest plans to compare, as shown in the table below:

	Microsoft 365 E3	Microsoft 365 E5
Windows 10 Enterprise E3	✔	
Windows 10 Enterprise E5		✔
Office 365 E3	✔	
Office 365 E5		✔
EMS E3	✔	
EMS E5		✔

Figure 73: Microsoft 365 Enterprise plans comparison

License assignment rules

There are no restrictions as to who can be assigned a Microsoft 365 E3/E5 license. However, the rights as to where and how Windows 10 Enterprise can be run differ dependent on the devices that a user uses, and whether or not they have a Qualifying Operating System.

Using Windows

A Microsoft 365 E3/E5 licensed user can run Windows 10 Enterprise E3/E5 locally on devices that have a Qualifying Operating System.

Licensing for virtual desktops

If a licensed Microsoft 365 E3/E5 user is the primary user of a device which has a Qualifying Operating System, then that user can access Windows 10 Enterprise virtual desktops hosted in the following environments:

- Azure Dedicated Host
- Azure multitenant infrastructure
- QMTH partner
- Windows Virtual Desktop service

If the licenses have been purchased through a Volume Licensing agreement (where available) then the user can also access virtual desktops hosted on the customer's own hardware or dedicated hardware provided by an Authorized Outsourcer.

If there is no Qualifying Operating System on the device, then licensed users are still eligible to access virtual desktops running on the Windows Virtual Desktop service in Azure.

There's a useful summary table in the section starting on page 369.

Use of the Office apps

Microsoft 365 Apps for enterprise is included in the Microsoft 365 E3/E5 licenses, and all the use rights for the users are exactly the same as described in the **Microsoft 365 Apps** section on page 178.

Step-up licenses

On the next page, some of the most useful Step-up licenses available in the Enterprise Agreement and/or the MPSA are listed. As usual, check the Product Terms website and the relevant price lists for exact availability, and to check that the step up you want to make is supported.

Original license	Step-up User SL
Microsoft 365 F3	Microsoft 365 E3
Microsoft 365 E3	Microsoft 365 E5
Office 365 E3	Microsoft 365 E3
Office 365 E5	Microsoft 365 E5
EMS E3	Microsoft 365 E3
EMS E5	Microsoft 365 E5
Windows 10 Enterprise E5	Microsoft 365 E5

Figure 74: Microsoft 365 Enterprise Step-up licenses

Add-on licenses (To-cloud)

There are To-cloud Add-on User SLs available in the Enterprise Agreement, enabling customers to purchase Microsoft 365 E3 or E5 Add-on User SLs for users already licensed with the Professional or Enterprise Desktop:

Qualifying license	Add-on User SL
Windows 10 Enterprise + Core CAL Suite User or Device + Office Professional Plus	Microsoft 365 E3 or Microsoft 365 E5
Windows 10 Enterprise + Enterprise CAL Suite User or Device + Office Professional Plus	Microsoft 365 E3 or Microsoft 365 E5

Figure 75: Microsoft 365 Enterprise To-cloud Add-on licenses

From SA licenses

From SA User SLs are available for customers to move from the Professional or Enterprise Desktop with Software Assurance to Microsoft 365 E3 or E5:

Qualifying license	From SA User SL
Windows 10 Enterprise + Core CAL Suite / Enterprise CAL Suite + Office Professional Plus	Microsoft 365 E3 or Microsoft 365 E5

Figure 76: Microsoft 365 Enterprise From SA licenses

Special rights to Office Professional Plus

When customers take advantage of the From SA license to move from the Professional/Enterprise Desktop to Microsoft 365 E3/E5 they stop paying for the Software Assurance on the qualifying licenses. In a perpetual agreement they retain ownership of the qualifying licenses and that means that they can use the then-current version of Office Professional Plus (or a previous version) for as long as they want to. However, as later versions of the traditional Office products are released, they can't install those versions since they no longer have Software Assurance. But they do have a special right – users licensed with Microsoft 365 E3/E5 From SA licenses are entitled to one installation of Office Professional Plus. This installation can be a current or previous version, but it may not be used in an RDS or VDI deployment, only locally.

There's a further right allowed for customers who have transitioned existing users using From SA User SLs and then acquire Microsoft 365 E3/E5 Full User SLs for new users who join the organization. These licensed users may also install Office Professional Plus on a local device. Note that the number of new User SLs which include these rights can't exceed the original number of From SA User SLs and all licenses must be purchased under the same agreement.

On-premises use rights

On-premises server access rights

The Microsoft 365 E3 and E5 User SLs include rights to access licensed on-premises servers equivalent to those for Office 365 E3/E5 and EMS E3/E5.

On-premises server installation rights

There is one other quirk with Microsoft 365 E3 and E5 User SLs, which is an additional right that is granted if the licenses are purchased through an Enterprise Agreement. This additional right allows the installation of some of the server products which may then be accessed by Microsoft 365 E3/E5 licensed users. The products are Exchange, SharePoint and Skype for Business Server and the rights allow unlimited installations of these products in both physical and virtual infrastructures, with rights to previous versions if required. The only restriction is that the installations must be on hardware dedicated to the customer – so not on shared servers in a Service Provider's server farm for example.

Home Use Program

Organizations that purchase 2,000 or more licenses for Microsoft 365 E3 and/or Microsoft 365 E5 through a Volume Licensing agreement or CSP are eligible for the Home Use Program. This means that their users can purchase Microsoft 365 Family or Personal subscriptions with a 30% discount. The individuals who purchase these licenses may continue to renew the subscriptions at the discounted price even if they no longer work for the company that made them eligible to purchase the licenses originally.

Availability of Microsoft 365 Enterprise plans

The Microsoft 365 E3 and E5 plans are available through CSP and the MPSA and EA.

Other interesting licenses

There are a couple of other licenses associated with Microsoft 365 E3/E5 that are worth mentioning at this point.

Microsoft 365 E3 – Unattended

The Microsoft 365 E3 – Unattended SL licenses a bot to run repetitive tasks in a Windows client or Office app without user intervention. A Microsoft 365 E3 – Unattended license must be assigned to each physical device or virtual machine on which an unattended bot is running.

This license is available through the Enterprise Agreement or CSP.

Skype for Business Plus CAL Add-on for Microsoft 365 E3

This User SL is designed for customers who are moving to the cloud and have purchased Microsoft 365 E3 licenses for their users, but still need to maintain an on-premises Skype for Business solution for enterprise telephony. These users need a Skype for Business Plus CAL which is not included in the on-premises use rights for Microsoft 365 E3, and this license enables them to purchase a subscription for as long as they need it.

The Skype for Business Plus CAL Add-on User SL is only available through the Enterprise Agreement.

VDA Add-on for Microsoft 365 E3/E5

This VDA Add-on User SL is an interesting one. It's used for users who are licensed with a Microsoft 365 E3/E5 User SL who don't have a primary device with a Qualifying Operating System, and it adds on for them a whole host of deployment options equivalent to those included with a VDA User SL. You can find a summary table with these options in the section starting on page 369.

The VDA Add-on User SL is only available through the Enterprise Agreement.

SharePoint Syntex

SharePoint Syntex uses advanced AI to automatically organize SharePoint content. All users who use the SharePoint Syntex capabilities need to be licensed via an In-cloud Add-on User SL which may be assigned to users already licensed with one of the following licenses:

- SharePoint Online Plan 1 or Plan 2
- Office 365 F3, E1, E3, or E5
- Microsoft 365 Business Basic, Standard or Premium
- Microsoft 365 F1, F3, E3 or E5

The SharePoint Syntex In-Cloud Add-on User SL is available through the Enterprise Agreement and the CSP program.

Viva Topics

Viva Topics is the first product in Microsoft's Employee Experience Platform category, which aims to give people knowledge directly within products like Office, Teams or SharePoint without them having to leave the products to search for it. All users to whom the Viva Topics capabilities will be available need to be licensed via an In-cloud Add-on User SL which may be assigned to users already licensed with one of the following licenses:

- SharePoint Online Plan 1 or Plan 2
- Office 365 F3, E1, E3, or E5
- Microsoft 365 Business Basic, Standard or Premium
- Microsoft 365 F1, F3, E3 or E5

The Viva Topics In-Cloud Add-on User SL is available through the Enterprise Agreement and the CSP program.

MICROSOFT 365 PLANS FOR SMB USERS

Microsoft 365 plans with the word "Business" in them are aimed at small and medium businesses since they are each limited to 300 users.

The table below gives an overview of the different plans. Customers should choose Microsoft 365 Apps for business if they need their users to install the Office apps, or choose Microsoft 365 Business Basic if they just need their users to use browser-based apps with Online Services like Exchange Online or Teams. Microsoft 365 Business Standard, in effect, combines these plans, and Microsoft 365 Business Premium adds on Windows 10 Business as well as further security tools and advanced Online Services:

	Microsoft 365 Apps for business	Microsoft 365 Business Basic	Microsoft 365 Business Standard	Microsoft 365 Business Premium
Install Office apps locally	✔		✔	✔
Use Office mobile apps and Office for the web	✔	✔	✔	✔
Exchange Online		✔	✔	✔
SharePoint Online		✔	✔	✔
Teams		✔	✔	✔
Further Online Services		✔	✔	✔
Windows 10 Business				✔
Advanced security				✔
Advanced Online Services				✔

Figure 77: Microsoft 365 Business plans comparison

License assignment rules

There are no restrictions as to who can be assigned one of the Microsoft 365 plans for SMB users.

Using Windows

Microsoft 365 Business Premium licenses include the rights to Windows 10 Business which is a set of cloud services and device management capabilities that build on Windows 10 Pro. The prerequisite for deploying Windows 10 Business is Windows 10 Pro, and a Microsoft 365 Business Premium license comes with an upgrade to Windows 10 Pro for devices licensed with Windows 7, 8 or 8.1 Pro. There are no downgrade or down-edition rights, or options to use a Long-Term Servicing Channel for Windows 10 Business.

Licensing for virtual desktops

Users licensed with Microsoft 365 Business Premium may access Windows 10 Enterprise virtual desktops running on the Windows Virtual Desktop service in Azure.

Use of the Office apps

Microsoft 365 Apps for business is included in the Microsoft 365 Business Standard and Microsoft 365 Business Premium licenses, and all the use rights for the users are exactly the same as described in the **Microsoft 365 Apps** section.

Step-up licenses

There are no Step-up licenses available for the Microsoft 365 Business plans.

Add-on licenses (To-cloud)

There's no equivalent traditional licensing position for the Microsoft 365 Business plans and thus there are no To-cloud Add-on licenses available for these plans.

From SA licenses

Again, the lack of an equivalent traditional licensing position for the Microsoft 365 Business plans also means that there are no From SA licenses available for these plans.

On-premises use rights

The Microsoft 365 Business plans do not include rights to access any licensed on-premises servers.

Availability of Microsoft 365 Business plans

All four Microsoft 365 Business plans are available through CSP, and all apart from Microsoft 365 Business Premium are available in the Open programs. As usual, check out the Product Terms website for specifics.

PLANS FOR FRONTLINE WORKERS

There are three plans for Frontline Workers as shown in the table below. Organizations choose Office 365 F3 when they want their users to use the Office mobile apps and Office for the web and to have a good level of access to Online Services such as Exchange and SharePoint Online. Microsoft 365 F3 licenses users for Office 365 F3, EMS E3 and Windows 10 Enterprise E3.

Organizations choose Microsoft 365 F1 when users need a pretty limited set of functionality. You can see in the table below that there's a gray tick for the Office apps – licensed users just have read-only access to documents. Additionally, these users have no email rights although, confusingly, there is actually an Exchange mailbox provisioned for users to enable the full Teams experience. Organizations that find that Microsoft 365 F1 would be the perfect solution if it only included email should additionally acquire an Exchange Online Plan 1 User SL for those users.

	Microsoft 365 F1	Microsoft 365 F3	Office 365 F3
Install Office apps locally			
Use Office Mobile apps/Office for the web	✔	✔	✔
Exchange Online (Kiosk)		✔	✔
SharePoint Online (Kiosk)	✔	✔	✔
Teams	✔	✔	✔
Further Online Services	✔	✔	✔
Windows 10 Enterprise E3		✔	
EMS E3	✔	✔	

Figure 78: Microsoft 365 Frontline Worker plans comparison

License assignment rules

There are some rules around the devices that a Frontline Worker may use. Firstly, if their primary work device is dedicated to them, then it must have a single screen smaller than 10.1". However, if they share their primary work device with other Frontline Workers during or across shifts, then this restriction is removed, as long as the other Frontline Workers also use this device as their primary work device.

Using Windows 10 Enterprise E3

If a device used by a licensed Microsoft 365 F3 user has a Qualifying Operating System, then Windows 10 Enterprise E3 can be installed and used locally on that device. However, there are no rights to use the Windows 10 Enterprise LTSC 2019 edition, or to install and use the MDOP tools.

Licensing for virtual desktops

If a device used by a licensed Microsoft 365 F3 user has a Qualifying Operating System, then that user can access Windows 10 Enterprise virtual desktops hosted in the following environments:

- Azure Dedicated Host
- Azure multitenant infrastructure
- QMTH partner
- Windows Virtual Desktop service

If the licenses have been purchased through a Volume Licensing agreement (where available) then the user can also access virtual desktops hosted on the customer's own hardware or dedicated hardware provided by an Authorized Outsourcer.

If there is no Qualifying Operating System on the device, then licensed users are still eligible to access virtual desktops running on the Windows Virtual Desktop service in Azure.

Use of the Office apps

Users licensed with Microsoft 365 F1 User SLs have read-only use of the Office Mobile apps and Office for the web. Users licensed with Office 365 F3 or Microsoft 365 F3 User SLs can use Office for the web with no restrictions and can sign into the Office Mobile apps with their organizational credentials on up to five smartphones and five tablets which have integrated screens measuring 10.1" diagonally or less.

Step-up licenses

The Step-up licenses enable users to move up through the Frontline Worker plans or to move to Microsoft 365 E3. As usual, check the Product Terms website and the relevant price lists for exact availability, and to check that the step-up you want to make is supported:

Original license	Step-up User SL
Office 365 F3	Microsoft 365 F3
Microsoft 365 F1	Microsoft 365 F3
Microsoft 365 F3	Microsoft 365 E3

Figure 79: Microsoft 365 Frontline Worker Step-up licenses

Add-on licenses (To-cloud)

There's no equivalent traditional licensing position for Frontline Workers and thus there are no To-cloud Add-on licenses available for the Frontline Worker plans.

From SA licenses

Again, the lack of an equivalent traditional licensing position for Frontline Workers also means that there are no From SA licenses available for the Frontline Worker plans.

On-premises use rights

Microsoft 365 F1 and F3 include EMS E3 and thus include rights to access licensed on-premises servers equivalent to those for EMS E3, as detailed on page 189.

Availability of Microsoft 365 plans for Frontline Workers

The plans for Frontline Workers are available through CSP, and the MPSA and EA. As usual, check out the Product Terms website for specifics.

SECURITY AND COMPLIANCE

Organizations who want to license their users for the complete set of Microsoft's advanced security and compliance tools would choose Microsoft 365 E5 licenses for all of their users. Organizations that want to license a subset of these tools can do so in a wide array of combinations. We'll take Lightshades of Grey as our customer in this section who are looking at licensing security and compliance components for their users.

Security and Compliance for Microsoft 365 E3 users

The first option we'll look at is where Lightshades of Grey have licensed some of their users with Microsoft 365 E3 and want to add on security and compliance components. In fact, there are two In-cloud Add-on User SLs for users already licensed with Microsoft 365 E3:

- Microsoft 365 E5 Security
- Microsoft 365 E5 Compliance

Lightshades of Grey can choose to purchase one or both of these licenses, dependent on their exact requirements. Here you can see that if you buy both of the Add-on licenses, the functionality is equivalent to the Microsoft 365 E5 license:

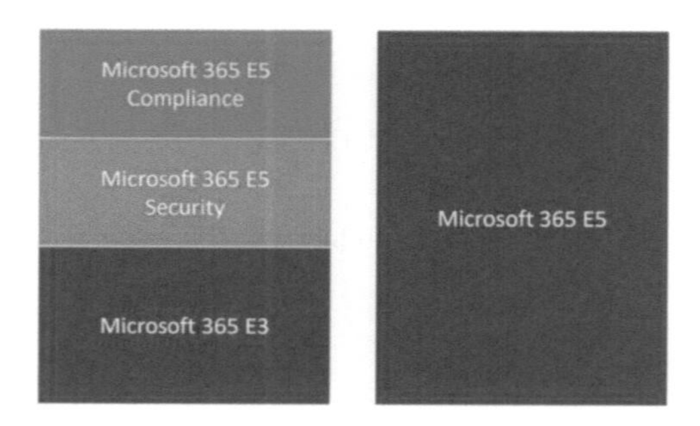

Figure 80: Security and Compliance Add-on licenses

Compliance mini suites

Customers who choose the Microsoft 365 E5 Compliance User SL are actually acquiring a single license for 3 individual suites of compliance licenses:

- Information Protection and Governance
- Insider Risk Management
- eDiscovery and Audit

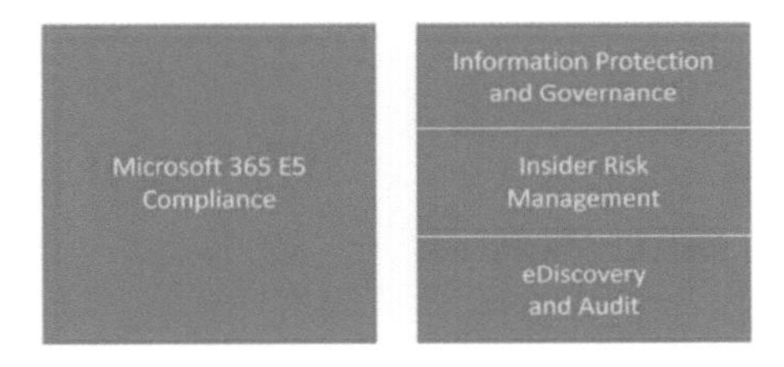

Figure 81: Compliance mini suites

If Lightshades of Grey have more specialized needs, then these suites are available as individual In-cloud Add-on User SLs. These can be assigned to any user already licensed with any Microsoft 365, Office 365, Exchange Online, SharePoint Online, or OneDrive for Business license. Users must also be licensed for Azure Information Protection or EMS to be eligible for the Information Protection and Governance license.

Security components

Customers who choose the Microsoft 365 Security User SL are actually acquiring a single license for these 5 security components:

- Azure Active Directory Premium
- Microsoft Defender for Endpoint
- Microsoft Defender for Office 365
- Microsoft Defender for Identity
- Microsoft Cloud App Security

Lightshades of Grey could choose any of these components as standalone licenses rather than the full Microsoft 365 E5 Security license. Some of these components are In-cloud Add-ons requiring qualifying licenses, and some are Full User SLs, as detailed in the next section.

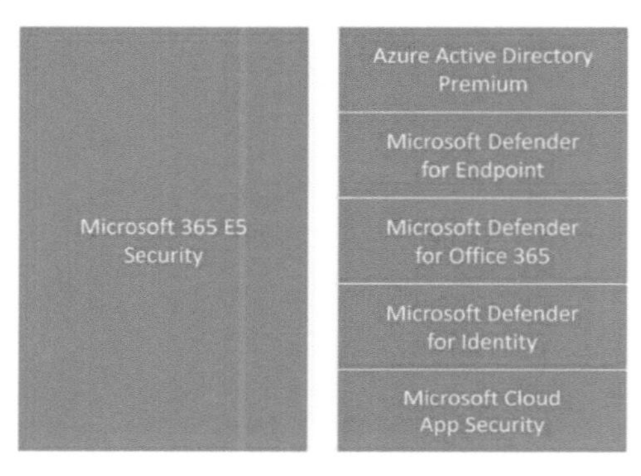

Figure 82: Security components

Azure Active Directory Premium

Azure Active Directory Premium is available as a Plan 1 or Plan 2 Full User SL. Azure Active Directory Premium Plan 2 is included in an EMS E5 user SL.

Microsoft Defender for Endpoint

Microsoft Defender for Endpoint is included in a Windows 10 Enterprise E5 User SL. Otherwise, it's available as a Full User SL, and licensed users are covered for up to 5 concurrent devices.

Microsoft Defender for Office 365

Microsoft Defender for Office 365 is available as a Plan 1 or Plan 2 In-cloud Add-on license which can be assigned to any user already licensed for any Microsoft 365, Office 365, Exchange Online, SharePoint Online, or OneDrive for Business license. Microsoft Defender for Office 365 Plan 2 is included in an Office 365 E5 User SL.

Microsoft Defender for Identity

Microsoft Defender for Identity is available as a Full User SL. Customers can also install and use Advanced Threat Analytics locally to manage client OSEs that are used solely by users to whom one of these licenses has been assigned. Microsoft Defender for Identity is included in an EMS E5 User SL.

There's also a To-cloud Add-on User SL available for users already licensed with an Advanced Threat Analytics 2016 Client Management License.

Microsoft Cloud App Security

Think of Microsoft Cloud App Security as the full Cloud App Security offering. A subset of features are licensed via Office 365 Cloud App Security which is included in an Office 365 E5 User SL.

The Microsoft Cloud App Security license is a Full User SL which allows an unlimited number of apps to be connected and protected for each user. Microsoft Cloud App Security is included in an EMS E5 User SL.

Microsoft 365 Defender

Microsoft Defender is Microsoft's Extended Detection and Response (XDR) solution for threat protection, and it's composed of two brands: Microsoft 365 Defender and Azure Defender. Azure Defender provides threat protection for workloads running in Azure, on premises, and in other clouds, while Microsoft 365 Defender works across endpoints, identities, email, and applications providing integrated protection against attacks. The licensing of the Azure Defender components is covered on page 371.

There are 3 Microsoft 365 Defender components:

- Microsoft Defender for Endpoint
- Microsoft Defender for Office 365
- Microsoft Defender for Identity

These components have already been mentioned in this section, but it's worth noting that Microsoft Defender for Endpoint is available for clients (above) and for servers (below).

Microsoft Defender for Endpoint Server

Microsoft Defender for Endpoint Server is sold as a subscription license and you need a license for every Operating System Environment you want to protect. Before a customer may acquire these server endpoint protection licenses, there's a requirement for them to have a combined minimum of 50 licenses for one of the following licenses:

- Microsoft Defender for Endpoint Client User SL
- Windows 10 Enterprise E5 User SL
- Microsoft 365 E5 User SL
- Microsoft 365 E5 Security User SL

Security and Compliance for Microsoft 365 F1/F3 users

And we end with a final offering for Lightshades of Grey and how they might want to license their Frontline Workers for security and compliance. There are three In-Cloud Add-on User SLs for users already licensed with Microsoft 365 F1 or F3:

- Microsoft 365 F5 Security
- Microsoft 365 F5 Compliance
- Microsoft 365 F5 Security + Compliance

Again, these licenses are collections of security/compliance components. Lightshades of Grey would choose to purchase either of the first two licenses, or the third license for the full set of security and compliance components.

TEAMS AND AUDIO SERVICES

In the on-premises section of this book we look at the licensing of Skype for Business Server (see page 75) and can see that it offers users presence information, instant messaging, web conferencing and enterprise telephony solutions. Originally the equivalent services in the cloud were sold as Skype for Business Online but this will officially be retired in July 2021. Teams will replace it, with the main services offered by Teams being chat, meetings, and calling, and a whole host of features for users to collaborate in, you guessed it, teams.

Teams is such an integral part of life for Office 365 and Microsoft 365 users that access to the Teams service is included in most licenses. Note, though, that there is a difference between the Teams service and the Teams app. The Teams app is installed with the Microsoft 365 Apps but if you've got a standalone license for the apps you won't be licensed for the Teams service and won't, for example, be able to set up meetings with your colleagues.

Once organizations have deployed Teams, they may want to extend the meetings and calling functionality that's available, and we'll take a look of the licensing of that in this section too. The availability of some of these additional services varies hugely between different parts of the world, so do check exactly what's available in your geography here: https://bit.ly/BOKRegionAvailability.

Chat

Users licensed for the Teams service can chat to users in their own organization, and, if external access is enabled for their tenant can chat to Teams users in other organizations too. This used to be known as federation, and there are no additional licensing requirements to chat to these users.

Meetings

There are two types of meetings that you can set up in Teams – a regular Teams meeting which supports up to 300 attendees, and a Teams Live event which enables you to schedule and produce events that stream to large online audiences of up to 10,000 attendees. There are no licensing requirements for attending either of these types of events, it's just the meeting organizers that need to be licensed and the following licenses include these rights:

	Set up a Teams meeting	Set up a Teams Live event
Microsoft 365 F1	✔	
Office 365 F3, Microsoft 365 F3	✔	
Office 365 E1	✔	✔
Office 365 E3/E5, Microsoft 365 E3/E5	✔	✔
Microsoft 365 Business Basic, Standard, Premium	✔	

Figure 83: licenses to set up Teams meetings and Teams Live events

Audio Conferencing

When you set up one of these meetings you typically send a meeting request which includes a link to join the meeting via the Teams app. If you want people to be able to join a meeting from a traditional telephone then you need to provide a dial-in number, and this requires an Audio Conferencing license.

Office 365 E5 and Microsoft 365 E5 licenses include rights to Audio Conferencing. Alternatively, the standalone license can be purchased as an

In-cloud Add-on and assigned to any user who is already licensed with any of the following licenses:

- Office 365 F3, Microsoft 365 F1/F3
- Office 365 E1/E3, Microsoft 365 E3
- Microsoft 365 Business Basic/Standard/Premium

When a user is licensed for Audio Conferencing, they are actually able to do three additional things in Teams meetings:

1. Send out a meeting request with a dial-in number
2. Send out a meeting request with a toll-free dial-in number
3. Dial out during a meeting and invite other callers into the Teams meeting

With the first option there are no further costs involved for the organization with the Audio Conferencing license since the person dialing in to the Teams meeting will be paying the call costs.

With the third option, there may not be costs involved for the licensed organization since each Audio Conferencing license (and Office 365/Microsoft 365 E5 license) provides 60 minutes per user per month (pooled at the tenant level) that can be used to dial out to non-premium numbers in certain countries, known as the Zone A countries. These countries include the US, many European countries, Australia, Brazil, Canada, China, Hong Kong, India, Japan, Malaysia, Mexico, New Zealand, Puerto Rico, Russia, Singapore, South Africa, South Korea, Taiwan, and Thailand. You can find the full list of countries here: https://bit.ly/BOKACZones.

However, there will be costs involved if users need to dial out to countries which are not included in the Zone A list (called the Pay-As-You-Go countries), and/or if they use up all the monthly included minutes. Organizations pay for these calls via Communication Credits which are described below.

The second option in the list above, where a meeting organizer wants to provide a toll-free number in a meeting request, is also paid for via Communication Credits, so let's take a look at those now.

Communication Credits

Communication Credits are a way of paying for calling minutes and are used with Audio Conferencing licenses as well as with Calling Plans which are covered in the next section.

You purchase Communication Credits in the Microsoft 365 Admin Center and you can add credits manually as you need them, or you can enable the Auto-recharge option which will add credit automatically when the balance falls below a threshold that you set. This is usually the preferred option, since if there is a zero-credit balance, licensed users won't be able to dial out from meetings to PAYG countries, and users won't be able to use the toll-free dial-in numbers to join a meeting.

Payment for the Communication Credits is, for many customers, via a credit card. However, an Enterprise Agreement customer can supply their Enrollment number to be billed via an invoice associated with their EA. Once Communication Credits have been purchased, they must be used within 12 months of purchase, otherwise they are lost.

Another important aspect of how Communication Credits work is that a free Communications Credits license must be assigned to any user who needs to make use of the calling minutes funded by Communication Credits. This is done, as you might expect, through the Microsoft 365 Admin Center.

Audio Conferencing Pay-Per-Minute licenses

There's an alternative way to license Audio Conferencing for Enterprise Agreement customers, which is a $0 Audio Conferencing Pay-Per-Minute license that can be assigned to a user to enable them for Audio Conferencing. All calls are paid for via Communication Credits and it means that an organization can be set up for Audio Conferencing without committing to a regular monthly payment.

Calling

It's easy for users of the Teams app to initiate a voice or video call with another user and beyond a requirement for an Internet connection, there are no additional licensing requirements or call costs. However, as we saw in the Meetings section, there are additional licenses which can be purchased to enhance the calling capability of an organization.

Phone System

Phone System is Microsoft's cloud PBX solution and is aimed at organizations that want to eliminate hardware PBX systems and to have their call management system in the cloud.

Office 365 E5 and Microsoft 365 E5 licenses include rights to Phone System. Alternatively, the standalone license can be purchased as an In-cloud Add-on and assigned to any user who is already licensed with any of the following licenses:

- Office 365 F3, Microsoft 365 F1/F3
- Office 365 E1/E3, Microsoft 365 E3
- Microsoft 365 Business Basic/Standard/Premium

Phone System Virtual User licenses

Auto Attendants and Call Queues require an associated Resource Account, and all Resource Accounts that need a phone number must be allocated a Phone System license. This can be a regular paid-for license, but there are also free Virtual User licenses available. Organizations that have at least one paid-for Phone System license, or a license that includes Phone System, get 25 Virtual User licenses. For each additional Phone System license added, another Virtual User license becomes available. Although these licenses are free, they must still be "purchased" through the Microsoft 365 Admin Center.

Calling Plans

Calling Plans enable users to call phone numbers outside their organization, and are always purchased as an In-cloud Add-on User SL. There are Domestic and International Calling Plans which essentially makes Microsoft your telecoms provider and provides you with calling minutes. A Domestic Calling Plan allows a user to make calls in the country to which his Office 365 license is assigned, and the International Calling Plan includes the Domestic country and 196 international destinations.

The number of calling minutes available with each Calling Plan varies with geography, but calling minutes are always pooled at the tenant level. For example, if there are 100 users who have been assigned a Domestic Calling Plan which includes 120 minutes, they share a pool of 12,000 minutes each month. If they run out of calling minutes, calls are billed on a per minute basis and paid for via Communication Credits, as described above.

Calling Plan User SLs must be assigned to users already licensed with a Phone System license – either one that is included as part of Office/Microsoft 365 E5, or the standalone license.

Microsoft 365 Business Voice

Microsoft 365 Business Voice is intended as a voice solution for SMB customers; the word "Business" in its name giving the hint that it's restricted to a maximum of 300 seats. It's a single license that combines Audio Conferencing, Phone System and a Calling Plan, and is available in the US and Canada with 3,000 domestic minutes and 600 international minutes, and in the UK with 1,200 domestic minutes and 600 international minutes. In other countries where Business Voice is available it's a "without Calling Plan" license, thus comprising just an Audio Conferencing and Phone System license.

A Microsoft 365 Business Voice In-cloud Add-on User SL can be assigned to any user licensed with one of the following licenses:

- Office 365 F3, Microsoft 365 F1/F3
- Office 365 E1/E3, Microsoft 365 E3
- Microsoft 365 Business Basic/Standard/Premium

The Microsoft 365 Business Voice licenses are only available through CSP.

Licensing Common Area Communication Devices

Microsoft define a Common Area Communication Device as a device which is shared by multiple users who use the device without logging in with their own Office 365 credentials. The device is intended to support calls, meetings and/or conferencing over voice, Voice over IP, and/or video.

A **Common Area Phone Device SL** is typically assigned to a Teams phone in an area, such as a lobby, where it may be used by guests to make and receive phone calls. The license includes Phone System which enables a phone number to be assigned to the device, but it doesn't include any calling service. Thus, organizations must either connect their existing telephony provider, or purchase a Calling Plan for the device.

The **Teams Rooms Standard and Premium Device SLs** are used for licensing meetings and calling functionality for meeting room devices. Both licenses include Teams, Phone System and Audio Conferencing components, with the Premium license additionally including use of the Microsoft Teams Rooms Managed Services where it's geographically available.

Advanced Communications

Advanced Communications is a collection of additional functionality for organizations that want to tailor and customize meetings and need tools to manage their communication policies.

It's licensed with an In-cloud Add-on User SL for users already licensed with one of the following licenses:

- Office 365 F3, Microsoft 365 F1/F3
- Office 365 E1/E3/E5, Microsoft 365 E3/E5
- Microsoft 365 Business Basic/Standard/Premium

VISIO ONLINE

Visio Online is Microsoft's online diagramming tool enabling users to create visuals such as flowcharts, org charts, network diagrams and floor plans.

Licensing Visio Online

There are two plans for Visio Online: Plan 1 and Plan 2, both licensed with User Subscription Licenses. A Visio Online Plan 1 User SL enables licensed users to create simple diagrams in a web app. Visio Online Plan 1 is also known as Visio for the web.

A User SL for Visio Online Plan 2 includes the functionality of Plan 1, including the right to use the web app. It also enables users to create more advanced diagrams, and to install the Visio desktop app. As you might expect, licensed users can install and activate this app on up to 5 devices.

The Visio desktop app is installed locally, and users don't need to be connected to the internet to use it. However, licensed users must connect to the internet at least once every 30 days so that the status of their license can be checked. If a license has been removed from a user, or the Visio Online Plan 2 subscription hasn't been renewed, then the app goes into Reduced Functionality Mode. In this mode users can open and view existing files but all features for editing or creating new diagrams are disabled.

Update Channels

One of the benefits of the Visio desktop app compared to the traditional Visio 2019 Standard and Professional applications is that new and updated features are provided on a regular basis. Organizations can control how often users get these new features by choosing an Update Channel.

There are three choices of Update Channel: Current, Monthly Enterprise, and Semi-Annual Enterprise, and they differ by the schedules by which feature, security, and non-security updates are delivered. The Update Channels are exactly the same as those for the Microsoft 365 Apps and are explained on page 178.

Shared Computer Activation

Visio Online Plan 2 also includes Shared Computer Activation rights if an organization wants to install the Visio desktop app on a shared device to be used by multiple licensed users. The ins and outs of Shared Computer Activation are described in the **Microsoft 365 Apps** section on page 179.

The Shared Computer Activation rights also allow organizations to install the Visio desktop app on a server to be delivered to users' devices. The same choices are available as for the Microsoft 365 Apps, and these are detailed on page 180.

Step-up licenses

There are Step-up licenses available to enable customers to move from Visio Online Plan 1 to Visio Online Plan 2. As usual, check the Product Terms website and the relevant price lists for exact availability.

Add-on licenses (To-cloud)

Customers with Software Assurance on Visio Standard or Professional licenses can purchase Visio Online Plan 2 Add-on User SLs to move to the cloud.

From SA licenses

The following From SA licenses are available for customers with active Software Assurance on their Visio Standard or Professional licenses who want to move to a Visio Online Plan:

Qualifying license	From SA User SL
Visio Standard	Visio Online Plan 1
Visio Professional	Visio Online Plan 1 or Visio Online Plan 2

Figure 84: Visio Online From SA licenses

Visio 2016 Standard/Professional deployment rights

Users licensed for Visio Online Plan 2 may install and use a copy of Visio 2016 Standard or Professional (or a prior version) on devices licensed for and running Office Standard or Professional Plus.

Viewing and printing rights

Users licensed with any Office 365 or Microsoft 365 plan which includes Office for the web may use Visio in Reduced Functionality Mode to view and print Visio diagrams.

Availability of Visio Online licenses

Visio Online Plan 1 and Plan 2 User SLs are available through the Volume Licensing agreements and CSP.

MICROSOFT PROJECT

There are two different cloud solutions for Project: Project for the web, and Project Online, which Microsoft collectively call **Microsoft Project**. Although they are separate applications, they can work together side by side, but Microsoft have stated that going forward they will focus on Project for the web innovations, while still making sure that Project Online receives key performance and security improvements.

Project Online

Project Online is the original solution, offering capabilities for Project Portfolio Management and used by all members of a project team – administrators, portfolio managers and viewers, project and resource managers, and team leaders and members.

There's a Project Online desktop client available for project managers and resource managers which can be used as a standalone application or connected to the Project Online service. It's the subscription version of the Project Professional 2019 product covered on page 114. Other members of the project team would use a web interface to perform task and time updates to projects managed in Project Online.

Project Online is built on the SharePoint platform and it stores data in the SharePoint data store. SharePoint Online is provisioned as part of Project Online but, as you might expect, rights to the SharePoint Online functionality are limited to storing and accessing data to support Project Online.

Project for the web

Project for the web is Microsoft's most recent offering for cloud-based work and project management. Project managers and team members can use Project for the web to plan and manage work.

Project for the web is built on the Power Platform, and Project for the web data is stored in Dataverse.

Licensing Microsoft Project

There are four User Subscription Licenses associated with licensing Microsoft Project, which license access to Project Online, Project for the web, and the Project Online desktop client, as shown in the table below:

	Essentials	Plan 1	Plan 3	Plan 5
Project for the web		✔	✔	✔
Project Online	✔	✔	✔	✔
Project Online desktop client			✔	✔

Figure 85: Microsoft Project licenses

Let's get a bit more detail on exactly what these licenses give access to, starting with Project Plan 1. As you can see, this gives access to features in both Project for the web and Project Online and would typically be used to license project team members. Project Plans 3 and 5 additionally give rights to the Project Online desktop client and would typically be used to license project and resource managers. Both licenses give rights to additional functionality in Project for the web and Project Online compared to Project Plan 1. As you might expect, Project Plan 5 gives access to more Project Online functionality than Project Plan 3.

That just leaves the Project Essentials license. This only gives limited access to Project Online functionality and would be an option to license project team members. However, it's a special type of license since it's only available for purchase by customers who have Project Plan 3 or Plan 5 User SLs. This restriction does not apply to Plan 1, which may be purchased without other licenses for use in an organization.

Deploying the Project Online client

Users licensed with Project Plan 3 or Plan 5 licenses may use the Project Online client on up to 5 devices. It may also be used via Shared Computer Activation on a shared device in the same way as the Microsoft 365 Apps, as described on page 179.

The Shared Computer Activation rights also allow organizations to install the Project Online client on a server to be delivered to users' devices. The same choices are available as for the Microsoft 365 Apps, and these are detailed on page 180.

Update Channels

One of the benefits of the Project Online desktop client compared to the traditional Project 2019 Standard and Professional applications is that new and updated features are provided on a regular basis. Organizations can control how often users get these new features by choosing an Update Channel.

There are three choices of Update Channel: Current, Monthly Enterprise, and Semi-Annual Enterprise, and they differ by the schedules by which feature, security, and non-security updates are delivered. The Update Channels are exactly the same as those for the Microsoft 365 Apps and are explained on page 178.

Project 2016 Standard/Professional deployment rights

Users licensed with Project Plan 3 or Plan 5 licenses are also licensed to install Project Standard or Professional 2016 on devices licensed for and running Office Standard or Professional Plus.

Step-up licenses

Back in 2019 there were some name changes of the Project licenses: Project Online Professional became Project Plan 3, and Project Online Premium became Project Plan 5. Because of that, you may find the names of Step-up licenses still incorporate these older names. However, using the new names, customers can step up, for example, using the following licenses. As usual, check the Product Terms website and the relevant price lists for exact availability:

Original license	Step-up User SL
Project Essentials	Project Plan 3
Project Plan 1	Project Plan 3
Project Plan 3	Project Plan 5

Figure 86: Microsoft Project Step-up licenses

Add-on licenses (To-cloud)

Customers with active Software Assurance on Project Standard, Project Professional or Project Server CAL licenses can purchase various Add-on User SLs for Project Plan 3 or Plan 5. Alternatively, a Project Essentials Add-on User SL can be purchased for a Project Server CAL;

Qualifying license	Add-on User SL
Project User or Device CAL	Project Essentials
Project User or Device CAL or Project Standard or Project Professional	Project Plan 3 or Project Plan 5

Figure 87: Microsoft Project To-cloud Add-on licenses

From SA licenses

Customers with active Software Assurance on their Project Server CALs and Project Standard/Professional licenses can choose the following From SA licenses to move to Project User SLs:

Qualifying license	From SA User SL
Project Standard + Project Server CAL	Project Plan 1
Project Professional + Project Server CAL	Project Plan 3 or Project Plan 5

Figure 88: Microsoft Project From SA licenses

On-premises use rights

All four of the Microsoft Project licenses we've been looking at in this section include access to a licensed on-premises Project Server:

- Project Essentials
- Project Plans 1, 3 and 5

Availability of Microsoft Project licenses

Microsoft Project User SLs are available through the Volume Licensing agreements and CSP.

DYNAMICS 365 CRM APPS

One of the key solution areas that Dynamics 365 delivers on is the area of Customer Relationship Management, enabling organizations to get a holistic view of what's happening across their customers. While it's useful to get insights across an organization, actual users working in different functional areas of the business need software specific to their roles. Thus, there are three main apps within the CRM solution: Sales, Customer Service, and Field Service, and you would license professionals who work in these areas with the relevant app. For example:

- A Territory Sales Manager managing sales pipelines and closing deals would be licensed for the **Sales** app
- A Customer Service Rep managing cases would be licensed for the **Customer Service** app
- A Field Technician managing site repairs and updating work orders would be licensed for the **Field Service** app

Professional and Enterprise licenses

For the Sales and Customer Service apps there are both Professional and Enterprise licenses available, where the Enterprise license gives access to a greater level of functionality. These licenses are NOT meant to be combined within an organization and you wouldn't, for example, license some people with Sales Professional licenses and others with Sales Enterprise licenses. You would decide, for the business as a whole, what functionality is required for a sales solution, and then purchase Sales Professional OR Sales Enterprise licenses for members of the sales team.

In a larger organization, if the head office needs the functionality of Sales Enterprise but a subsidiary only needs Sales Professional, then the applications must be deployed in separate environments.

User and Device Subscription Licenses

As you know, the usual model for licensing Microsoft's Online Services is with User Subscription Licenses, but there are some Device Subscription Licenses also available for the CRM apps as shown below:

App	User SL	Device SL
Sales Enterprise	✔	✔
Sales Professional	✔	
Customer Service Enterprise	✔	✔
Customer Service Professional	✔	
Field Service	✔	✔

Figure 89: CRM apps User and Device Subscription License availability

The User and Device SLs give access to exactly the same functionality and are there as a choice for a customer: if they have several users sharing a device then it's probably attractive to license with a Device SL, whereas if users may use several devices, then a User SL is a better choice. In terms of price, a Device SL is about 50% more expensive than a User SL. Customers are free to mix User and Device SLs as works best for them. Users licensed with a User SL use their own credentials to use any device to access the apps, while shared devices are used by any user with a shared login.

Base and Attach licenses

If there are users within an organization who need to be licensed for more than one app then there's a cost-effective way of doing this with the Dynamics 365 licensing model. The first license that you assign to a user is known as a Base license and the second (and subsequent) licenses are called

Attach licenses. Attach licenses are much cheaper than the original Base licenses – they could be as little as a fifth of the cost.

There are rules about how you combine Base and Attach licenses: the table below shows the possible combinations for the applications we've talked about so far and, in all cases, the Base license must be the most expensive license:

Base license	Eligible Attach licenses
Sales Enterprise	Customer Service Enterprise or Professional, Field Service
Sales Professional	Customer Service Professional
Customer Service Enterprise	Sales Enterprise or Professional, Field Service
Customer Service Professional	Sales Professional
Field Service	Sales Enterprise or Professional, Customer Service Enterprise or Professional

Figure 90: CRM apps Base and Attach license combinations

Although some of the apps may be available to be licensed via Device SLs, Base and Attach licenses are always User SLs.

Team Members licenses

So far we've talked about licenses for the three CRM apps, but there's another license – a Team Members license. This is a User Subscription License costing around 10% of the cost of one of the Enterprise licenses we've been talking about, and it's used to license users who only need light access to the CRM functionality. Someone with this license can read Dynamics 365 CRM data across all of the apps, but can only create, update or delete data in a specific set of limited scenarios. There is some flexibility in customizing these scenarios with up to 15 additional tables.

All of the CRM app licenses also include Team Members rights which means that if, for example, a user is licensed with a Sales Enterprise User SL then they also have light access to the Customer Service and Field Service parts of the solution.

At this point it's probably worth considering how you'd assign the right license to a user – how do you know exactly what they're going to be allowed to do? The Dynamics 365 Licensing Guide is a very useful resource for situations like this and you can find it here: http://bit.ly/D365LicensingGuide.

The snippet below is taken from the Licensing Guide and you can see a list of functionality for the Customer Service app at the left-hand side (it's just the start of a very long list!) and then the indicators at the right-hand side show which license (Team Members, Customer Service Professional, or Customer Service Enterprise) gives access to that functionality:

Customer Service use rights

Use Rights	Team Members	Customer Service	
		Pro	Ent
Access			
Dynamics 365 for Outlook and Dynamics 365 App for Outlook[1]	•	•	•
Dynamics 365 Mobile Client Application	•	•	•
Microsoft Dynamics 365 for iPad & Windows	•	•	•
Microsoft Dynamics 365 Web application	•	•	•
Read			
All Dynamics 365 application data	•	•	•
Custom table data	•	•	•
Approve			
Finance functionality: time, expense, and invoices	•	•	•
Tables: Create, Update, Delete			
Accounts		•	•
Activities	•	•	•
Announcements	•	•	•
Calendar: share	•	•	•
Case/Incident		•	•
Contacts	•	•	•
Custom tables (see Appendix D)	15 max[2]	15 max	•
Embedded Intelligence			•
Entitlements		•	•
Facilities/Equipment			•
Leads (create only)		•	•

Figure 91: choosing the right CRM app licenses

Licensing external users

Limited external user access is included with the licenses purchased for internal users. An external user could be an end customer of the organization buying the licenses, or a supplier – perhaps a supply chain vendor, or an IT help desk vendor who services multiple organizations.

If business processes are outsourced to external contractors, then these people need to be licensed as internal users.

Microsoft Relationship Sales Solution Plus

The Microsoft Relationship Sales Solution Plus User SL is a single license for organizations wanting to license users for both the Dynamics 365 Sales Enterprise app and LinkedIn Sales Navigator Enterprise. It is only available through the Enterprise Agreement where a minimum purchase of 10 licenses is required. Note that although the product is classed as an Additional Product in the Enterprise Agreement, licenses can't be reduced at anniversary.

Since the Microsoft Relationship Sales Solution Plus license includes Sales Enterprise it qualifies as a Base license with the same Attach license purchases permitted shown in the first row in the table on page 226. However, because a Microsoft Relationship Sales Solution Plus license is significantly more expensive than a Sales Enterprise license, it does qualify as a Base license for a couple of the Dynamics 365 ERP apps too, and you can find a table with details on page 244.

Included entitlements for other Dynamics apps

The Sales Enterprise, Customer Service Enterprise and Field Service licenses include 2,000 **Customer Voice** responses per tenant per month.

Organizations with Customer Service Enterprise licenses may also install and use **Unified Service Desk** for licensed users. Unified Service Desk enables organizations to quickly build applications for call centers so that agents can get a unified view of customer data.

Dataverse capacity

Default capacity

The first Base license of certain Dynamics 365 apps enables default Dataverse capacities across the whole tenant. For the CRM apps, it's any of the licenses that we've been talking about: Sales Professional or Enterprise, Customer Service Professional or Enterprise, and Field Service. In common with most of the other Dynamics 365 apps, these default capacities are:

- Dataverse Database capacity: 10 GB
- Dataverse File capacity: 20 GB
- Dataverse Log capacity: 2 GB

Accrued capacity

In addition, Sales Enterprise, Customer Service Enterprise and Field Service Base licenses accrue additional capacity for each license acquired:

- Dataverse Database capacity: 250 MB
- Dataverse File capacity: 2 GB
- Dataverse Log capacity: None

For example, if Ochre Poker purchase 10 x Sales Enterprise User SLs they will be entitled to:

- Dataverse Database capacity
  10 GB + 10 x 250 MB = 12.5 GB
- Dataverse File capacity
  20 GB + 10 x 2 GB = 40 GB
- Dataverse Log capacity
  2 GB

It's just Base licenses that accrue the additional capacity, including those offers that include Sales Enterprise such as Sales Premium (see below) and Microsoft Relationship Sales Solution Plus licenses.

Additional capacity

Customers requiring further capacity can purchase Dataverse Database, File and/or Log Capacity Add-ons in increments of 1 GB.

Add-on licenses (In-cloud)

Users licensed with Sales Enterprise, Customer Service Enterprise and Field Service licenses are eligible for a number of In-cloud Add-on licenses as detailed below. It doesn't matter if the qualifying licenses are Base or Attach licenses.

Sales Enterprise

Customers with Sales Enterprise licenses have access to the standard features of **Sales Insights** functionality which includes, for example, the Assistant. This analyzes customer-interaction data in Dynamics 365 Sales and Microsoft 365 databases, and advises sellers on their best course of action to build stronger relationships with their customers and to close more deals. Organizations that want to access the premium features of Sales Insights, such as predictive forecasting and pipeline intelligence, can purchase Sales Insights User SLs and assign them to users already licensed with a Sales Enterprise User SL. Users licensed with Microsoft Relationship Sales Solution Plus User SLs would also be eligible to be licensed with these Sales Insights User SLs.

An alternative license, the **Sales Premium** User SL, is a cost-effective way for organizations to license a single user for both Sales Enterprise and Sales Insights. The Sales Premium license also qualifies as a Base license in the same way as the Microsoft Relationship Sales Solution Plus license, and again, due to its higher price it also qualifies as a Base license for some of the ERP apps as shown on page 244.

Conversation Intelligence in Sales Insights assists sales managers to analyze the calls of individual call center sellers and to help them improve with targeted coaching. There are 3 hours of call analysis included in each Sales Insights User SL, pooled at the tenant level, and additional hours can be purchased via the **Call Intelligence** Add-on license providing an additional 1,000 hours per tenant per month.

Customer Service Enterprise

Users licensed with Customer Service Enterprise User SLs have access to **Customer Service Insights** functionality which was once a standalone license. There are also two Add-on User SLs to license further, optional functionality for these users. The first, **Chat for Customer Service**, enables customer service agents to engage with customers in real time to resolve issues faster. The second, **Digital Messaging**, includes Chat for Customer Service as well as support for third party SMS and additional messaging channels. Both Add-on User SLs include an entitlement to 1,000 Power Virtual Agent chat sessions at the tenant level. Additional chat sessions can be purchased, as detailed on page 289.

Field Service

Resource Scheduling Optimization automatically schedules jobs to the people, equipment, and facilities best equipped to complete them. The Resource Scheduling Optimization Add-on license may be purchased when an organization has one or more Field Service licenses. One license is required for each resource whose schedules will be optimized. Resources can be either a person or a non-human asset.

Step-up licenses

Some of the most useful Step-up licenses for the CRM apps are shown on the next page.

Original license	Step-up User SL
Team Members	Sales Professional or Enterprise, Customer Service Professional or Enterprise, Field Service
Sales Professional	Sales Enterprise
Customer Service Professional	Customer Service Enterprise
Sales Enterprise	Sales Premium or Microsoft Relationship Sales Solution Plus

Figure 92: CRM apps Step-up licenses

There are also Step-up licenses available when an EA customer has, in error, purchased an Attach license rather than a Base license for a product:

Original license	Step-up User SL
Sales Professional Attach	Sales Professional Base
Sales Enterprise Attach	Sales Enterprise Base
Customer Service Professional Attach	Customer Service Professional Base
Customer Service Enterprise Attach	Customer Service Enterprise Base
Field Service Attach	Field Service Base

Figure 93: CRM apps Attach to Base Step-up licenses`

From SA licenses

In October 2019 Microsoft announced a simplification of the licensing for customers moving from an on-premises Dynamics 365 solution to an online one. They decided that, rather than having Add-on AND From SA licenses, they would just have From SA licenses for customers with either active Software Assurance in a Volume Licensing agreement or an active Enhancement Plan when buying through the Dynamics Price List (DPL). In addition, they also decided to have just one From SA license regardless of the licensing starting point. Thus, a Customer Service Professional From SA User SL may be purchased for a user licensed with a Team Members CAL, a Sales CAL or a Customer Service CAL, for instance.

These licenses were made available through CSP and the EA. There are also From SA Attach licenses available, and these are used to purchase licenses for the second and further apps that a user needs to be licensed for.

On-premises use rights

On-premises server access rights

The Dynamics 365 Sales Enterprise, Customer Service Enterprise, and Team Members Subscription Licenses allow users to access and use equivalent functionality in Dynamics 365 Server which is the on-premises Dynamics 365 CRM product.

Server installation rights

Dynamics 365 Server is licensed with the Server/CAL model (see page 81) albeit a slightly strange one since there is no Server license you can buy – the CALs allow you to install the server software. The Sales Enterprise, Customer Service Enterprise, and Field Service SLs allow you to install the on-premises server software too, in the same way as the CALs do. Customers may choose to exercise downgrade rights and deploy CRM Server 2016.

Availability of Dynamics 365 CRM apps licenses

Licenses for the Dynamics 365 CRM apps are available through CSP and the EA and MPSA Volume Licensing agreements. As usual, check out the Product Terms website for specifics.

DYNAMICS 365 MARKETING

Dynamics 365 Marketing is a marketing automation application helping users to automate the marketing process to generate, score and qualify leads for a sales team.

Licensing Dynamics 365 Marketing

The Marketing app is licensed via a single license that is purchased for a tenant and enables the Marketing functionality for an organization. Customers who have ten of any one of the following licenses are eligible to purchase the Marketing Attach license. Note that you can't combine licenses to meet minimums – you do need ten licenses of any ONE of these app licenses:

- Sales Enterprise or Sales Professional
- Customer Service Enterprise or Customer Service Professional
- Field Service
- Finance, Supply Chain Management, Commerce or Project Operations

Customers who don't qualify for the Marketing Attach license must buy the more expensive Marketing Standalone license for which there are no prerequisites.

Marketing contacts

Once a Marketing license is acquired – either the Attach or Standalone variety – then all contacts that will be used for a marketing activity need to be licensed. Both Marketing licenses include an initial capacity of 10,000 Marketing contacts per tenant per month, and then organizations need to cover additional contacts according to how many contacts they will be marketing to each month.

To identify a Marketing contact, the Marketing app monitors the interactions of contacts, and any contact that performs one or more of these key interactions is flagged as a Marketing contact and counts against the

Marketing contact total:

- Contact used in customer journey
- Marketing email sent
- Marketing or LinkedIn form submitted
- Event registration or check-in

Once a contact has been counted as a Marketing contact, it doesn't matter how many of these actions they perform, they are still just counted as a single Marketing contact. Contacts that aren't involved in any of the above interactions do not count towards the Marketing contacts' total.

Additional Marketing contacts

For customers who need less than 50,000 additional contacts, there are packs of 5,000 contacts to purchase, and a customer simply purchases as many of these packs as required.

For customers who need 50,000 or more additional contacts there are packs of 50,000 contacts to purchase which are arranged in four tiers. There is decreasing pricing and increasing minimums to meet as you go through the tiers. You'll notice there is no Tier 1 shown – that's the packs of 5,000 contacts I mentioned in the previous paragraph, and for which a minimum purchase of 1 pack applies:

Tier	Additional contacts required	Minimum packs
2	50,000 – 99,999	1
3	100,000 – 249,999	2
4	250,000 – 499,999	5
5	500,000 +	10

Figure 94: Marketing Additional Contacts SKUs

Let's see how this works in a customer scenario, and we'll take a look at Maroon Balloons who have purchased the Marketing Standalone license since they don't have any existing Dynamics 365 licenses to qualify for the Marketing Attach license. They intend to market to 300,000 contacts each month. Now, they have access to 10,000 contacts included in the Marketing Standalone license and thus they need to cover 290,000 additional contacts.

What do they do? They use the table above and find where the 290,000 contacts that they need to cover fits into the ranges shown. They're eligible for Tier 4 pricing since 290,000 is between 250,000 and 499,999. The packs for these tiers are in multiples of 50,000 so they divide their requirement of 290,000 contacts by this number to give the number of SKUs they should buy. The answer here is 5.8, which of course you can't transact, so they will need 6 of the Tier 4 packs which, as you can see, is in line for the minimums for that tier.

As usual, they need to commit to these SKUs either for a 12-month period in programs like CSP, or up until anniversary in the Enterprise Agreement.

Licensing Marketing users

As we've seen, the Marketing app is not licensed by user, but two things need to be in place before a user can use the features and functionality of the Marketing app.

First of all, they do need some sort of license – either a Dynamics 365 Sales, Customer Service or Field Service license, or a free Marketing User license. These licenses are acquired through the Microsoft 365 Admin Center and assigned to users in the usual way.

Secondly, an IT admin needs to assign the relevant security roles and privileges to a user to ensure that they can access the Marketing features they need.

Dataverse capacity

Default capacity

The Marketing Standalone license includes default Dataverse capacities which are shared per tenant, as shown below:

- Dataverse Database capacity: 10 GB
- Dataverse File capacity: 20 GB
- Dataverse Log capacity: 2 GB

Purchasing additional Marketing applications

Organizations may purchase additional production or non-production Marketing applications. No additional marketing contact capacities are included in these purchases and the total marketing contacts used is counted across both production and non-production applications on a tenant.

Included entitlements for other Dynamics apps

The Marketing Standalone license includes 2,000 **Customer Voice** responses per tenant per month.

Availability of Dynamics 365 Marketing licenses

The Dynamics 365 Marketing licenses are available through CSP and the EA and MPSA Volume Licensing agreements. As usual, check out the Product Terms website for specifics.

DYNAMICS 365 CUSTOMER INSIGHTS

Dynamics 365 Customer Insights is part of Microsoft's Customer Data Platform that helps businesses unify all of their customer data to give a single view of all customer information. An organization can then use these insights to drive customer-centric experiences and processes.

Dynamics 365 Customer Insights app licenses

Customer Insights is licensed in a similar way to the Marketing app – a customer purchases a single tenant license that enables Customer Insights functionality for an organization. Customers who have any of the following licenses are eligible to purchase the Customer Insights Attach license:

- 20 x Sales Enterprise
- 20 x Customer Service Enterprise
- 1 x Marketing Standalone

Customers who don't qualify for the Customer Insights Attach license are obliged to buy the more expensive Customer Insights Standalone license for which there are no prerequisites.

Dynamics 365 Customer Insights profiles

A Customer Insights profile is a report for a single customer that is created by collecting data from multiple sources. The Customer Insights Standalone and Attach licenses include an initial capacity of 100,000 profiles per tenant per month, and then organizations need to cover additional profiles according to how many customers they have.

There is a Customer Insights Additional Profiles license available for customers to purchase, with each license adding 100,000 profiles to the tenant each month. As usual, they need to commit to these SKUs either for a 12-month period in programs like CSP, or up until anniversary in the Enterprise Agreement.

Included entitlements for other Dynamics apps

The Customer Insights Standalone license includes 2,000 **Customer Voice** responses per tenant per month.

Dataverse capacity

Default capacity

Acquiring a Customers Insights Standalone license enables the following default Dataverse capacities across the whole tenant:

- Dataverse Database capacity: 15 GB
- Dataverse File capacity: 20 GB
- Dataverse Log capacity: 2 GB

Availability of Dynamics 365 Customer Insights licenses

The Dynamics 365 Customer Insights licenses are available through CSP and the EA and MPSA Volume Licensing agreements. As usual, check out the Product Terms website for specifics.

DYNAMICS 365 CUSTOMER VOICE

Dynamics 365 Customer Voice is an Enterprise Feedback Management solution that enables organizations to develop custom surveys to collect feedback from customers and employees.

Licensing Dynamics 365 Customer Voice

Customer Voice is licensed per tenant with capacity allowances based on the number of responses that distributed surveys receive.

The following licenses include 2,000 Customer Voice responses per tenant per month:

- Sales Enterprise
- Customer Service Enterprise
- Field Service
- Marketing Standalone
- Customer Insights Standalone
- Human Resources

Alternatively, there is a Customer Voice Standalone license available which also includes 2,000 Customer Voice responses per tenant per month.

Licensing Customer Voice users

Like the Marketing app, Customer Voice is licensed by tenant rather than by user, but internal users do need some sort of license before they can start using Customer Voice to create and distribute surveys. If users are licensed with a Sales Enterprise, Customer Service Enterprise, or Field Service license, then Customer Voice is already available to those users.

Other users need to have a Customer Voice User license assigned to them. These are free licenses but need to be "purchased" through the Microsoft 365 Admin Center and then assigned to a user.

Licensing for additional Customer Voice responses

Organizations already licensed with the Customer Voice Standalone license, or one of the other licenses listed, can purchase Customer Voice Additional Responses licenses to add a further 1,000 responses per tenant per month for each license purchased. Customer Voice responses are enforced annually.

In programs like CSP customers may (if their partner permits it) pay for licenses monthly. However, Customer Voice responses are still consumed against the annual commitment. For example, if Honeydew Hatters purchase 2 of the Customer Voice Additional Responses licenses, then they have 2 x 1,000 x 12 = 24,000 responses that can be used through the year. They're not restricted to just using 2,000 responses a month, they can use them as required. If they run out of responses in the eleventh month then Customer Voice will stop receiving new responses and won't allow new surveys to be created. Naturally, Honeydew Hatters will need to purchase further Customer Voice Additional Response licenses at that point. If they have unused responses at the end of the year, these responses are not carried over to the next year.

Availability of Dynamics 365 Customer Voice licenses

The Dynamics 365 Customer Voice licenses are available through CSP and the EA and MPSA Volume Licensing agreements. As usual, check out the Product Terms website for specifics.

DYNAMICS 365 ERP APPS

Enterprise Resource Planning is the other key area that Dynamics 365 delivers on, enabling an organization to manage processes and departments within and across the entire organization. Again, people working in the business will need software specific to their roles and thus there are five main apps that form the ERP solution: Commerce, Finance, Supply Chain Management, Project Operations and Human Resources, and you would license professionals who work in these areas with the relevant app. For example:

- Users who work in the headquarters of a retail operation would be licensed for the **Commerce** app
- Users working in a central finance department would be licensed for the **Finance** app
- Users in operations roles at manufacturers, distributors, and retailers would be licensed for the **Supply Chain Management** app
- Project managers, project assistants and project accountants responsible for accelerating project delivery would be licensed for the **Project Operations** app
- An HR professional or a recruiter would be licensed for the **Human Resources** app

User Subscription Licenses

Licenses for the main apps detailed above are all User Subscription Licenses, assigned to individual users, following all the usual rules.

Base and Attach licenses

As with the CRM apps, if there are users within an organization who need to be licensed for more than one app then Base and Attach licenses are a cost-effective way of doing this. In the CRM section we considered just the CRM apps in terms of Base and Attach licenses and the various combinations that are allowed. In reality, however, there are further combinations permitted, mixing the CRM and ERP apps. I've already mentioned how useful the

Dynamics 365 Licensing Guide is, and this snippet from it shows the allowable Base and Attach license combinations:

Dynamics 365 base licenses per user	Dynamics 365 attach licenses per user										
	Commerce	CS Ent	CS Pro	Field Svc	Finance	HR	Proj Oper.	RA	Sales Ent	Sales Pro	SCM
Business Central Essentials			•							•	
Business Central Premium			•							•	
Commerce		•	•	•	•	•	•		•	•	•
Customer Service Enterprise (CS)				•					•	•	
Customer Service Professional (CS)											
Field Service		•	•					•	•	•	
Finance	•	•	•	•		•	•		•	•	•
Guides											
Human Resources (HR)		•	•	•			•		•	•	
Microsoft Relationship Sales solution Plus (MRSs Plus)		•	•	•		•	•				
Project Operations (Proj Oper.)		•	•	•		•			•	•	
Remote Assist (RA)											
Sales Enterprise		•	•	•							
Sales Premium		•	•	•		•	•				
Sales Professional			•								
Supply Chain Management (SCM)	•	•	•	•	•	•	•		•	•	

Figure 95: CRM and ERP Base and Attach license combinations

You may notice from the table that it's always the ERP apps that are the Base licenses and the CRM apps which are the Attach licenses in a combined solution; this is due to the cost of the app licenses – the ERP ones are always more expensive than the CRM ones and thus must be the Base licenses. The exceptions are the Sales Premium and Microsoft Relationship Sales Solution Plus licenses which incorporate Sales Enterprise with Sales Insights and LinkedIn Sales Navigator Enterprise respectively, and qualify as Base licenses due to their higher price.

Minimum purchasing requirements

There are some minimum purchasing requirements tied to the five ERP app licenses, as listed below:

- 20 x Commerce
- 20 x Finance
- 20 x Supply Chain Management
- 20 x Project Operations
- 5 x Human Resources

In an Enterprise Agreement, you may combine licenses to meet the minimums in two ways. Firstly, you could combine any numbers of licenses of the first four apps to meet the 20-license minimum: 10 x Commerce + 10 x Finance, for example.

Secondly, the Operations-Device SLs (see page 252) can be used to satisfy the minimums of the first four apps with a ratio of 2.5 to 1. Thus, 50 x Operations-Device SLs would be sufficient to meet the 20-license minimum for Commerce, Finance, Supply Chain Management, or Project Operations.

In CSP it's not possible to combine licenses in any way – the initial order for each of the five apps needs to be for the full minimum amount.

Team Members licenses

Team Members User Subscription Licenses are also available for the same sort of users detailed in the CRM section, and they have similar use rights – someone with this license can read Dynamics 365 ERP data across all of the apps, but can only create, update or delete data in a specific set of limited scenarios. As before, customization is possible with an additional 15 tables, and users licensed with the full ERP app licenses also have Team Members rights across the other ERP apps.

Note there is just a single Team Members license which allows users to work across both the CRM and ERP solutions.

Human Resources licenses

Organizations that want to license their users for Human Resources functionality will use the Human Resources app license for their HR professionals and recruiters, but then have a choice as to how they license users who need to interact with HR functionality as a secondary part of their role. It could be a manager who needs to be up to date with how recruitment for a role is going, or a regular user who wants to submit vacation requests or view their benefits.

If the users will only use HR functionality, then there is a Human Resources Self Service User SL which licenses them for the light HR tasks just mentioned. However, if they need to access other parts of a Dynamics 365 solution then a Team Members license would be a better fit since it includes all the rights of the Human Resources Self Service license as well as access across the other solution areas. A Human Resources Self Service license is half the price of a Team Members license to put this into perspective.

Licensing external users

Limited external user access is included with the licenses purchased for internal users. An external user could be an end customer of the organization buying the licenses, or a supplier – perhaps a supply chain vendor, or an IT help desk vendor who services multiple organizations.

If business processes are outsourced to external contractors, then these people need to be licensed as internal users.

Included entitlements for other Dynamics apps

Commerce, Finance, Supply Chain Management, and Project Operations licenses include 100 **Electronic Invoicing** transactions per tenant per month.

Commerce licenses include transactions for **Fraud Protection**:

- 20,000 x Account Protection
- 2,000 x Purchase Protection
- 8,000 x Loss Prevention.

Human Resources licenses include 2,000 **Customer Voice** responses per tenant per month.

Dynamics ERP apps capacity

Dataverse capacity

The first Base license of one of the ERP apps that we've considered in this section (Commerce, Finance, Supply Chain Management, Project Operations and Human Resources), enables default Dataverse capacities across the whole tenant. In common with the CRM apps, these default capacities are:

- Dataverse Database capacity: 10 GB
- Dataverse File capacity: 20 GB
- Dataverse Log capacity: 2 GB

However, unlike the CRM apps further capacity is not accrued for each license purchased. Customers requiring further Dataverse capacity must purchase Dataverse Database, File and Log Capacity Add-ons in increments of 1 GB.

Operations capacity

The first license of the ERP apps also enables Operations Database and Operations File capacity for the tenant as below:

- Operations Database capacity: 20 GB
- Operations File Capacity: 40 GB

In addition, some licenses accrue additional capacity as shown in the table on the next page. For the Commerce, Finance, Supply Chain Management, and Project Operations (but not Human Resources*) licenses the accrued amounts are per SL, for Operations-Activity licenses the accrued amounts are per 4 SLs, and for Operations-Device licenses the accrued amounts are per 2.5 SLs:

Capacity type	ERP apps*	Operations-Activity	Operations-Device
Operations Database capacity	500 MB/SL	500 MB/4 SL	500 MB/2.5 SL
Operations File capacity	4 GB/SL	4 GB/4 SL	4 MB/2.5 SL

Figure 96: ERP apps Operations capacity

For example, if Aisle of White Paints have purchased 20 x Commerce licenses, 16 x Operations-Activity, and 20 x Operations-Device licenses, they will have the following Operations capacity available to them:

- Operations Database capacity
  20 GB + 20 x 500 MB + (16/4) x 500 MB + (20/2.5) x 500 MB = 36 GB
- Operations File capacity
  40 GB + 20 x 4 GB = (16/4) x 4 GB + (20/2.5) x 4 GB = 168 GB

Operations Database Capacity and File Capacity Add-ons are also available in increments of 1 GB.

Environments

Commerce, Finance, Supply Chain Management and Project Operations licenses enable an Application Object Server (AOS) production environment which comes with Disaster Recovery and high availability and is monitored 24/7 for service health. Additional production environments are not available.

These licenses also include a Tier 2 Sandbox environment, and additional Tier 2, Tier 3, Tier 4 and Tier 5 Sandbox environments may be purchased as required.

Human Resources licenses come with 2 Dataverse environments and 2 AOS environments, only 1 of which may be in production at a time. Additional Human Resources Sandbox environments may be purchased as required.

Step-up licenses

Here are some of the most useful Step-up licenses available for the ERP apps:

Original license	Step-up User SL
Human Resources Self Service	Team Members
Team Members	Commerce, Finance, Supply Chain Management, Project Operations, Human Resources, or Operations-Activity
Operations-Activity	Commerce, Finance, Supply Chain Management, Project Operations, or Human Resources

Figure 97: ERP apps Step-up licenses

There are also Step-up licenses available when an EA customer has, in error, purchased an Attach license rather than a Base license for a product:

Original license	Step-up User SL
Commerce Attach	Commerce Base
Finance Attach	Finance Base
Supply Chain Management Attach	Supply Chain Management Base
Project Operations Attach	Project Operations Base
Human Resources Attach	Human Resources Base

Figure 98: ERP apps Attach to Base Step-up licenses

From SA licenses

In October 2019 Microsoft announced a simplification of the licensing for customers moving from an on-premises Dynamics 365 solution to an online one. They decided that, rather than having Add-on AND From SA licenses, they would just have From SA licenses for customers with either active Software Assurance in a Volume Licensing agreement or an active Enhancement Plan when buying through the Dynamics Price List (DPL). In addition, they also decided to have just one From SA license regardless of the licensing starting point. Thus, a Supply Chain Management From SA User SL may be purchased for a user licensed with a Team Members CAL, an Operations Activity CAL or an Operations User CAL, for instance.

These licenses were made available through CSP and the EA. There are also From SA Attach licenses available, and these are used to purchase licenses for the second and further apps that a user needs to be licensed for.

On-premises use rights

On-premises server access rights

The licenses we've considered in this section allow users to access and use equivalent functionality in Dynamics 365 for Operations Server which is the on-premises Dynamics 365 ERP product.

If you look at the diagram on page 85 you can see that the on-premises product is licensed with the Server/CAL model and there are four different CALs. The table on the next page shows which Online Services license is equivalent to which on-premises CAL. The * in the table means that these users don't have full access to all parts of the on-premises solution – for instance, a user licensed with a Finance User SL can only use the Dynamics 365 on-premises security roles associated with Finance.

Dynamics 365 online license	Equivalent on-premises CAL
Operations-Device SL	Operations Device CAL
Operations-Activity User SL	Operations Activity User CAL
Team Members User SL	Team Members User CAL
* Commerce, Finance, Supply Chain Management, Project Operations User SL	* Operations User CAL

Figure 99: ERP apps on-premises CAL equivalents

On-premises server installation rights

Dynamics 365 for Operations Server is licensed with the Server/CAL model and users licensed with Commerce, Finance, Supply Chain Management, and Project Operations User SLs may install the server software. Customers may choose to exercise downgrade rights and install and use Dynamics AX 2012 R3 Server.

Availability of Dynamics 365 ERP apps licenses

Licenses for the Dynamics 365 ERP apps are available through CSP and the EA and MPSA Volume Licensing agreements. As usual, check out the Product Terms website for specifics.

DYNAMICS 365 COMMERCE

In the Dynamics 365 ERP apps section I said that users who work in the headquarters of a retail operation would be licensed with the Commerce app. In this section we'll consider how the other parts of the retail operation would be licensed: the users who work in stores or a call center, and the eCommerce part of the business.

Licensing stores and call centers

There are two licenses aimed at licensing stores and call centers – the Operations-Device license and the Operations-Activity license. The Operations-Device license (as its name indeed suggests) is a device license, and the Operations-Activity license is a user license. However, they are not equivalent alternatives as they are for the user and device licenses for the CRM apps covered on page 225. The Operations-Device license is aimed at a specific set of scenarios for licensing Point of Sale devices, and shop floor or warehouse devices.

The Operations-Activity license allows access to all the functionality that the Operations-Device license does with some additional functionality, such as reviewing and approving bank reconciliations, for example. The Operations-Activity license is about two thirds of the price of the Operations-Device license and thus, if several users are sharing a device in a store it certainly makes sense to license that store device with an Operations-Device license. Equally, if a single user needs to use several devices, then an Operations-Activity license is a good idea.

CRM users using a device licensed with a Device SL use a shared login, but users who use a device licensed with an Operations-Device license can either use a shared login or use their existing credentials to use that device. An IT administrator will have assigned security roles to users such that when they log in to a store or warehouse device, they will have access to the right parts of the application to do their jobs.

Licensing eCommerce solutions

The Dynamics 365 eCommerce solution is licensed by tenant, and enabled when an organization purchases an eCommerce Tier license. Each eCommerce Tier license includes a certain number of transactions, and there are overage SKUs associated with each tier to enable further transactions. Just to add to the excitement of choosing the right tier, there are also bands which you need to choose based on expected Average Order Value – the result of dividing a customer's total revenue by the number of transactions.

Let's take a snippet from the Dynamics 365 Licensing Guide and do a scenario to make sure all is clear.

	# of monthly transactions per SKU					
	BAND 1 AOV<$50	BAND 2 AOV $50-$150	BAND 3 AOV $150-$500	BAND 4 AOV $500-$2K	BAND 5 AOV $2K-$5K	BAND 6 AOV $5K+
Tier 1	4,700	2,400	1,100	480	275	200
Tier 1 overage	780	365	170	80	45	30
Tier 2	29,000	12,000	5,500	2,900	1,700	1,160
Tier 2 overage	1,250	540	230	125	75	50
Tier 3	86,000	38,750	15,500	8,600	5,065	3,400
Tier 3 overage	1,400	625	250	140	85	55

Figure 100: eCommerce Tiers and Overage SKUs

Xanthic Tractors are interested in transacting via the eCommerce solution and to choose the right licenses they need to be armed with two pieces of information – the number of transactions they are expecting to carry out each month over a 12-month period, and the Average Order Value (AOV). After research and discussion, they decide that their AOV is likely to be around $3,000 and they would expect 500 orders for most months of the year, but up to 750 orders in July to September. This equates to 9 x 500 + 3 x 750 = 6750 orders for the year, or 562.5 orders a month.

Then they consult the table above to find the right band for their expected AOV of $3,000, which you can see fits into Band 5. So far, so good. Their 562.5 orders a month isn't enough for Tier 2 pricing, so they need to purchase a Band 5 Tier 1 eCommerce SKU. This covers 275 transactions of the required 562.5 and so they need to pay for 288 through overage. Tier 1 Overage for

Band 5 is in increments of 45, so they need 288/45 = 6.4 or 7 of these Overage SKUs each month too.

In common with many of the Dynamics 365 products the transactions are purchased monthly but enforced on an annual basis. Thus, the calculations that Xanthic Tractors have done in good faith are likely to work for them during the year but there may be a shortfall to make up at the end of the year via additional Overage SKUs. They will be notified if there is any shortfall to be paid.

We need to touch again on minimums as we consider the eCommerce solution. In the **Minimum purchasing requirements** section on page 245 you can see that the minimum purchase of Commerce licenses is 20. However, if an organization just wants to use the eCommerce solution, a single eCommerce Tier license also satisfies the minimums, and they would just need a single Commerce license to support the solution. This flexibility is only available for customers purchasing through an Enterprise Agreement – in CSP customers cannot purchase an eCommerce Tier license without first meeting the minimum of 20 Commerce licenses.

Commerce Scale Units

A default Commerce Scale Unit is provisioned when an organization purchases 20 Commerce licenses and one or more Operations-Device licenses. This Commerce Scale Unit only supports device transactions. Equally, if an organization purchases an eCommerce Tier license a Commerce Scale Unit is also provisioned which is used to support eCommerce transactions.

Customers can acquire additional Commerce Scale Units when they want additional cloud environments of the commerce service for co-location, performance, additional redundancy, or customization purposes.

Customers requiring additional Commerce Scale Units to support eCommerce transactions simply purchase an additional eCommerce Tier license. Customers who want an additional Commerce Scale Unit to support device transactions purchase a Commerce Scale Unit license, choosing from three levels dependent on how many devices they want to support:

- Basic: up to 65 devices
- Standard: up to 225 devices
- Premium: up to 500 devices

The Commerce Scale Unit, in effect, includes those numbers of Operations-Device licenses and organizations can acquire further Operations-Device licenses as required. For instance, to cover 100 devices, Xanthic Tractors would purchase a Basic Commerce Scale Unit (which includes 65 devices) and 35 x Operations-Device licenses.

Ratings and Recommendations

There are two additional solution areas that Commerce customers may license for their eCommerce website. The first is **Commerce Recommendations** which helps customers find the products they want, and the second is **Commerce Ratings and Reviews** which enables the retailer to capture product reviews and ratings from their customers.

Both of these licenses are tenant licenses and Add-ons to a Commerce license, and they include capacity which may be consumed at any time during the 12-month Subscription. Commerce Recommendations includes 240,000 transactions, and Commerce Ratings and Reviews provides up to 250,000 active ratings and reviews.

If customers want more capacity, then they just purchase additional units of these licenses – there is no separate additional capacity license.

Availability of Dynamics 365 Commerce licenses

Licenses for the Dynamics 365 Commerce solution are available through CSP and the EA and MPSA Volume Licensing agreements. As usual, check out the Product Terms website for specifics.

DYNAMICS 365 FRAUD PROTECTION

Dynamics 365 Fraud Protection helps customers to block fraudulent activity with a set of three protection and prevention capabilities:

- **Account Protection**
  To assess online account events for fraud or abuse
- **Purchase Protection**
  To assess online payment transactions for fraud
- **Loss Prevention**
  To protect online or in-store transactions by identifying potential fraud on returns and discounts

Licensing Dynamics 365 Fraud Protection

Single workloads

Customers licensing Dynamics 365 Fraud Protection first of all choose a Base offer – this is the workload from the list above which is of primary interest to them. All of the Base offers include a certain number of transactions for the workloads per month, and then customers who need to use more transactions purchase Overage Add-ons which allow additional transactions per month.

Here's the table for the Base offers with the included transactions, and you can see that each workload as a Base offer includes transactions for the other two workloads as well:

Included transactions	Base offers: Account Protection	Base offers: Purchase Protection	Base offers: Loss Prevention
Account Protection	100,000	20,000	20,000
Purchase Protection	2,000	10,000	2,000
Loss Prevention	4,000	4,000	20,000

Figure 101: Dynamics 365 Fraud Protection Base offers

Using the table, you can see that the Account Protection Base offer includes 100,000 Account Protection transactions as well as 2,000 Purchase Protection and 4,000 Loss Prevention transactions per month.

Here's the table for the Overage Add-ons:

	Account Protection	Purchase Protection	Loss Prevention
Included transactions	20,000	2,000	4,000

Figure 102: Dynamics 365 Fraud Protection Overage Add-ons

So, what should customers purchase each month to cover the transactions they need? Well, they need to estimate the transactions for the year, and from there work out the average transactions per month. This means that they can even out any seasonality since unused transactions do, in effect, carry forward between months. As usual, they need to commit to these SKUs either for a 12-month period in programs like CSP, or up until anniversary in the Enterprise Agreement.

Let's take an example to make sure this all makes sense! Sienna Blenders are interested in the capabilities of Account Protection and estimate that they will use 250,000 transactions in February and March, and 190,000 transactions in the other months. They need to total all their estimated transactions: 2 x 250,000 + 10 x 190,000 = 2,400,000, and then divide by 12 = 200,000 to give the required transactions per month. They will purchase the Account Protection Base offer which will give them the included 100,000 transactions per month, and thus will need the remaining 100,000 transactions covered by 100,000 / 20,000 = 5 Overage Add-ons per month.

There's just one other detail to know: there is some advantageous Tier 2 pricing available if customers can reach the minimum transactions per month shown in the table below:

	Account Protection	Purchase Protection	Loss Prevention
Minimum transactions	2,000,000	500,000	250,000

Figure 103: Tier 2 minimum transactions for Overage Add-ons

The calculations work in exactly the same way; customers are just eligible for the Tier 2 level pricing for their Overage Add-ons. For our example here let's consider Fuchsia Fancy Dress Hire who are estimating 700,000 Purchase Protection transactions each month. They will purchase the Purchase Protection Base offer which will give them the included 10,000 transactions per month (from Figure 101), leaving 690,000 transactions to be covered by Overage Add-ons. This number of transactions makes them eligible for Tier 2 pricing (Figure 103) and to calculate the required number of Overage Add-ons they divide their requirement by the number of transactions in the Purchase Protection Overage Add-on (from Figure 102). This gives a requirement for 690,000 / 2,000 = 345 Overage Add-ons per month.

Multiple workloads

Let's now take a look at what happens to the licensing if a customer is interested in multiple workloads, and we'll choose Periwinkle Packaging Solutions for this example. They are estimating that they will use 40,000 Purchase Protection transactions per month and 12,000 Loss Prevention transactions.

So what should they buy? Customers only ever buy one Dynamics 365 Fraud Protection Base offer and Periwinkle Packaging Solutions choose their primary workload for this. Thus, they purchase the Purchase Protection Base offer with its included transactions of 10,000 for Purchase Protection and

4,000 for Loss Prevention. This leaves them a shortfall of 40,000 – 10,000 = 30,000 transactions for Purchase Protection, and 12,000 – 4,000 = 8,000 transactions for Loss Prevention which they need to cover with Overage Add-ons. Note that any of the Overage Add-ons can purchased with any of the base offers. If we refer back to Figure 102 we see that the Overage Add-on for Purchase Protection includes 2,000 transactions so they would need 15 of those licenses for the shortfall that we calculated. In addition, they would need 2 x Loss Prevention Overage Add-on licenses to cover the extra 8,000 transactions that they need for that workload too.

Licensing Dynamics 365 Fraud Protection with Commerce

The final part of our Dynamics 365 Fraud Protection licensing story is what's available to customers who want to license both Dynamics 365 Fraud Protection and Dynamics 365 Commerce.

When customers buy the Commerce licenses (see page 252) they are entitled to some included Fraud Protection transactions as shown in the table below. Note that this is a single allocation – if a customer has 40 Commerce licenses, they still just receive the initial transactions shown below:

Workload	Transactions per month
Account Protection	20,000
Purchase Protection	2,000
Loss Prevention	8,000

Figure 104: Fraud Protection transactions included in Commerce licenses

The Commerce license is also considered to be a Base license for the Fraud Protection solution, which means that the Overage Add-ons that we considered earlier in this section can be added on to the Commerce license as required.

Let's see how this works for Ultramarine Swim Wear. They have 25 Commerce licenses and have estimated that they will require 50,000 Account Protection transactions per month. Their Commerce licenses give them 20,000 Account Protection transactions each month which leaves 30,000 to be covered by the Overage Add-ons. An Account Protection Overage Add-on provides 20,000 transactions per month, so they would purchase 2 of these licenses.

Availability of Fraud Protection licenses

The Dynamics 365 Fraud Protection licenses are available through CSP and the EA and MPSA Volume Licensing agreements. As usual, check out the Product Terms website for specifics.

DYNAMICS 365 ELECTRONIC INVOICING

Electronic Invoicing enables organizations to create and present invoice documents in an electronic format. It aims to prevent tax evasion and is gaining in popularity in both business-to-government and business-to-business scenarios.

Included capacity

Commerce, Finance, Supply Chain Management, and Project Operations licenses include 100 Electronic Invoicing transactions per tenant per month.

Additional capacity

Organizations that have licenses for one of the apps listed above and who need additional Electronic Invoicing transactions are eligible to purchase Dynamics 365 Electronic Invoicing Add-on licenses. These licenses provide an additional 1,000 Electronic Invoicing transactions per month.

Any unused transactions do not carry forward between months and customers should license for peak capacity. As usual, they need to commit to these SKUs either for a 12-month period in programs like CSP, or up until anniversary in the Enterprise Agreement.

Availability of Electronic Invoicing licenses

The Dynamics 365 Electronic Invoicing Add-on licenses are available through CSP and the EA and MPSA Volume Licensing agreements. As usual, check out the Product Terms website for specifics.

DYNAMICS 365 BUSINESS CENTRAL

Dynamics 365 Business Central is an ERP solution aimed at smaller business helping them to automate and streamline their business processes.

Business Central Essentials and Premium licenses

A bit like the Dynamics 365 Sales and Customer Service apps there are two levels of functionality with Business Central: Essentials and Premium. Customers must choose one or the other to license users in the organization, dependent on what functionality is required across the business.

A Business Central Essentials User SL gives a named user access to the following functionality: financial management, supply chain management, customer relationship management, human resources management, project management and warehouse management. A Business Central Premium User SL additionally gives access to service management and manufacturing functionality.

Business Central Device license

In addition to the Business Central Essentials and Premium User SLs there is also a Business Central Device SL which gives access to a subset of Business Central capabilities. It's a pretty similar set of functionality to that which the Dynamics 365 Operations-Device license gives access to, and it's used for licensing Point of Sale devices, and shop floor or warehouse devices.

Users who use a device licensed with a Business Central Device license can either use a shared login or use their existing credentials to use that device. An IT administrator will have assigned security roles to users such that when they log in to a store or warehouse device, they will have access to the right parts of the application to do their jobs.

Business Central Team Members license

In common with the Dynamics 365 CRM and ERP apps there is a Business Central Team Members User SL for users who just need to have read access across the Business Central solution and to participate in a limited set of scenarios. As with the Dynamics 365 Team Members solution, there's customization allowed with up to 15 additional tables.

Note that the Business Central Team Members license is a completely separate license to the Dynamics 365 Team Members license.

Base and Attach licenses

With the CRM and ERP apps, if there are users within an organization who need to be licensed for more than one app then Base and Attach licenses are a cost-effective way of doing this. Within the Business Central solution there's no need for Base and Attach licenses since we know that organizations choose either Essentials or Premium licenses.

However, both these licenses are also eligible Base licenses for the Sales Professional and Customer Service Professional Attach licenses if customers want to extend their solution to these areas.

Using Business Central with other Dynamics 365 apps

The Business Central solution doesn't work with all of the other Dynamics 365 apps. It DOES work with Sales Professional and Customer Service Professional, as described above, and Business Central customers may also choose to purchase a Marketing Standalone license and/or Fraud Protection Base offers and Overage Add-ons.

Licensing external users

Limited external user access is included with the licenses purchased for internal users. An external user could be an end customer of the organization buying the licenses, or a supplier – perhaps a supply chain vendor, or an IT help desk vendor who services multiple organizations.

If business processes are outsourced to external contractors, then these people need to be licensed as internal users.

Business Central includes 3 External Accountant licenses for customers who have external accountants who need to connect to their Business Central application. These are $0 SKUs which the partner needs to transact so that they can be assigned to external accountant users.

Business Central capacity

The first Business Central Essentials or Premium license includes a default capacity of 80 GB of Business Central Database storage. Customers requiring further capacity can purchase Business Central Database Capacity Add-ons in increments of 1 GB. As usual, they need to commit to these SKUs for a 12-month period.

That first license also includes a single production environment and 3 Sandbox environments. If required, customers can purchase the Business Central Additional Environment Add-on which comes with 1 additional production environment and 3 more Sandbox environments, and 4 GB of Business Central Database storage.

Step-up licenses

There are no Business Central Step-up licenses available. Since Business Central is aimed at a smaller business the licenses are not available in an Enterprise Agreement where Step-up licenses are required to move from a lower edition to a higher edition.

From SA licenses

In October 2019 Microsoft announced a simplification of the licensing for customers moving from an on-premises Dynamics 365 solution to an online one. They decided that, rather than having Add-on AND From SA licenses, they would just have From SA licenses for customers with either active Software Assurance in a Volume Licensing agreement or an active

Enhancement Plan when buying through the Dynamics Price List (DPL). In addition, they also decided to have just one From SA license regardless of the licensing starting point. Thus, a customer can buy Business Central From SA licenses from a variety of on-premises licensing positions.

These new licenses were made available through CSP and the EA. There are also From SA Attach licenses available to purchase licenses for the second and further apps that a user needs to be licensed for.

On-premises use rights

Organizations licensed with Business Central SLs are licensed to install and access the Dynamics 365 Business Central on-premises server solution. The rights are to install the current released version with downgrade rights to the previous three versions.

Availability of Business Central licenses

All of the Business Central licenses are only available through CSP. As usual, check out the Product Terms website for specifics.

DYNAMICS 365 GUIDES

Dynamics 365 Guides is a mixed-reality application that provides users with on-the-job guidance via holographic instructions. HoloLens-wearing users see instruction cards showing what needs to be done, and where, helping them to carry out new or unfamiliar tasks.

Licensing Dynamics 365 Guides

Dynamics 365 Guides is licensed with User Subscription Licenses.

Base and Attach licenses

With the CRM and ERP apps, if there are users within an organization who need to be licensed for more than one app then Base and Attach licenses are a cost-effective way of doing this. The Dynamics 365 Guides license is a unique kind of license in the sense that it sits between a Base and an Attach license. Strictly speaking it IS a Base license, but there are no Attach licenses that can be acquired with it, and it can't be the Attach license to any other product. Thus if, for example, a user needs to be licensed for Sales Enterprise and Dynamics 365 Guides, then a Base license for each product would be required.

Licensing external users

In common with the Dynamics 365 CRM and ERP apps there are no licensing requirements for external users for Dynamics 365 Guides. Have a look at the CRM section for examples of users who are external users and those who are not, on page 228.

Dataverse capacity

Default capacity

Acquiring a Dynamics 365 Guides license enables default Dataverse capacities across the whole tenant. In common with most of the other Dynamics 365 apps, these default capacities are:

- Dataverse Database capacity: 10 GB
- Dataverse File capacity: 20 GB
- Dataverse Log capacity: 2 GB

Additional capacity

Unlike the CRM apps, further capacity is not accrued for each license purchased. Customers requiring further Dataverse capacity must purchase Dataverse Database, File and Log Capacity Add-ons in increments of 1 GB.

Availability of Dynamics 365 Guides licenses

Licenses for Dynamics 365 Guides are available through CSP and the EA and MPSA Volume Licensing agreements. As usual, check out the Product Terms website for specifics.

DYNAMICS 365 REMOTE ASSIST

Dynamics 365 Remote Assist is a mixed-reality application which enables users to get on-the-job help from experts. The user wears a HoloLens and contacts an expert for help via a Teams video call. The expert can see everything the user sees and can provide assistance by holographically drawing and annotating whatever the user is working on.

Licensing Dynamics 365 Remote Assist

Dynamics 365 Remote Assist is licensed with User Subscription Licenses. Licensed users may make and receive Teams calls without a separate Teams license, but the expert they contact for remote assistance does need to be licensed for Teams.

Base and Attach licenses

With the CRM and ERP apps, if there are users within an organization who need to be licensed for more than one app then Base and Attach licenses are a cost-effective way of doing this. The Dynamics 365 Remote Assist product can be acquired as an Attach license for a Field Service Base license but can't itself be used as a Base license for any other products. Thus if, for example, a user needs to be licensed for Customer Service Enterprise and Dynamics 365 Remote Assist, then a Base license for each product would be required.

Licensing external users

In common with the Dynamics 365 CRM and ERP apps there are no licensing requirements for external users for Dynamics 365 Remote Assist. Have a look at the CRM section for examples of users who are external users and those who are not, on page 228.

Dataverse capacity

Default capacity

Acquiring a Dynamics 365 Remote Assist license enables default Dataverse capacities across the whole tenant. In common with most of the other Dynamics 365 apps, these default capacities are:

- Dataverse Database capacity: 10 GB
- Dataverse File capacity: 20 GB
- Dataverse Log capacity: 2 GB

Additional capacity

Unlike the CRM apps, further capacity is not accrued for each license purchased. Customers requiring further Dataverse capacity must purchase Dataverse Database, File and Log Capacity Add-ons in increments of 1 GB.

Availability of Dynamics 365 Remote Assist licenses

Licenses for Dynamics 365 Remote Assist are available through CSP and the EA and MPSA Volume Licensing agreements. As usual, check out the Product Terms website for specifics.

POWER PLATFORM

Power Platform is the collective term for four products which all begin with the word "Power" – Power BI, Power Apps, Power Automate, and Power Virtual Agents.

POWER BI

We've probably all looked at a very large spreadsheet of figures and had no real idea of what the trends are, what we should worry about, or indeed what we should celebrate in the figures. Power BI is a tool to analyze data, and it uses visualizations to help users turn data into information. Some examples of visualizations are shown below and these make it easy to see, for example, if targets are met, the relationships between different sets of data, and upward or downward trends.

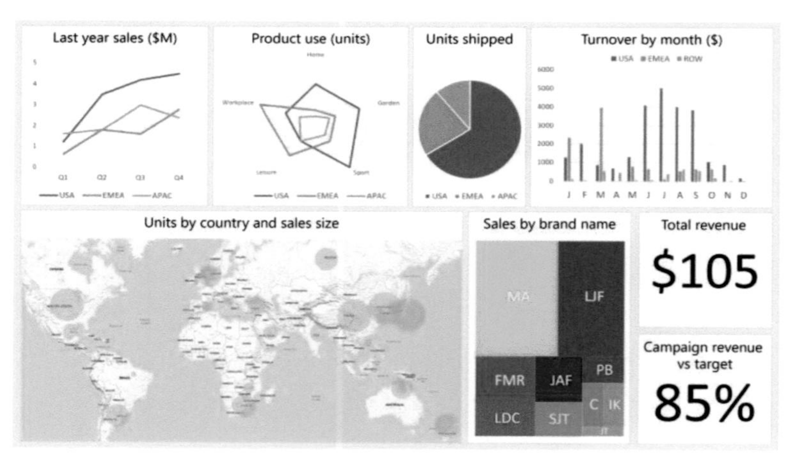

Figure 105: Power BI example visualizations

A Power BI user creates dashboards (single pages) and reports (multiple pages) consisting of these visualizations, and they often then share that information with other users in an organization.

Licensing users to create Power BI content

Power BI Desktop is a free application, installed locally, that enables a user to connect to his data sources and then transform that data into visualizations on a report. If the user then wants to create a dashboard or to share his report with other users he uses the Power BI Service which is the online part of Power BI. A user needs a license to use the Power BI Service and there are two licenses to choose between. First of all, there's the Power BI (free) license which, as its name suggests, is a free license. This allows a user to use the service but does not allow him to share any of his reports or dashboards with other users. To share content with other users a user must be licensed with a Power BI Pro User Subscription License. This is available as a standalone license and is included in the Office 365 E5 and Microsoft 365 E5 plans too.

Licensing users to consume Power BI content

Power BI content can be shared in a variety of ways, and that dictates the licensing for the consumers of the shared content. If content is shared via the Power BI Service as we discussed above, then the consumer of the content also needs to be licensed with a Power BI Pro license. Licensed users will be able to interact with the content.

Alternatively, Power BI content can be shared via an embedded report in Teams or SharePoint Online but, again, consumers of the content need to be licensed with a Power BI Pro license. Dashboards and reports can also be bundled into an app that users consume on their mobile device using the Power BI Mobile apps. These apps are free to download but, again, all users need to be licensed with Power BI Pro licenses. A user working on a report can annotate and share it with anyone via email, and if the recipient is licensed with a Power BI Pro license, they can go to the actual report on the Power BI service.

In fact, there are only two situations when a consumer of Power BI content does not need to be licensed. If the content is printed or shared as a PDF or other type of static file, then there are no licensing implications. Equally if information is shared online via the "Publish to the Web" option then there is no requirement to license consumers. Note with this last option though that there is no facility to restrict access to the online reports – any and all users across the Internet will be able to see the information published.

Power BI Premium capacity

We know that users licensed with Power BI Pro licenses have access to the Power BI Service, and this is the public service for Power BI. This public service is restricted for all users to a certain extent so that no individual organization can monopolize the service to the detriment of other businesses. However, if an organization wants dedicated Power BI Service capacity, then they can buy an annual subscription to Power BI Premium.

These are licenses like any other Online Services license in that a customer commits to a 12-month Subscription (or up to their Anniversary in an EA) for the licenses that they need. A technical team needs to do a certain amount of work to estimate the capacity they will need to buy for Power BI Premium, based upon, for example, the number of users they have and how frequently they are likely to use the service.

Firstly, they may consider the Power BI Premium P licenses, and you can see that they differ in the number of virtual cores that are provided for the service:

Node	Virtual cores
Power BI Premium P1	8
Power BI Premium P2	16
Power BI Premium P3	32
Power BI Premium P4	64
Power BI Premium P5	128

Figure 106: Power BI Premium P licenses

In the previous section we looked at the ways that Power BI content can be shared, and these licenses for Power BI Premium allow reports to be embedded in Teams or SharePoint Online, and dashboards and reports to be shared via the Power BI Service or to be bundled into apps. These licenses are available through the EA and CSP program.

There may be organizations who have a lesser requirement in terms of both the power of the capacity, and the sharing functionality, and for them the Power BI Premium EM licenses may be attractive:

Node	Virtual cores
Power BI Premium EM1	1
Power BI Premium EM2	2
Power BI Premium EM3	4

Figure 107: Power BI Premium EM licenses

An EM1 license is about an eighth of the price of a P1 license – with an eighth of the capacity – and only allows the sharing of Power BI content via an embedded report in either Teams or SharePoint Online. These licenses are available through the EA, but not through CSP.

When organizations choose to purchase Power BI Premium capacity there's also another benefit – not only do you get dedicated capacity for the Power BI Service, there's also no requirement to license the consumers of the content. You can imagine that there will certainly be businesses that want to take advantage of the dedicated capacity of the Power BI Service via Power BI Premium, but probably just as many who want a cost-effective way of licensing the users who will consume the Power BI content in their organization.

Let's consider an example here: Mellow Yellow Sounds have 50 users who will create Power BI content, and 3,500 users who will consume it. If we just use Power BI Pro licenses then Mellow Yellow Sounds will need to purchase a Power BI Pro license for all users. These licenses are $10 per user per month, and so the monthly costs are 3,550 x $10 = $35,500.

Alternatively, the IT department could calculate how many Power BI Premium virtual cores would be suitable to support their solution. Then, Mellow Yellow Sounds could just buy Power BI Pro licenses for the users who create the content and license the rest via Power BI Premium capacity licenses. Perhaps the IT department have decided that they need 3 x Power BI Premium P1 licenses – these cost $4,995 per month and so licensing this way would mean costs of: Power BI Pro (50 x $10 = $500) + Power BI Premium (3 x $4,995) = $15,485.

This represents a good saving on the Power Bi Pro-only licensing solution. Of course the figures are hugely dependent on the number of users and the virtual cores needed, but it's an interesting licensing alternative for an organization to consider.

Power BI Premium per User

Then, in April 2021, Microsoft announced a new way of licensing Power BI Premium – by user. Power BI Premium has more features than the regular Power BI Service, and this new option is a way of licensing users for premium features over and above those which Power BI Pro-licensed users have access to.

Users already licensed with a Power BI Pro license are eligible for the Power BI Premium Add-on User SL which, as its name suggests, gives users access to the additional Power BI Premium features. As I mentioned earlier, Power BI Pro is included in Office 365 E5 and Microsoft 365 E5 and so these are eligible qualifying licenses too. This In-cloud Add-on license is available through the EA and CSP program, and costs $10 per user per month.

Alternatively, there's a Power BI Premium per User license. This is a standalone license and includes access to both Power BI Pro and Power BI

Premium features. It's available through the EA and CSP program, and costs $20 per user per month.

Organizations can combine Power BI Pro, Power BI Premium capacity and Power BI Premium per User licenses in any way that works for them.

Power BI Report Server

Another element of Power BI licensing is the availability of Power BI Report Server. This was originally aimed at organizations who wanted to distribute interactive Power BI reports to their users, but to do it within the boundaries of their own firewall, rather than using the Power BI Service.

Power BI Report Server is not available as a product to buy; the rights to use it are granted to customers who have:

- Active Software Assurance on SQL Server Enterprise Core licenses
- Active Server Subscriptions for SQL Server Enterprise Core licenses
- Active Power BI Premium licenses for any of the P SKUs

Customers may actually deploy Power BI Report Server in an Azure virtual machine as an alternative to using their own dedicated hardware, and they're allowed to deploy it on as many cores as they have qualifying licenses. For example, if they have active SA on 24 SQL Server Enterprise Core licenses, they can deploy Power BI Report Server across 24 cores.

In terms of the other licenses required, the usual Power BI Pro licenses are required for users who will create content, but there are no additional licenses required for content consumers when using Power BI Report Server.

Licensing Power BI Embedded apps

There's one more topic to touch on in the licensing of Power BI, and that's the licensing of Power BI Embedded apps. This is another flavor of Power BI that's intended for application developers, or ISVs, who are building apps and want to embed visuals into those apps without having to build an analytics solution from scratch.

Power BI Embedded is sold as an Azure consumption service where the ISV pays for what they use, as they use it, with no commitment to use the service. They can scale the service up and down using the various nodes below and they can even pause the service while it's not in use.

Node	Virtual cores
Power BI Embedded A1	1
Power BI Embedded A2	2
Power BI Embedded A3	4
Power BI Embedded A4	8
Power BI Embedded A5	16
Power BI Embedded A6	32

Figure 108: Power BI Embedded A SKUs

As far as the licensing of the content creators and the content consumers goes, it's the usual story: a Power BI Pro license is required for the content publisher, and there are no additional licenses required for content consumers.

Availability of Power BI licenses

Power BI Pro licenses are available through most of the Volume Licensing agreements and CSP. Power BI Premium capacity licenses are not available through the Open programs or Select Plus. and availability through the other ways to buy varies. Power BI Premium per User licenses are available through the EA and CSP. As usual, check out the Product Terms site for exact availability.

POWER APPS

The Power Apps product enables users of all technical abilities to create apps for an organization so that they can improve efficiency by perhaps taking time out of a process or creating an app to replace a paper-based process.

Licensing Power Apps

When an app is created, it is assigned to an environment. An environment is a place to store, manage and share an organization's apps, and it's also a container to separate apps that might have different security requirements or target audiences. Power Apps automatically creates a single default environment for each tenant, and additional environments can be created as required. When apps are created and assigned to environments, they are then shared with users, who need to be licensed via either a Per User or a Per App license.

Per User licenses

A Per User license is assigned to a user via the Microsoft 365 Admin Center and allows the licensed user to access any app in any environment across the organization.

Per App licenses

A Per App license, on the other hand, is not assigned to a user but to an environment via the Power Platform Admin Center. Let's imagine that Goldfinger Foods have assigned a Per App license to the Finance environment that has a single app that a user, James, needs to access. The app has been shared with James but he's not licensed with a Per User license. In this situation the Per App license is automatically assigned to James and he can then successfully access the app. Slightly oddly, this is not actually a "Per App" license but a "Per Two Apps" license since if James needs access to another app in the same environment, then the first Per App license assigned to him also allows him to access the second app.

If James needs access to a third app in the Finance environment then the IT department must assign a further Per App license to that environment, and if he also needs access to apps in the Training environment then, likewise, sufficient Per App licenses must be assigned to that environment.

As per Microsoft's public website: https://bit.ly/BOKPApPricing, as of May 2021, the price of a Per User license is $40 per user per month and a Per App license is $10 per user per month. Thus, you can imagine that the more apps that James needs to access across multiple environments the more attractive a Per User license will be. Organizations may mix and match licenses as required.

Licensing Power Apps Portals

A Power Apps Portal is typically a self-service, interactive website developed for external users, although it could equally be some sort of employee self-service app.

There are no licensing requirements for provisioning a Power Apps Portal, it's the user access that is licensed, and this varies dependent on the type of user.

Internal, authenticated users

Internal, authenticated users are covered with the Power Apps Per User and Per App licenses covered in the earlier section. A Per User license allows the user to access an unlimited number of Portals across any environments, and a Per App license allows the user to whom the license has been allocated to access one Portal in the environment to which the license was assigned. If the user needs to access further Portals, then further licenses must be allocated to the relevant environments.

External, authenticated users

An external, authenticated user could be authenticated by any one of a wide variety of authentication providers (Microsoft account, Facebook, LinkedIn etc.) when they access a Power Apps Portal. These users are licensed via a Power Apps Portal Login Capacity Add-on license.

Organizations purchase logins in groups of 100 logins, where a single authenticated user is allowed to log in multiple times within a 24-hour period and it just counts as a single billable login.

Again, referring to Microsoft's public pricing page, this login capacity is available in three different pricing tiers with a minimum purchase attached to each SKU as shown below:

Tier	Minimums	Price per rmonth
Tier 1	100 logins/1 SKU	$200/SKU
Tier 2	1,000 logins/10 SKUs	$100/SKU
Tier 3	5,000 logins/50 SKUs	$70/SKU

Figure 109: Power Apps Portals Login Capacity Add-on licenses

Customers need to estimate their monthly requirements and then make sure that they are licensed for peak capacity. So, for example, if Goldfinger Foods estimate that they will have 6 months where 3,000 logins will be required, and 6 months where 3,500 logins will be required, they must license the full term of 12 months for 3,500 logins. This would equate to 35 x Tier 2 SKU = 35 x $100 = $3,500 per month. Note that the minimum purchase for Tier 3 is 50 x $70 = $3,500 so, in this case, it would probably be best for them to make that order since they could take advantage of an extra 1,500 logins per month.

Clearly it is extremely unlikely that a customer's usage will exactly match what they have estimated and purchased. Unused logins do not carry over between months, but what happens if a customer occasionally needs more logins that they have purchased – does everything stop working when the logins for a particular month are used? Actually, nothing bad happens and Microsoft's official line is that while occasional and reasonable overages will be tolerated, customers exceeding purchased capacity should adjust their purchase quantity as per standard Microsoft terms to remain in compliance.

Anonymous users

Anonymous or unauthenticated users, either internal or external, are licensed via a Power Apps Portal Page View Capacity Add-on license. Each Add-on license gives access to 100,000 page views per month, and customers purchase, again, as many Add-ons as would be required for peak capacity. For example, if Goldfinger Foods anticipate 375,000 page views per month, then they should purchase 4 Add-on licenses.

Power Apps rights included in other licenses

Limited Power Apps use rights are included with certain Office 365 and Dynamics 365 licenses. For the scope of this book, I've just included a summary below – if you need to know the (quite complicated) details of the specific rights included in specific licenses then you should refer to Microsoft's Power Platform Licensing Guide.

Office 365

Limited Power Apps use rights are included with most Office 365 and Microsoft 365 licenses with the aim of allowing users to customize and extend Office 365 for productivity scenarios. You're limited in the type of apps you can run and the connectors you can use, and you should note that Microsoft 365 F1 does not include these rights at all.

Dynamics 365

Again, limited Power Apps use rights are included in many Dynamics 365 licenses with the same objective – to allow users to customize and extend Dynamics 365 applications. Use of the Power Apps capabilities can only be within the context of the licensed Dynamics 365 application and are only included within the same environment as the licensed Dynamics 365 application. Use rights vary between licenses for the Enterprise apps (such as Sales Enterprise, Finance etc.) and the other licenses (such as Team Members, Sales Professional, Human Resources Self Service, for example).

Dataverse capacity

Default capacity

The first Power Apps Per User or Per App license purchased enables default Dataverse capacities across the whole tenant as shown below:

Capacity type	Per User	Per App
Dataverse Database capacity	10 GB	5 GB
Dataverse File capacity	20 GB	20 GB
Dataverse Log capacity	2 GB	2 GB

Figure 110: Power Apps default Dataverse capacity

Accrued capacity

In addition, for each Power Apps Per User or per App license there is additional capacity added to the tenant as shown below:

Capacity type	Per User	Per App
Dataverse Database capacity	250 MB	50 MB
Dataverse File capacity	2 GB	400 MB
Dataverse Log capacity	-	-

Figure 111: Power Apps accrued Dataverse capacity

For example, if Goldfinger Foods purchase 10 x Power Apps Per User and 20 x Power Apps per App licenses they will be entitled to:

- Dataverse Database capacity
  10 GB + 10 x 250 MB + 20 x 50 MB = 13.5 GB
- Dataverse File capacity
  20 GB + 10 x 2 GB + 20 x 400 MB = 48 GB
- Dataverse Log capacity
  2 GB

Additional capacity

Customers requiring further capacity can purchase Dataverse Database, File and/or Log Capacity Add-ons in increments of 1 GB.

Availability of Power Apps licenses

The Power Apps licenses are available through CSP and the EA and MPSA Volume Licensing agreements. As usual, check out the Product Terms website for specifics.

POWER AUTOMATE

The Power Automate product is all about automating business processes. It enables organizations to automate processes across modern systems with APIs, where users can create **flows** by connecting easily to hundreds of applications and making use of the many triggers and actions that are available. This is often known as Digital Process Automation (DPA).

Older, legacy apps probably don't have APIs but Power Automate still enables users to create **desktop flows** by recording their keystrokes across the applications via something called Robotic Process Automation (RPA). The licensing of Power Automate differs dependent on the type of process automation that's required.

Licensing DPA flows

When a DPA flow is created it is assigned to an environment. In common with Power Apps, an environment is a place to store, manage and share an organization's flows, and it's also a container to separate flows that might have different security requirements or target audiences. Power Automate automatically creates a single default environment for each tenant, and additional environments can be created as required. Flows are then shared with users, who need to be licensed to use those flows. DPA flows are licensed via either a Per User or a Per Flow license.

Per User licenses

A Per User license is assigned to a user via the Microsoft 365 Admin Center and allows the licensed user to access any flow in any environment across the organization. These users can also create unlimited flows for their own needs.

Per Flow licenses

A Per Flow license is assigned to one particular flow via the Power Platform Admin Center. When a flow is shared with a user who does not have a Per User license, that user may use the flow as long as there is a Per Flow license assigned to it. A Per Flow license allows an unlimited number of users in an organization to use the licensed flow.

If a flow is triggered by another flow it is known as a child flow and does not need to be separately licensed,

As per Microsoft's public website at May 2021 (https://bit.ly/BOKPAuPricing) the price of a Per User license is $15 per user per month and a Per Flow license is $100 per flow per month with a minimum purchasing requirement of 5 licenses per month. Organizations will choose licenses depending on how their users will use the flows that they have created: if they have a large number of users using a small number of flows, then Per Flow licensing is attractive, while if they have a small number of users using a large number of flows, then Per User licensing is likely to be the best option for them.

Licensing RPA desktop flows

RPA flows are known as desktop flows, executed by bots, and can be run as attended or unattended processes. Attended desktop flows run on a user's device and are initiated by the user, whereas unattended desktop flows can run on any device and the bot operates independently of a user.

Power Automate Per User with Attended RPA licenses

There's a Power Automate Per User with Attended RPA User SL to license users who need to create and use attended desktop flows. It includes the full capabilities of the Power Automate Per User plan so they can create flows or desktop flows as required and don't need to buy the Power Automate Per User license separately. The desktop flow must run on that user's device, and if there's a need to run multiple desktop flows then the bot must run one after another, in series.

Power Automate Unattended Add-on licenses

Unattended desktop flows are licensed via the Power Automate Unattended Add-on license. As the name suggests, it's a license that needs a qualifying base license and that can be either the Power Automate Per User with Attended RPA license or a Power Automate Per Flow license.

These Add-on licenses are assigned to a specific environment so that unattended flows can run within the environment. If multiple bots need to run in parallel in a single environment, then multiple Add-on licenses must be assigned to the environment, although only a single qualifying base license is needed.

Note that if the bot makes use of Windows or the Office applications, then the Microsoft 365 E3 – Unattended license must also be purchased, which is detailed on page 195.

Power Automate Desktop

Power Automate Desktop is a free download and enables users to automate tasks by recording actions such as mouse and keyboard clicks across multiple applications, and then replaying them when needed. Users who then want to share flows across an organization and to take advantage of additional capabilities will need to be licensed with a Power Automate with Attended RPA User SL.

Power Automate rights included in other licenses

Limited Power Automate use rights are included with licenses for other products. For the scope of this book, as for the Power Apps section, I've just included a summary below – if you need to know the (quite complicated) details of the specific rights included in specific licenses then you should refer to Microsoft's Power Platform Licensing Guide.

Office 365

Limited Power Automate use rights are included with most Office 365 and Microsoft 365 licenses with the aim of allowing users to customize and extend Office 365 for productivity scenarios. You're limited in the type of flows you can run and the connectors you can use, and you should note that Microsoft 365 F1 does not include these rights at all.

Dynamics 365

Again, limited Power Automate use rights are included in many Dynamics 365 licenses with the same objective – to allow users to customize and extend Dynamics 365 applications. Use of the Power Automate capabilities can only be within the context of the licensed Dynamics 365 application. Use rights vary between licenses for the Enterprise apps (such as Sales Enterprise, Finance etc.) and the other licenses (such as Team Members, Sales Professional, Human Resources Self Service, for example).

Power Apps

Power Apps Per User and Per App licenses include limited Power Automate use rights to allow users to automate workflows associated with Power Apps applications. As you might expect, the use rights are confined to the context of the Power Apps application.

Power Virtual Agents

The Power Virtual Agents Standalone license includes limited Power Automate use rights. As usual, the use rights are restricted to the context of the Power Virtual Agents bot.

Dataverse capacity

Default capacity

The first Power Automate license purchased enables default Dataverse capacities across the whole tenant as shown below:

Capacity type	Per User	Per Flow	RPA Per User
Dataverse Database capacity	10 GB	5 GB	10 GB
Dataverse File capacity	20 GB	2 GB	20 GB
Dataverse Log capacity	2 GB	200 MB	2 GB

Figure 112: Power Automate default Dataverse capacity

Accrued capacity

In addition, for each type of Power Automate license there is additional Dataverse Database and File capacity added to the tenant as shown below:

Capacity type	Per User	Per Flow	RPA Per User
Dataverse Database capacity	250 MB	50 MB	250 MB
Dataverse File capacity	2 GB	200 MB	2 GB
Dataverse Log capacity	-	-	-

Figure 113: Power Automate accrued Dataverse capacity

Additional capacity

Customers requiring further capacity can purchase Dataverse Database, File and/or Log Capacity Add-ons in increments of 1 GB.

Availability of Power Automate licenses

The Power Automate licenses are available through CSP and the EA and MPSA Volume Licensing agreements. As usual, check out the Product Terms website for specifics.

POWER VIRTUAL AGENTS

The Power Virtual Agents product enables users of all technical abilities to create a bot which could be used, for example, to answer customer questions without having to wait for a human agent, or to give employees access to information at any time they might need it.

Bots are made available to employees or customers by deploying them in a channel which could be Teams, a website, or Facebook, or a whole host of other channels. Where the bot is deployed changes the licensing, so let's take a look at that now.

Creating and deploying a bot in Teams

Power Virtual Agents is available as an app within Microsoft Teams, useful if you want to create a bot to answer questions posed by other employees or team members.

Anyone who is licensed with one of the following licenses is eligible to create and use a bot in Teams:

- Office 365 E1, E3, E5, F3
- Microsoft 365 E3, E5, F3
- Microsoft 365 Business Basic, Standard, Premium

When a bot is deployed in Teams, a user chats to it in the same way they would chat to a human user. Microsoft's intention is to allow unlimited chat sessions although there are (high) throttles in place to make sure that service levels remain high for all organizations using the service.

Licensing Power Virtual Agents Standalone

Deploying a bot outside of Teams, to a website, for example, requires that the organization is licensed with the Power Virtual Agents Standalone license. This is a tenant-wide license shown on the price list as a monthly price to which you make the usual 12-month commitment.

Licensing bot creators

Licenses also need to be acquired for any users who will create and manage bots. These Power Virtual Agents per User licenses are $0 licenses but do need to be ordered and then assigned to bot creators through the Microsoft 365 Admin Center.

Licensing chat sessions

The Power Virtual Agents Standalone license includes the capacity for 2,000 chat sessions with any bots that are deployed. A chat session is a conversation between the bot and a human user, and counts as one unit of consumption when:

- the user's questions are answered, or
- the conversation exceeds 60 minutes, or
- the conversation exceeds 100 "turns"

A turn is one exchange between the user and the bot, and if the conversation does exceed 60 minutes or 100 turns, there's no impact on the end user, it just counts as another unit of consumption.

Additional capacity

If 2,000 chat sessions are not enough, then there are Chat Session for Virtual Agents Add-on licenses available which license another 1,000 chat sessions per tenant per month. There is the same 12-month commitment when you buy these Add-on licenses and chat sessions don't roll over from month to month, so you need to make sure you're licensed for peak capacity.

For your reference, the Licensing Guide states that "while occasional and reasonable overages will be tolerated, customers exceeding purchased capacity should adjust their purchase quantity per standard Microsoft terms to remain in compliance".

Power Virtual Agents rights included in other licenses

Office 365

As mentioned above, most Office 365 and Microsoft 365 licenses give rights to create and use a bot in Teams.

Dynamics 365

The **Chat for Customer Service** and **Digital Messaging** Add-on licenses for Dynamics 365 Customer Service Enterprise include 1,000 Power Virtual Agents chat sessions per month. In line with Power Virtual Agents licensing, the unused sessions don't carry forward between months, and additional capacity can be purchased via the usual Chat Session for Virtual Agents Add-on licenses.

Dataverse capacity

Default capacity

When a Power Virtual Agents Standalone license is purchased, the usual Dataverse capacities are enabled across the whole tenant:

- Dataverse Database capacity: 10 GB
- Dataverse File capacity: 20 GB
- Dataverse Log capacity: 2 GB

Additional capacity

Customers requiring further capacity can purchase Dataverse Database, File and/or Log Capacity Add-ons in increments of 1 GB.

Availability of Power Virtual Agents licenses

The Power Virtual Agents licenses are available through CSP and the EA and MPSA Volume Licensing agreements. As usual, check out the Product Terms website for specifics.

DATAVERSE

Dataverse, previously known as the Common Data Service, is where you securely store and manage data that's used by the Dynamics 365 and Power Platform products.

Default capacity

The first Base license of most Dynamics 365 CRM/ERP apps and Power Platform apps purchased enables default Dataverse capacities across the whole tenant. Typically, the amounts are as shown below, but check the individual product sections to confirm which licenses enable these default capacities, and what the included amounts are:

Capacity type	Default
Dataverse Database capacity *(Stores and manages table definitions and data)*	10 GB
Dataverse File capacity *(Stores attachments to notes or emails)*	20 GB
Dataverse Log capacity *(Records table and attribute data changes over time for use in analysis and reporting)*	2 GB

Figure 114: typical Dataverse capacities

Accrued capacity

For some of the products, the first license of a solution initiates the allocation of the default Dataverse capacities as above, and then additional capacity is accrued as further licenses are purchased. Again, check the individual product sections for full details.

Additional capacity

Customers requiring further capacity can purchase Dataverse Database, File and/or Log Capacity Add-ons in increments of 1 GB. As usual, they need to commit to these SKUs either for a 12-month period in programs like CSP, or up until anniversary in the Enterprise Agreement.

BUYING ONLINE SERVICES: EA

In this section we take a look at all of the different options that a customer has for buying Online Services through their Enterprise Agreement. We'll start with the two Enterprise Enrollments where they can add User SLs as Additional Products to an existing, traditional Enterprise Enrollment; or they can sign a new Enterprise Enrollment with User SLs for Enterprise Online Services only; or they can start to move their licensing to the cloud by opting for a hybrid enterprise-wide commitment consisting of traditional device licenses and User SLs for Online Services. User SLs can also be added to a Server and Cloud Enrollment as Additional Products.

Buying Online Services through the Enterprise Enrollments

Product availability

The vast majority of the Online Services are available through the Enterprise Enrollments with the only exceptions being those products which are aimed at smaller businesses: for instance, the Microsoft 365 Business licenses and the Dynamics 365 Business Central licenses aren't available, shown by the gray ticks below:

Products	
Windows 10 Enterprise User SLs	✔
Office 365 User SLs	✔
EMS User SLs	✔
Microsoft 365 User SLs	✔ (gray)
Dynamics 365 User SLs	✔ (gray)
Power Platform User SLs	✔

Figure 115: availability of Online Services products in the Enterprise Enrollments

License type availability

All of the different license types are available through the Enterprise Enrollments:

License types	
Full User SLs	✔
Step-up User SLs	✔
In-cloud Add-on User SLs	✔
To-cloud Add-on User SLs	✔
From SA User SLs	✔

Figure 116: availability of Online Services license types in the Enterprise Enrollments

Minimums

If a customer has made an enterprise-wide commitment to the on-premises products in a traditional Enterprise or Enterprise Subscription Enrollment, then they can order Full User Subscription Licenses for the Online Services as Additional Products. In this case, they can order as little as a single User SL, and they only have to commit to the products up until the next anniversary.

Adding Online Services licenses

Customers may add licenses for Online Services at any time in their Enrollment. This is typically done through a process known as License Reservation where a customer orders licenses for the relevant Online Services, which are activated for them at that time, but are paid for at anniversary for the preceding months.

Reducing Online Services licenses

At anniversary, any licenses for Online Services Additional Products may be reduced – to zero if required.

Pricing and price protection

The price level of Online Services added as Additional Products is the same as for the Enterprise Products in the same pool, and the pricing for products on the Customer Price Sheet is fixed for the term of the Enrollment.

Enterprise Online Services-only Enrollment

As an alternative to making an enterprise-wide commitment to the on-premises products, a customer may choose to sign an Enterprise or Enterprise Subscription Enrollment with an order for 500 User SLs of certain Online Services called the **Enterprise Online Services** which are these products:

- Office 365 E1, E3 or E5
- EMS E3 or E5
- Microsoft 365 E3 or E5

The minimum of 500 User SLs must be composed of licenses within a single bullet point in the list above. For example, 250 x Office 365 E1 + 150 x Office 365 E3 + 100 x Office 365 E5 is an acceptable initial order, but 250 x Office 365 E3 + 250 x EMS E3 is not.

Starting an Enterprise Enrollment in this way is known as an Enterprise Online Services-only Enrollment and once the initial requirement of the 500 User SLs is met, licenses for Additional Products can be acquired – either Online Services or the traditional, on-premises products. If a customer has signed an Enterprise Subscription Enrollment, then licenses for any on-premises products will be subscription licenses.

Pricing

There are four different price levels available for an Enterprise Online Services-only Enrollment customer, with discounts increasing between the levels. A customer's price level depends on the number of Enterprise Online Services User SLs on the initial order, as shown on the next page, and is set for the duration of the 3-year term of their Enterprise Enrollment:

User SLs	Price level
500	A
2,400	B
6,000	C
15,000	D

Figure 117: Enterprise Online Services-only Enrollment price levels

Price protection

Prices for the chosen Enterprise Online Services are fixed for the three-year term of the enrollment.

Adding and reducing Online Services licenses

Licenses for Online Services may be added at any time and there is a commitment to pay the monthly fee for the licenses at least until the anniversary. At anniversary any licenses for Online Services Additional Products may be reduced (to zero if required) and those for Enterprise Online Services to the program minimum of 500 User SLs.

Hybrid enterprise-wide commitment

If customers want to buy the Enterprise Products (Windows 10 Enterprise, Office Professional Plus 2019, and the Core or Enterprise CAL Suites) then they need to commit to them enterprise wide as described on page 127. But what of the customer who wants to license some of his estate with the traditional device licenses and some with User SLs?

The rules are, that if you want to license any of the Enterprise Products you MUST commit enterprise wide. However, you can meet the enterprise-wide commitment with either user or device licenses, as long as devices are either covered by device licenses or only used by users licensed with user licenses.

Let's take Windows 10 Enterprise as an example which is available both as a device license (Windows 10 Enterprise) and a user license (Windows 10 Enterprise E3). Peach Snaps Cameras have 300 users who sit at the same desktop device every day, and 300 users who use 2 or 3 devices every day. They've decided that device licenses would be ideal for the first group of users and user licenses would be better for the second group of users. They could sign an Enterprise Enrollment with Windows as their Enterprise Product with an initial order of 300 x Windows 10 Enterprise device licenses + 300 x Windows 10 Enterprise E3 User SLs.

You can imagine that a commitment to Office is very similar – you could combine the traditional device-licensed Office Professional Plus 2019 licenses and Microsoft 365 Apps for enterprise User SLs as long as, again, devices are either covered by device licenses or only used by users licensed with user licenses. And, because Office 365 E3/E5 and Microsoft 365 E3/E5 User SLs include Microsoft 365 Apps for enterprise, they too can be used to satisfy the enterprise-wide commitment for Office. In fact, there is a whole host of combinations that are allowed which are detailed on the Enterprise Enrollment Product Selection Form.

Moving to the cloud

So far in this section we've looked at options for adding Online Services as Additional Products or starting a new Enterprise Enrollment with Enterprise Online Services only. There's a further option for customers with an existing on-premises solution who want to move to the cloud. These customers would purchase either From SA or To-cloud Add-on User SLs. These are available for customers with existing Software Assurance and recognize the fact that the customer has made an investment in Microsoft licenses. Note that "To-cloud Add-on" is a term we've invented to indicate the job that the Add-on is doing – it's added on to existing on-premises licenses to take customers to the cloud. This term is introduced on page 169.

Let's take Apple and Pears Stairlifts who are an Enterprise Agreement customer with the full Desktop Platform (Office Professional Plus,

Core/Enterprise CAL Suite, and Windows 10 Enterprise licenses) and are now interested in moving to Microsoft 365 E3. As I said, they could buy the Full User SL but that wouldn't recognize their existing investment. Their best choices are a To-cloud Add-on User SL which they buy in addition to the existing traditional licenses with SA, and which adds on access to all the additional Microsoft 365 E3 functionality. Alternatively, with a From SA User SL, Apple and Pears Stairlifts stop paying for the original licenses and move to a single User SL for the Microsoft 365 E3 services. You can compare these options below:

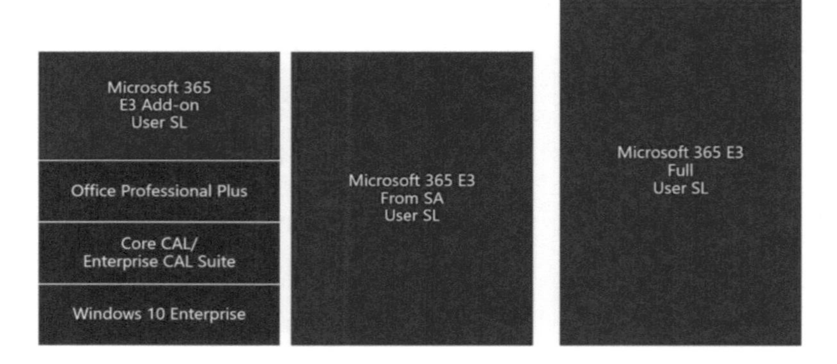

Figure 118: options for moving to the cloud

The height of the bars gives a rough indication of pricing – using Add-ons or the From SA licenses is more cost effective that buying the Full User SLs.

Let's get some more detail now on how these licenses work in an Enterprise Agreement.

Add-on User SLs (To-cloud)

The Add-on User SLs at the left-hand side of the picture above are an option for Apple and Pears Stairlifts to license their users for the cloud services of Microsoft 365. What do they buy though? Let's assume that there are (conveniently) 1,000 users and 1,000 devices in this organization. They have already purchased 1,000 Windows, Office and Enterprise CAL Suite device licenses and these are considered to be qualifying licenses for the Add-ons.

Add-ons are licensed by user and so they buy 1,000 Microsoft 365 E3 Add-on User SLs giving them the licensing position shown in the first column. They continue to pay SA on the underlying licenses but they now have cloud rights as if they had purchased the Full User SLs at the right-hand side.

In a slightly more realistic scenario where there aren't the same number of users and devices, you can only buy Add-on User SLs up to the number of underlying qualifying licenses. So if Apple and Pears Stairlifts had 1,000 devices licensed with the Desktop Platform, and 1,200 users, then they could only buy 1,000 Add-on User SLs and would need to license the remaining users with 200 Full User SLs.

Add-on User SLs are transacted as Additional Products within an Enterprise Agreement and so there is no requirement to buy an Add-on User SL for all users across the organization. They can be added at any time during the year and Apple and Pears Stairlifts must pay for complete months up until the anniversary. At the anniversary, the number of Add-on User SLs may be reduced if needed, and then an upfront payment is made for the required number of User SLs for the next 12 months.

We've talked about the Microsoft 365 E3 Add-on User SLs so far, but there are more To-cloud Add-on User SLs available. The diagram on the next page shows the traditional licenses for the Enterprise Products that Apple and Pears Stairlifts have in their Enterprise Agreement and the variety of different Add-on User SLs they could choose to purchase, and what the effect of that would be in terms of accessing cloud services.

Down the left-hand side are the workloads that can be licensed in an Enterprise Agreement and the first column shows the traditional licenses that Apple and Pears Stairlifts have bought and which particular rights they give – the Office Professional Plus license licensing the Office applications, the Core or Enterprise CAL Suite licensing access to the Productivity Servers (Exchange, SharePoint and Skype for Business) and to the Core Infrastructure Servers (Windows Server and System Center), and a Windows 10 Enterprise device license licensing the Windows client operating system.

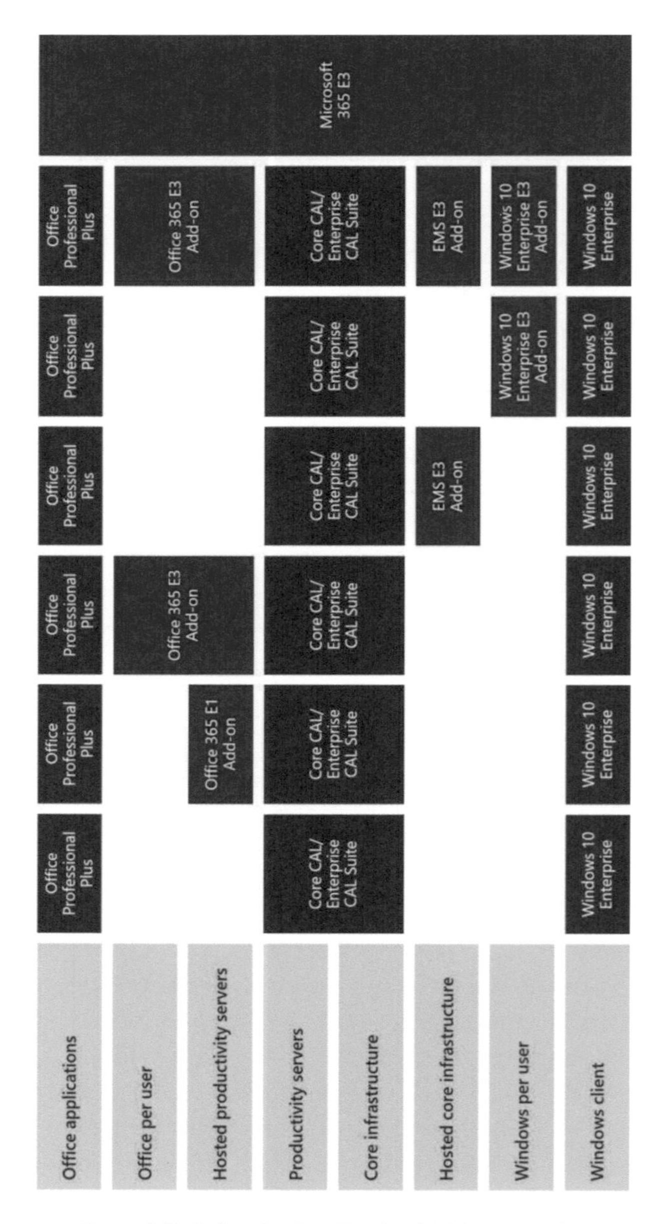

Figure 119: Online Services To-cloud Add-on User SLs

The spaces show what this collection of licenses doesn't license and that's where Apple and Pears Stairlifts can buy individual To-cloud Add-ons to fill in the gaps. In the second column, Apple and Pears Stairlifts could use their Core CAL Suite as a qualifying license to purchase the Office 365 E1 Add-on and in this situation the Core CAL Suite license would continue to license the on-premises productivity servers, with the E1 Add-on licensing the equivalent services in the cloud. In the third column they could use their Office Professional Plus license and Core CAL Suite as the qualifying licenses to purchase an Office 365 E3 Add-on User SL and you can see that that would add Office licensed per user (via Microsoft 365 Apps for enterprise) and access to the Office 365 hosted services.

The EMS E3 Add-on is added on to the Core or Enterprise CAL Suite in the fourth column giving access to cloud security and management tools, and a Windows 10 Enterprise E3 Add-on is added on to a Windows 10 Enterprise device license in the fifth column allowing Windows to be licensed per user. The sixth column shows the effect of adding all three Add-ons which are purchased as the Microsoft 365 E3 Add-on User SL which we started this section with.

The final column shows that the traditional licenses plus all the Add-ons give access to the same services as if the Full Microsoft 365 E3 User SL had been acquired.

From SA User SLs

So, with Add-on User SLs Apple and Pears Stairlifts keep their existing licenses and purchase these additional licenses as required. This is very convenient and easy for customers but does give rise to a slightly complicated licensing position – you have up to three underlying licenses, at least two of which will be device licenses and an Add-on license which is user based. To-cloud Add-on User SLs are great for trying the cloud services and to easily license the additional services at any time in an agreement, but at renewal it's often the case that a customer opts to simplify their licensing position by moving to From SA User SLs. In this case, they stop paying for the underlying licenses and just have a single User SL for their users.

From a transactional perspective, there are some rules concerning when the From SA User SLs may be purchased by a customer: the customer must fully own the underlying licenses and the From SA User SLs can only be transacted at anniversary or renewal. This means that a customer can't buy these licenses in the first 3-year term of an Enterprise Enrollment. If a customer wanted to move to the cloud during the second 3-year term, it's generally easier to transact Add-ons during the enrollment term, and then change to From SA User SLs at the start of the third 3-year term. Note that Enterprise Subscription Enrollment customers are eligible for From SA User SLs too as long as they have paid for the qualifying licenses for a period of three consecutive years. Customers may renew their From SA User SLs at the start of the next term – they don't need to start transacting Full User SLs after one term of From SA licenses.

If you look at the sixth column in Figure 119 and compare it to the last column then the licensing position is very similar, but with an Add-on User SL you retain the original Office Professional Plus license. This means that you retain the rights to install this traditional product and/or downgrade to a previous version of Office. You don't get this right with Microsoft 365 Apps for enterprise acquired through a Microsoft 365 E3 User SL. However, there are some special rights for customers who move to the Microsoft 365 E3 From SA User SL; they are also allowed one installation of Office Professional Plus for the use of the licensed user. This installation can be a current or previous version, but it may not be used in an RDS or VDI deployment.

Server and Cloud Enrollment

There is no option to sign a Server and Cloud Enrollment with just Users SLs for the Online Services, but they may be added as Additional Products once a commitment to one of the server components has been made. They then follow the rules for buying Online Services through the Enterprise Enrollments as detailed in the previous section.

BUYING ONLINE SERVICES: MPSA

Product availability

Most of the Online Services are available through the MPSA. Notable exceptions are those products which are aimed at smaller businesses: for instance, the Microsoft 365 Business licenses and the Dynamics 365 Business Central licenses aren't available, shown by the gray ticks below.:

Products	
Windows 10 Enterprise User SLs	✔
Office 365 User SLs	✔
EMS User SLs	✔
Microsoft 365 User SLs	✔ (gray)
Dynamics 365 User SLs	✔ (gray)
Power Platform User SLs	✔

Figure 120: availability of Online Services products in the MPSA

License type availability

Generally speaking, there are different types of Online Services licenses available in the MPSA which license customers starting out with cloud solutions (Full User SLs), who need to move between editions (Step-up User SLs) and who want to try the cloud (To-cloud Add-on User SLs) but there's not the complete range of products and options compared to the Enterprise Agreement, and that's why there are some gray ticks in the table on the next page. In addition, some of the newer In-cloud Add-on User SLs are not being made available in the MPSA – SharePoint Syntex and Viva Topics User SLs, for example:

License types	
Full User SLs	✓
Step-up User SLs	✓
In-cloud Add-on User SLs	✓
To-cloud Add-on User SLs	✓
From SA User SLs	

Figure 121: availability of Online Services license types in the MPSA

Points and pools

Licenses for Online Services are placed in product pools and given a points value in the same way as the licenses for on-premises products. Typically, these User SLs are assigned a points value of 1, and the minimums for a product pool are changed to just 250 points if only User SLs are being ordered. For more information on MPSA points and pools see page 143.

Payment

The MPSA enables the signing organization and its affiliates to buy under a single agreement, with Purchasing Accounts allowing an organization to structure themselves exactly as they want with regards to purchasing their licenses. You can find out more about Purchasing Accounts on page 142.

Each Purchasing Account has its own anniversary which is important for the alignment of purchases for Online Services. If Blacken White Solicitors want to purchase 100 Office 365 E3 User SLs 6 months before their Purchasing Account anniversary a Subscription is created for the Office 365 E3 licenses which aligns to the next Purchasing Account anniversary. Online Services licenses are priced monthly and always paid for upfront in an MPSA. So, Blacken White Solicitors will pay upfront for 6 months of the licenses. The

Subscription will then renew on the Purchasing Account anniversary and they will pay upfront for the next 12 months at that time.

Price protection

There is fixed price protection for Online Services in an MPSA: in the previous example Blacken White Solicitors ordered 100 Office 365 E3 licenses and paid upfront for those licenses at the current price list price. If they then add more Office 365 E3 licenses within the term of the Subscription, they are charged at the same price – regardless of the current price list price.

BUYING ONLINE SERVICES: SELECT PLUS

Customers cannot buy licenses for Online Services through a Select Plus agreement.

BUYING ONLINE SERVICES: OPEN PROGRAMS

We'll consider the Open License program, and the Open Value and Open Value Subscription agreements in one section here since the Online Services work (just about) the same way in all of them.

The Open License program will retire at the end of December 2021. Licenses for Online Services purchased through the Open License program won't suddenly stop working at the end of 2021, a customer just won't be able to purchase more licenses through their existing agreement. After this date, if they want to purchase or renew licenses for Online Services, they can do that through one of the Open Value agreements, or through CSP.

Product availability

Some of the Online Services products are available through the Open programs, but by no means all, as you can see from the table below. Windows 10 is only available as a device license, and none of the Dynamics 365 User SLs are available.

Products	
Windows 10 Enterprise User SLs	
Office 365 User SLs	✓
EMS User SLs	✔
Microsoft 365 User SLs	✓
Dynamics 365 User SLs	
Power Platform User SLs	✓

Figure 122: availability of Online Services products in the Open programs

There are gray ticks for some of the categories indicating only partial availability:

- Office 365: Office 365 E5 and Office 365 F3 are not available
- Microsoft 365: Only Microsoft 365 Business Basic and Microsoft 365 Business Standard are available
- Power Platform: only Power BI Pro is available

License type availability

Generally speaking, it's the Full User SLs for available products that are sold through the Open programs, but there are a couple of the In-cloud Add-on User SLs available such as the Audio Conferencing and Phone System User SLs. For customers who have made an organization-wide commitment there are also some To-cloud Add-on licenses available – see the section further down for details.

License types	
Full User SLs	✔
Step-up User SLs	
In-cloud Add-on User SLs	✔ (gray)
To-cloud Add-on User SLs	✔ (gray)
From SA User SLs	

Figure 123: availability of Online Services license types in the Open programs

Minimums

An Open License agreement may be started with as little as 1 User SL, and a single User SL can be purchased in an existing agreement. The same is true of starting an Open Value non Organization-Wide agreement. Once the organization-wide commitment has been met in an Open Value or Open Value Subscription agreement, a single User SL for Online Services may be purchased.

Commitment

Orders for Online Services are always for 12 months. However, the 12-month period doesn't necessarily start immediately as it does in other agreements and programs. Let's imagine that Copper Feel Fabrics need 5 Office 365 E3 licenses which they purchase through their existing Open or Open Value agreement. They receive an Online Services Activation (OSA) key for the 5 licenses which they can activate at any time within 5 years of the purchase date. This could happen long after their Open or Open Value agreement has expired and that would be fine. When the OSA key is used, the 12-month period starts.

In the diagram below you can see that Copper Feel Fabrics purchased the Office 365 E3 licenses at the beginning of the second quarter of their agreement and activated them 3 months later at the start of the second quarter which is when the 12-month Subscription starts:

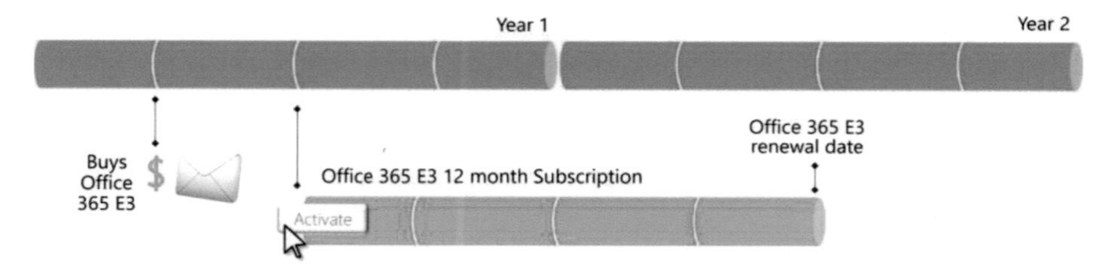

Figure 124: buying Online Services in the Open programs

Payment

Payment for Online Services licenses is always in full at the time of purchase. This may mean, of course, that a customer could have paid for licenses that they don't activate and assign to users for some months.

Pricing and price protection

Each Online Services license purchase is an individual event in the Open programs and that means that the price for each purchase is taken from the current price list and there is no notion of price protection for a particular Online Service.

Adding and reducing licenses

There is no mechanism in the Open programs for reducing licenses; the payment for licenses is upfront, in full and a customer would simply not renew the license if they no longer wanted to access the service.

Of course, customers may add licenses whenever they like, and the new licenses will have a 12-month term from the moment they are activated. If Copper Feel Fabrics purchase 5 more Office 365 E3 licenses, there is the potential for having a lot of different renewal dates to work with. The system actually takes care of this by blending the end dates of Subscriptions for the same Online Service. In the diagram below you can see that the original Subscription has been extended slightly, and the new Subscription is not for the full 12 months, so that they now both have the same renewal date:

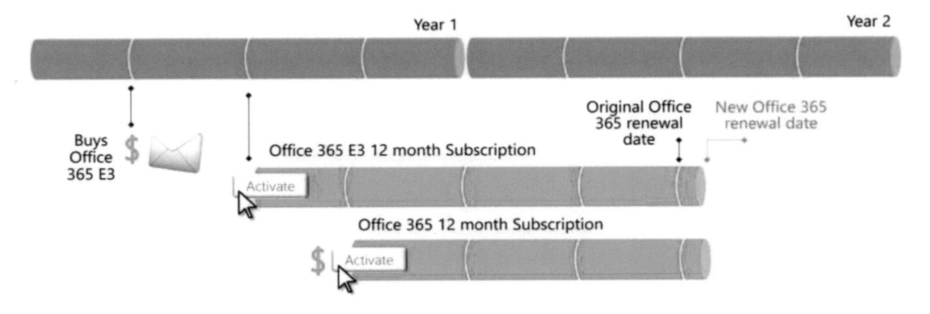

Figure 125: blended end dates in the Open programs

Add-on licenses (To-cloud)

Customers who have made an organization-wide commitment to the on-premises products through either an Open Value Organization-Wide agreement or an Open Value Subscription agreement can purchase Add-on User SLs to license their users for the Online Services. These To-cloud Add-on User SLs are cheaper than the corresponding Full User SLs, recognizing the customer's existing commitment.

The table below shows the qualifying licenses that a customer needs at the left-hand side, and the Add-ons that they may purchase to the right:

	Office 365 E1	Office 365 E3	EMS E3	EMS E5
Office Professional Plus		✔		
Core CAL Suite	✔		✔	✔
Enterprise CAL Suite			✔	✔

Figure 126: To-cloud Add-on User SLs available

The diagram on the next page is useful to see the effect of acquiring these Add-on licenses. Down the left-hand side are the workloads that can be licensed in the Open programs and the first column shows the traditional licenses that customers can buy and which particular rights they give – the Office Professional Plus license licensing the Office applications, the Core or Enterprise CAL Suite licensing access to the Productivity Servers (Exchange, SharePoint and Skype for Business) and to the Core Infrastructure Servers (Windows Server and System Center), and a Windows 10 Enterprise device license licensing the Windows client operating system. These are the Enterprise Products that a customer must commit to one or more of in an organization-wide agreement.

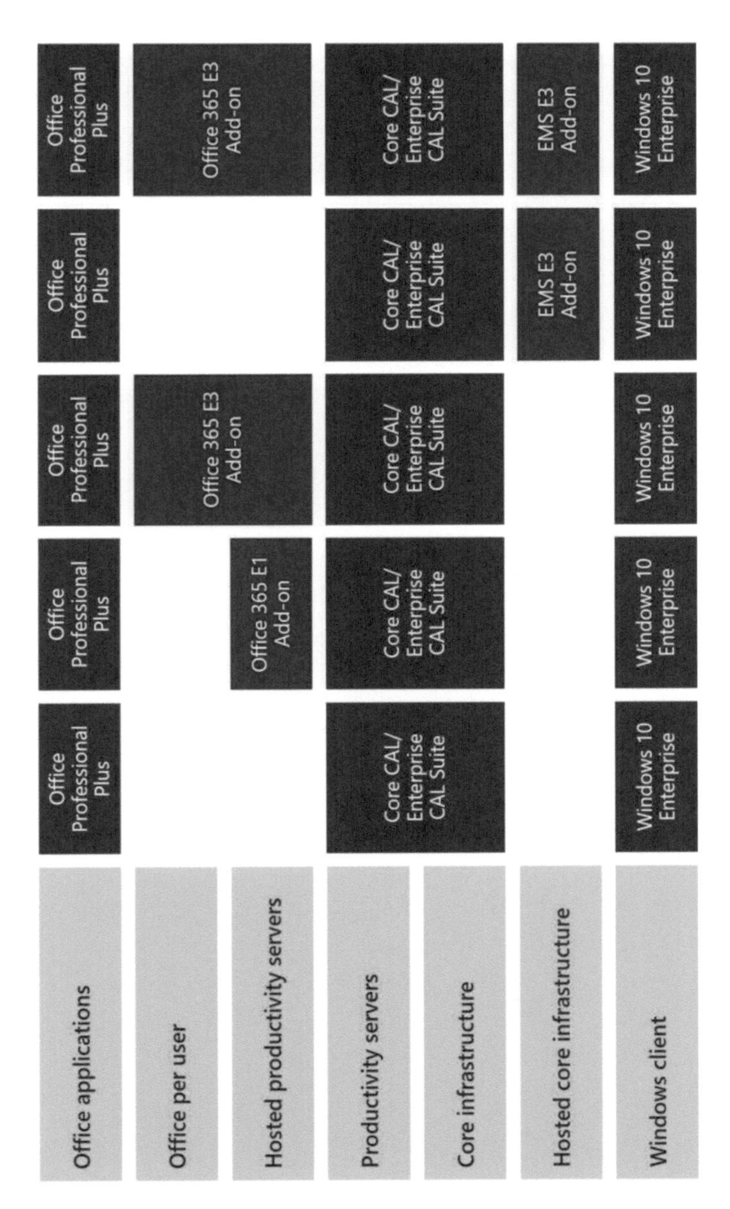

Figure 127: Online Services To-cloud Add-on User SLs

As a customer starts to think about moving to the cloud, the spaces show what this collection of licenses doesn't license, and that's where To-cloud Add-ons are available to fill in the gaps. In the second column, Mauve Stoves could use their Core CAL Suite as a qualifying license to purchase the Office 365 E1 Add-on and in this situation the Core CAL Suite license would continue to license the on-premises productivity servers, with the E1 Add-on licensing the equivalent services in the cloud. In the third column they could use their Office Professional Plus license as the qualifying license to purchase an Office 365 E3 Add-on User SL and you can see that that would add Office licensed per user (via Microsoft 365 Apps for enterprise) and access to the Office 365 hosted services.

In the same way, they could choose the EMS E3 Add-on to add on to the Core or Enterprise CAL Suite in the fourth column, or choose both the EMS E3 Add-on and the Office 365 E3 Add-on in the final column.

Mauve Stoves must maintain the qualifying licenses to be compliant in purchasing the Add-on User SLs. When they come to renew their underlying agreement, they may choose to purchase the Full User SLs rather than the Add-ons if they want to move fully to the cloud.

BUYING ONLINE SERVICES: CSP

In this section we'll cover what's available to the partner to sell and how they are invoiced for it, knowing that it's up to the partner what solutions and payment terms are actually offered to the customer.

Product availability

There is availability of almost all of the Online Services in CSP. Notable exceptions include Microsoft 365 Apps for enterprise Device SLs (only available in the EA) and Relationship Sales Solution User SLs (also only available in the EA):

Products	
Windows 10 Enterprise User SLs	✔
Office 365 User SLs	✔
EMS User SLs	✔
Microsoft 365 User SLs	✔
Dynamics 365 User SLs	✔
Power Platform User SLs	✔

Figure 128: availability of Online Services products in CSP

License type availability

The main license types for the Online Services available through CSP are Full User SLs and the In-cloud Add-on User SLs. The To-cloud Add-on and From SA User SLs are mainly a purchasing mechanism for Enterprise Enrollment customers, although From SA User SLs are available for Dynamics 365.

Step-up User SLs are a necessary license type in the Enterprise Enrollments to allow customers to move midterm from a lower license (Microsoft 365 E3 for example) to a higher one (Microsoft 365 E5 for example). In CSP, to achieve the same thing, a partner would reduce the number of Microsoft 365 E3 licenses in a Subscription and transact some new Microsoft 365 E5 licenses to assign to the users who need to use the additional services. Thus, although Step-up User SLs are not available in CSP, they are not actually needed.

License types	
Full User SLs	✔
Step-up User SLs	
In-cloud Add-on User SLs	✔
To-cloud Add-on User SLs	
From SA User SLs	✔

Figure 129: availability of Online Services license types in CSP

Minimums

There is no minimum order in CSP, a partner may order just one User SL if that's all that's required for a customer. Don't take this to mean that CSP is only aimed at smaller businesses, this rule is just to remove any barrier to sale, so that businesses of any size with any requirement for Online Services with partner support can purchase through CSP.

Commitment

When a partner orders User SLs for a customer they set up a Subscription for that Online Service. This is essentially a container to which they add licenses. So, if The Papaya Hire Company want 25 Office 365 E3 licenses then an Office 365 E3 Subscription is set up with 25 licenses in it. Most Subscriptions have a duration of 12 months, although there are 36-month Subscriptions available for some products.

Adding and reducing licenses

Partners can add and reduce licenses to an existing Subscription at any time. If the original order for The Papaya Hire Company was for 25 Office 365 E3 licenses and they want another 5 licenses in the middle of the month then the partner just adds those licenses to the Subscription and then they are billed, on a pro-rated daily basis, for the extra licenses at the beginning of the next billing period, as well as for the total of 30 Office 365 E3 licenses for the next month.

Licenses may also be reduced at any time. If the same customer wanted to reduce their 30 licenses to 27 a couple of months later, then the partner would just reduce the number of licenses in the Subscription. No fees are currently charged to partners for making these changes.

Payment

Partners are billed upfront for Online Services licenses and can choose for each Subscription whether this is on a monthly or an annual basis. So, in our example above, the partner would be billed for 25 Office 365 E3 licenses at the start of their monthly billing period, and again at the start of the next one. As we've said, the partner is under no obligation to bill The Papaya Hire Company in this way – they could bill upfront quarterly, for example – but monthly billing is an attractive option that they are easily able to offer their customers.

Pricing

Pricing is, of course, determined by the partner. Microsoft's intention is that CSP pricing is the same as Level A pricing of an EA, or if a customer purchases through the Microsoft website. There is only one price level in CSP.

Price protection

When a Subscription is set up it has a duration of 12 or 36 months, and this is the term through which the price of the licenses will be fixed. If The Papaya Hire Company need more Office 365 E3 licenses, then the partner knows what the price will be to them and so they can guarantee a fixed price for the duration of the Subscription to their customers if they want to. At the end of the Subscription term it will automatically renew taking the current price list price which will remain fixed for the next 12 months.

BUYING ONLINE SERVICES: ENTERPRISE MCA

The Online Services are not available to be purchased through this channel.

LICENSING AZURE

The Azure services are an ever-growing collection of thousands of Microsoft-hosted cloud services. Typical examples of these services could be virtual machines running on Microsoft's servers, hosting an application there, or even just using it as an off-site data storage facility.

The Azure services are sold in two main ways. Firstly, customers can buy a User Subscription License which is assigned to a user who is then licensed to use the associated Azure service while their subscription is active. This is very much the way that Office 365 and Microsoft 365 licenses work – see the **Licensing Online Services** section on page 166 for information on how customers buy these services.

There are just a handful of the Azure services licensed in this way and while you should always check the Product Terms website for the most up-to-date information, these were the services licensed in this way in May 2021:

- Azure Active Directory Premium Plan 1 and Plan 2
- Azure Information Protection Premium Plan 1
- Microsoft Defender for Identity

All of the other services are sold on a consumption basis which means that if a customer is using a service they pay for it, and if they stop using it, they don't incur any charges. The consumption services are the main focus of this section of the book, and we look at the most popular services as well as how customers buy them through all the different ways to buy.

Partners can create solutions around the Azure services which they can then sell through the Azure Marketplace. Again, there are only two ways that customer buy these solutions: as a User Subscription License, or as a consumption service. There's information on Azure Marketplace at the end of this section on page 381.

AZURE CONSUMPTION SERVICES

The majority of this part of the book is devoted to specific solutions based on the Azure consumption services – virtual machines for example. This first section gets you up to speed with some fundamental principles that work across all of the consumption services.

The Azure Pricing Calculator

When customers are considering deploying a solution based on the Azure consumption services, they need some idea of how much the solution will cost, and the Azure Pricing Calculator is an excellent tool to assist with this. You can find it here: http://bit.ly/AzurePricingCalculator.

Let's imagine that the IT Manager at Tangerine Truckers is interested in a D2 v3 Windows Server virtual machine in the North Europe region. This is the estimate he would see using the Azure Pricing Calculator: if the VM is running for 730 hours in the month (the total number of hours in a year divided by 12) then his monthly costs will be $145.27:

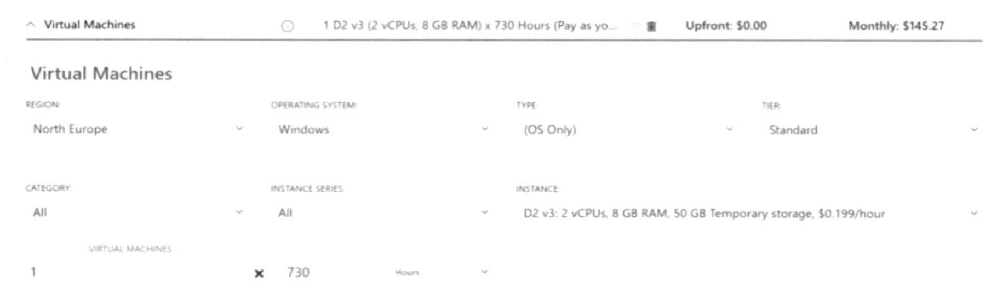

Figure 130: Azure Pricing Calculator – virtual machine estimate

The Azure Pricing Calculator is also very good at alerting you to where savings could be made and if you look at the Savings Options section in the picture below you can see the costs have been split out between the compute part of the VM and the operating system. The initial estimate of $145.27 is composed of $78.11 compute costs and $67.16 operating system costs. However, there are further options you could choose, which are to purchase a Reservation for the compute part and to take advantage of the Azure

Hybrid Benefit to reduce costs for the operating system part. These concepts are explained on page 322 and it's worth looking out for these savings options as you use the Azure Pricing Calculator.

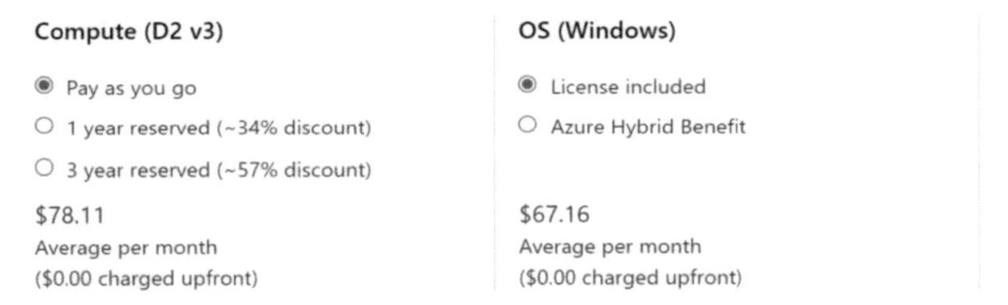

Figure 131: Azure Pricing Calculator – Savings Options

Another way of saving money is to use Dev/Test pricing where it's appropriate, and the Azure Pricing Calculator has an option towards the bottom where you can show Dev/Test pricing for your estimate.

Figure 132: Azure Pricing Calculator – showing Dev/Test pricing

For some services, such as storage, there is graduated pricing available which means that the more of a service you use each month, the cheaper the unit price becomes. Graduated pricing is applied automatically to the estimates in the Azure Pricing Calculator.

The Azure Management Portal

The Azure Management Portal at https://portal.azure.com is used by two types of users. Firstly, technical people use it to set up the resources such as virtual machines. Volume Licensing customers and those buying through the Enterprise MCA have direct access to this portal, but the default behavior in

CSP is that partners have access on behalf of their customers, although they can grant access to customers if required.

Secondly, users with a particular interest in the costs incurred by their Azure solutions use this portal. An extensive set of functionality called Azure Cost Management helps customers to gain visibility into their costs and to optimize their Azure spend.

Azure Advisor is an interesting part of the tools available; it analyzes the resource configuration and usage telemetry and then recommends solutions that can help a customer improve (among other things) the cost effectiveness of the Azure resources. For instance, it can recommend that you resize or shut down underutilized virtual machines or buy a Reservation for a virtual machine if you're currently paying on an ad hoc basis.

You may also know about the Azure Enterprise Portal at https://ea.azure.com. This portal is exclusively for Enterprise Agreement customers and their partners and is also used to track usage and spend of the Azure consumption services. However, these days the Azure Cost Management functionality in the Azure Management Portal offers a more sophisticated set of tools, and many customers use this portal in preference to the original Azure Enterprise Portal.

Azure Subscriptions

The last topic we need to cover in this overview section is the notion of an Azure Subscription. An Azure Subscription is a container to which resources are assigned as they are created. It is always linked to a billing mechanism – the EA, CSP etc. and it needs to be created before any resources can be provisioned on Azure.

Some customers have several (or many) Subscriptions. They are useful if you want to split spend by budget, department, subsidiary or project, for example, and they also give you an easy way to control who has access to which resources.

The structure of an Azure Subscription is shown below. There are one or more Resource Groups grouping Resources and it's Role Based Access Control that helps you to manage who has access to which Resources and what they can do with those Resources: For instance, Erich may have Owner rights on the Subscription and can thus do anything with any Resource within the Subscription; Katrin may have Contributor rights on a Resource Group and has more restricted rights on just the Resources in that Resource Group; and Martijn has Reader rights on a single Resource which means he can see but can't make changes to that Resource.

Figure 133: Azure Subscription

LICENSING AZURE VIRTUAL MACHINES

Apparently, the first workload that many customers try in Azure is a virtual machine, so it seems a good consumption service to start with.

Options for licensing Windows Server virtual machines

When you buy a Windows Server virtual machine in Azure you need to pay for two components of the VM: the infrastructure, or compute, costs, and the cost for the Windows Server operating system component. As a customer you can choose to pay for these two components in a transactional, or Pay-As-You-Go, way, or in a committed way. If you can make a commitment, then you will get the best possible price for the virtual machine.

Note that whichever way you choose to license a Windows Server virtual machine in Azure, there is no requirement for Windows Server CALs for users or devices accessing those virtual machines.

The Pay-As-You-Go option works via an all-inclusive cost for the virtual machine: you simply decide on the resources you want the virtual machine to have in terms of the number of cores and the amount of RAM etc. in much the same way you would if you went to a hardware supplier and ordered a physical machine. As you would expect, the higher specification the Azure virtual machine has, the more it costs. It's offered on an hourly rate, with per-minute billing, which means organizations only pay for the virtual machine while it's up and running. The diagram below represents the all-inclusive virtual machine, where a single meter runs to charge for both components of the VM:

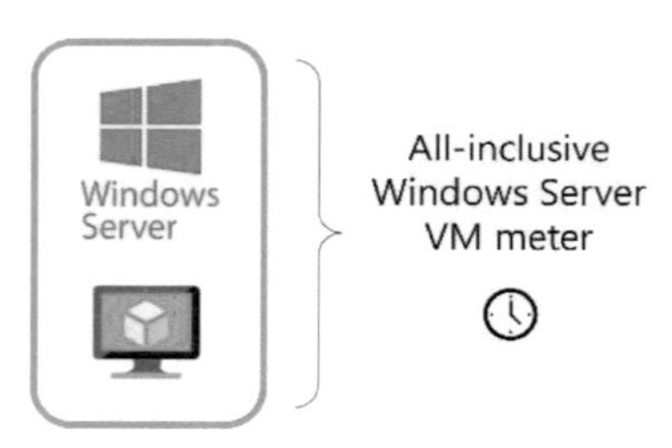

Figure 134: all-inclusive Windows Server virtual machine

This way of paying for a virtual machine offers the greatest flexibility, allowing you just to pay for what you use, but it is the most expensive way of running virtual machines in Azure. To get the best possible pricing you need to split the two components and pay for them separately, not on a meter, but by making a commitment. You buy something different for each component as shown below:

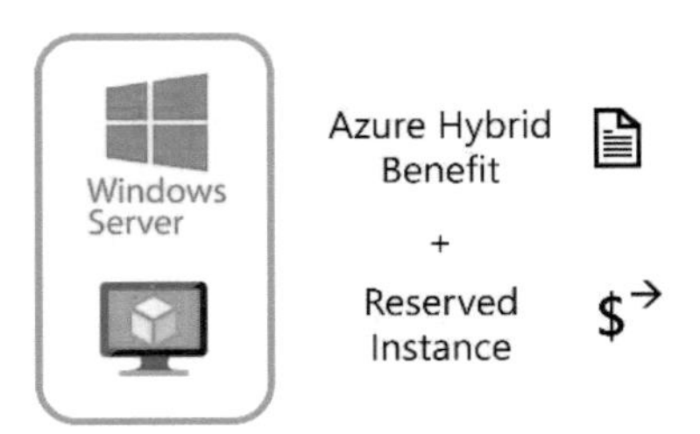

Figure 135: Windows Server VM – Reserved Instance + Azure Hybrid Benefit

You need to buy a Reserved Instance for the compute component and make use of the Azure Hybrid Benefit for the Windows Server component. The following sections give an overview of how these different things work, with full details on page 333 onwards.

Reserved Instances

A Reservation is a way of making a duration-based commitment to one of the Azure services to get attractive pricing. If you commit to the compute part of a virtual machine, then that's called a Reserved Instance. When you buy a Reserved Instance, you choose the VM type and the Azure data center region: a D16 v3 virtual machine in the West US region, for example.

There are 1 and 3-year Reserved Instances with, perhaps not surprisingly, the biggest discounts available for the 3-year commitment. You can choose to pay upfront or monthly for Reserved Instances and there are no penalties (in terms of higher costs) for choosing a monthly option.

Once a customer has acquired a Reserved Instance, they don't need to manually assign it to a virtual machine. If there is already a virtual machine running which matches both the type of virtual machine of the Reserved Instance (D16 v3) and the region (West US), then the Reserved Instance is automatically applied to the virtual machine. This will immediately change the way the virtual machine is charged, removing any costs for the base compute component.

If a customer creates a new virtual machine using an image in the Azure Management portal, then the Reserved Instance will automatically be applied to that virtual machine as long as, again, it matches the type of virtual machine and the region.

If a customer's Reserved Instances requirements change, then they have a number of options. If they need to run a different virtual machine type in the same family (a D8 v3 for example) then the existing Reserved Instance is automatically applied to any virtual machines of the same family. This is called **instance size flexibility** and you can read more about it on page 337.

If the customer needs to change the Azure region, the term, or the virtual machine family, then they can exchange the Reserved Instance. If they want to cancel the Reserved Instance altogether then refunds are also available. You can find full details of **Exchanging Reservations** and **Canceling Reservations** on page 335 onwards.

Azure Hybrid Benefit: Windows Server

The Azure Hybrid Benefit is essentially a way of being allowed to bring your own licenses to license the Windows Server part of an Azure virtual machine. Customers are eligible for the Azure Hybrid Benefit if they have active Software Assurance on Windows Server Standard or Datacenter Core licenses purchased through any Volume Licensing agreement, or if they have purchased Server Subscriptions for Windows Server Standard Core licenses through CSP.

Either of these license types can be used to license on-premises servers following the rules detailed on page 18, and either license type can be used to license an Azure virtual machine, following a different set of rules.

Here we follow the "groups of 8" rule. Licenses must be kept together in groups of 8 and assigned to Azure virtual machines based on the number of cores that they have. Thus, a 1-, 2-, 4- or 8-core virtual machine will all need 1 group of 8 Core licenses, and a 16-core virtual machine will need 2 groups of 8 licenses.

We saw that Reserved Instances actively search for a matching virtual machine and when a match is found, the compute charges for the virtual machine stop. However, you need to manually activate the Azure Hybrid Benefit for both new and existing virtual machines. It's not tricky to do and you can find details on page 344.

LICENSING AZURE SQL SOLUTIONS

Microsoft use the term **Azure SQL** to group together the options that customers have for running SQL Server in Azure, and we'll see that there are three main deployment options.

Firstly there's an Infrastructure as a Service, or IaaS, solution, and this is SQL Server running in an Azure virtual machine. The infrastructure and the host are managed by Azure, and the customer manages the operating system and the SQL Server.

Then there are two Platform as a Service, or PaaS, types of offerings where Azure manages more of the solution compared to an IaaS solution. The first option is Azure SQL Managed Instance, where Azure manages both the infrastructure and the operating system, and the customer is just responsible for the SQL Server. And in the second option, Azure SQL Database, Azure manages the infrastructure, the operating system and the SQL Server, and the customer just focuses on their individual database apps.

If you're interested in a Microsoft view of when you would use one option rather than another from a technical perspective, then it's worth taking a look at a very useful article which you can find here: http://bit.ly/SQLOptions.

LICENSING SQL SERVER VIRTUAL MACHINES

Options for licensing SQL Server virtual machines

When you buy a SQL Server virtual machine in Azure you need to pay for three components of the VM: the infrastructure, or compute, costs and the costs for software: Windows Server and SQL Server. As a customer you can choose to pay for these three components in a transactional, or Pay-As-You-Go, way, or in a committed way. If you can make a commitment, then you will get the best possible price for the virtual machine.

The Pay-As-You-Go option works via an all-inclusive cost for the virtual machine: you simply decide on the resources you want the virtual machine to have in terms of the number of cores and the amount of RAM etc. in much the same way you would if you went to a hardware supplier and ordered a physical machine. As you would expect, the higher specification the Azure virtual machine has, the more it costs. It's offered on an hourly rate, with per-minute billing, which means organizations only pay for the virtual machine while it's up and running. The diagram below represents the all-inclusive virtual machine, where a single meter runs to charge for all three components of the VM:

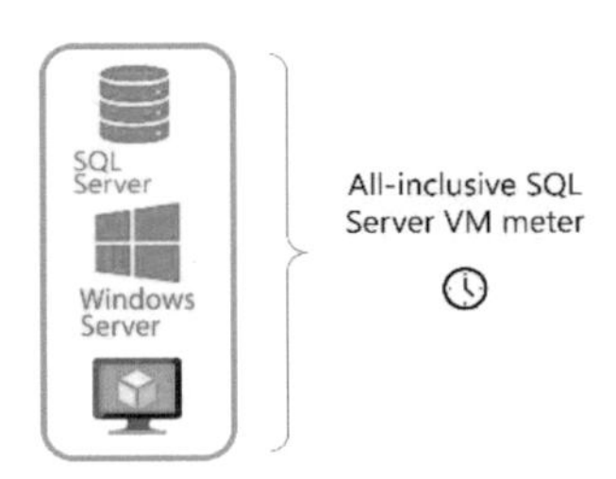

Figure 136: all-inclusive SQL Server virtual machine

This way of paying for a virtual machine offers the greatest flexibility allowing you just to pay for what you use, but it is the most expensive way of running virtual machines in Azure. To get the best possible pricing you need to split the three components and pay for them separately, not on a meter, but by making a commitment. You buy something different for each component as shown below:

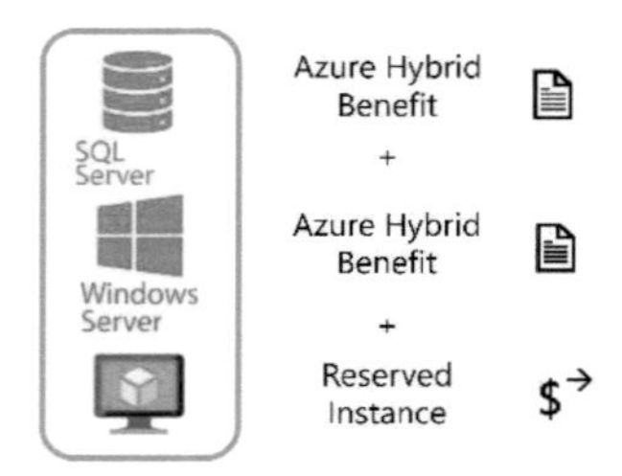

Figure 137: SQL Server VM - Reserved Instance + Azure Hybrid Benefit

You need to buy a Reserved Instance for the compute component and make use of the Azure Hybrid Benefit for the Windows Server and SQL Server components. Now, the virtual machine that we've been talking about is, effectively, SQL Server running in a Windows Server virtual machine, and the section which covers the licensing of Windows Server virtual machines in Azure on page 322 covers how to acquire the Reserved Instance and to use the Azure Hybrid Benefit for the Windows Server part of this virtual machine. So we just need to focus on the remaining part of this virtual machine – using the Azure Hybrid Benefit for SQL Server.

Azure Hybrid Benefit: SQL Server

The Azure Hybrid Benefit is essentially a way of being allowed to bring your own licenses to license the SQL Server part of the Azure virtual machine. Customers are eligible for the Azure Hybrid Benefit if they have active Software Assurance on SQL Server Standard or Enterprise Core licenses purchased through a Volume Licensing agreement, or if they have purchased Server Subscriptions for SQL Server Standard or Enterprise Core licenses through CSP.

Either of these license types can be used to license on-premises servers or to license Azure virtual machines, and the rules are the same: you count the virtual cores assigned to the virtual machine and assign that number of licenses to the virtual machine, making sure that you meet the minimum of 4 licenses.

In the **Licensing Azure virtual machines** section we cover the fact that Reserved Instances actively search for a matching virtual machine and when a match is found, the compute charges for the virtual machine stop. However, you need to manually activate the Azure Hybrid Benefit for both Windows Server and SQL Server, and you can find out more about this on page 347.

LICENSING SQL SERVER PaaS SOLUTIONS

The two SQL Server PaaS offerings – Azure SQL Managed Instance and Azure SQL Database – follow the same sort of purchasing rules as a SQL Server virtual machine. There's an option for customers who need a flexible, commitment-free PAYG solution, and another for customers who are willing to commit for the best possible pricing:

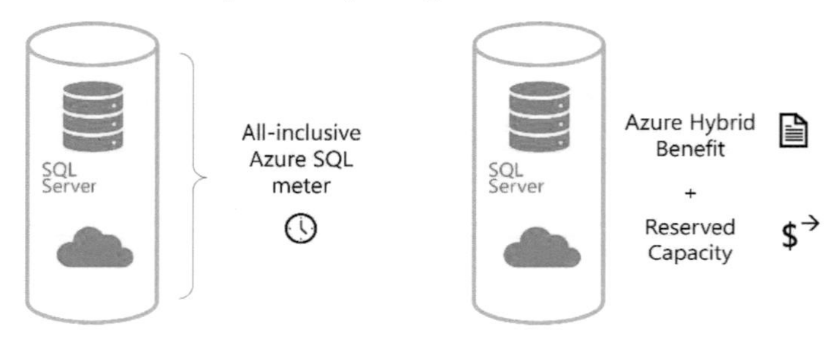

Figure 138: purchasing options for SQL PaaS solutions

The left-hand side option is the all-inclusive cost for the solution, running on a meter. As usual, this offers the greatest flexibility, with customers just incurring costs while the workload is running, but it is the most expensive option. To get the best possible pricing you again need to split the components of the solution. The Azure Hybrid Benefit will allow customers to use their existing SQL Server licenses to cover the SQL Server part of the solution. The infrastructure costs for an Azure virtual machine are covered with a purchase of a particular Reservation, called a Reserved Instance, and in this solution another type of Reservation is used, called Reserved Capacity. The following sections give an overview of how these different things work, with full details on page 333 onwards.

Reserved Capacity

A Reservation is a way of making a duration-based commitment to one of the Azure services to get attractive pricing. If you commit to the infrastructure part of an Azure SQL Managed Instance or Azure SQL Database solution then that's called Reserved Capacity. There are 1 and 3-year options to purchase

Reserved Capacity with, perhaps not surprisingly, the biggest discounts available for the 3-year commitment.

Aside from the choice of duration, you make some other choices when you purchase Reserved Capacity. Firstly, you choose the Deployment Type (Azure SQL Managed Instance or Azure SQL Database) and the Performance Tier (General Purpose, Business Critical or Hyperscale) and the Azure region. Then you choose the scope, which is where you want the Reserved Capacity to be used. The final part of the purchase is the number of virtual cores, or vCores, that you need.

Once a customer has acquired Reserved Capacity, they don't need to manually assign it to a specific database. If there is already a workload running which matches the Performance Tier and Azure region then the Reserved Capacity is automatically applied to it. This will immediately change the way the deployment is charged, removing any costs for the infrastructure component.

If a customer creates a new Azure SQL Managed Instance or Azure SQL Database, then the Reserved Capacity will automatically be applied to that solution as long as, again, it matches the Performance Tier and Azure region.

Azure Hybrid Benefit

In the Azure Hybrid Benefit section on page 328 we saw that customers with eligible SQL Server licenses can choose to use those licenses either with on-premises or Azure virtual machines. Actually, there's a third option for customers – they can choose instead to use the licenses to cover the SQL Server costs for an Azure SQL Managed Instance or Azure SQL Database solution.

Eligible SQL Server Standard or Enterprise Core licenses cover a certain number of vCores for either Azure SQL Managed Instance or Azure SQL Database solutions, dependent on the tier that is chosen, as shown below:

Edition	**General Purpose/ Hyperscale**	**Business Critical**
Standard	1 license = 1 vCore	4 Core licenses = 1 vCore
Enterprise	1 Core license = 4 vCores	1 Core license = 1 vCore

Figure 139: Azure Hybrid Benefit rights to Azure SQL vCores

As we have seen before, the Azure Hybrid Benefit is not enabled automatically. However, it's a simple task for an administrator to adjust a database's configuration settings to turn this option on for any database.

RESERVATIONS

A Reservation is a way of making a duration-based commitment to one of the Azure services, or to a Software Plan, to get attractive pricing. The term of a Reservation is typically 1 or 3 years with, perhaps not surprisingly, the biggest discounts available for the 3-year commitment.

Types of Reservations

As of May 2021, there were 21 different categories of Reservations available. In this section we'll focus on a few of the most common ones, looking first at rules that apply to all Reservations, and then the specifics of the following types:

Azure services:

- Virtual Machines
- Azure Dedicated Host
- Azure SQL
- Azure Storage

Software Plans:

- SUSE Linux

Availability

Reservations are available through the Enterprise Agreement, CSP, the Enterprise MCA, and through azure.com.

Transacting Reservations

Assigning a Reservation

When a Reservation is purchased, you make some choices. This could include the type of virtual machine family, the Performance Tier of an Azure SQL Database solution, and your required Azure region.

You also choose a scope for it, which is where you want it to be used. You can choose to assign it to a specific Resource Group, or to a specific

Subscription, or to all Subscriptions. Once the transaction is complete, the Reservation looks for a match with the selected attributes within the chosen scope and it's then applied automatically to that workload, without interruption, and stops the associated charges. If within the scope there are several workloads that match, a customer has no control over which workload the Reservation is assigned to. If this level of control is required then you would make use of the more granular Resource Group approach. The scope of a Reservation can easily be changed at any time after it has been purchased.

For these Reservations that I've chosen to focus on, the advantageous pricing works on a use-it-or-lose-it basis. Thus, if there are no matching resources for an hour the benefit is lost and doesn't carry forward to future hours where there are perhaps multiple matching resources.

Payment options

For the four Azure Reservations listed you can choose to pay upfront or monthly and there are no penalties (in terms of higher costs) for choosing a monthly option. For the SUSE Linux Software Plan, only the upfront payment option is available.

If Reserved Instances are purchased through a CSP partner then the partner could compile any payment terms (annual, for example) that are acceptable to, or desired by, their customer. If a Reserved Instance is purchased through an Enterprise Agreement, then it is paid for from the Azure Prepayment balance (see page 384), or, if that is at zero, as an overage payment on the next monthly bill.

Automatic renewal

Reservations do not automatically renew, but customers are sent notifications about upcoming Reservation expiration, and can choose to opt in to automatically renew the Reservation at any time. This will purchase a new Reservation at the relevant time rather than extending the term of an existing one. If a Reservation is not set to automatically renew then there is no interruption to the workload, it just starts being charged at regular metered prices. As soon as another Reservation is purchased it is automatically applied to the relevant workload.

Exchanging Reservations

The scope of a Reservation can be changed at any time, but for all other attributes – the term, the data center, the virtual machine family etc. – an Exchange needs to be carried out. You can exchange a Reservation within the same type – from one virtual machine family (Dv4) to another (Ev4), for example – but you can't exchange a virtual machine Reservation for a SQL Database one.

When an Exchange is made, credit is calculated for the remaining term of the Reservation and refunded to the customer. The existing Reservation is canceled, and the new purchase is processed. The cost of the new Reservation must be equal to or greater than the returned Reservation's remaining commitment.

As an example, let's imagine that World of Magnolia have paid $6,000 upfront for a 3-year Reservation. After 9 months they choose to exchange it for a $5,000 1-year Reservation. They will be credited $4,500 as a prorated amount for the existing Reservation and billed $5,000 for the new Reservation. This is an eligible refund since the cost of the new Reservation ($5,000) is greater than the remaining amount of the existing Reservation ($4,500).

The same rules are applied if World of Magnolia had chosen to pay monthly for their original Reservation - the total lifetime cost of the new purchase must be greater than the leftover payments that are canceled for the returned Reservation.

Exchanges can also be used to change the billing frequency of a Reservation. If World of Magnolia had chosen to pay for their original Reservation upfront, they could exchange it for a monthly-paid one, or vice versa. Note, however, that in each case a full new term of a Reservation starts, rather than changes being made to the existing one.

There's no limit on the number of Exchanges that can be made, and there are no fees charged. Exchanges don't contribute to the cap on refunds as described below.

Note however, that you can't exchange a SUSE Linux Software Plan.

Canceling Reservations

If World of Magnolia's needs change so much that they no longer need any sort of Reservation, they can cancel it, if required.

Credit is again calculated for the remaining term and an early termination fee of 12% is deducted, and then the balance is refunded. At the time of writing (May 2021) Microsoft do not charge the early termination fees for refunds. They state on their website: "We might charge the fees for refunds made in the future. We currently don't have a date for enabling the fee." You can find the current status of that text here: https://bit.ly/BOKRefundNotice.

If the original Reservation had been purchased through an Enterprise Agreement, it is refunded to the original mechanism used to purchase it: if Azure Prepayment was used, it is returned to the available balance, and if overage was used then it shows as a credit on the monthly overage invoice. If the Reservation was purchased through CSP then it is the partner's account that is refunded, and they credit their customer according to their own agreed terms and conditions.

Refunds are capped at $50,000 in a 12-month rolling window, and this is per customer in the Enterprise Agreement or Enterprise MCA, and per partner in CSP.

SUSE Linux Software Plans aren't eligible for refunds.

Virtual machines: Reserved Instances

Purchasing a Reserved Instance

When you purchase a Reservation to prepay for the base compute cost of a virtual machine it's known as a Reserved Instance. At the time of purchase you choose the VM type and the Azure data center region: a D16 v3 virtual machine in the West US region, for example. You also choose the scope across which it will be used in common with the other Reservations: a single Subscription or all Subscriptions, or a Resource Group, as well as the term (1 or 3 years), and the payment option (monthly or annually). Reserved Instances are automatically applied to matching virtual machines in the same Azure region, and charges for the base compute part of the virtual machine are stopped.

If the virtual machine is running Windows Server and/or SQL Server, then the Reserved Instance does not cover the cost for this software – the most cost-effective way of paying for the software is to take advantage of the Azure Hybrid Benefit as described on page 343. If you don't bring your own licenses via this method, then the software costs will be charged on a meter while the virtual machine is running.

Instance size flexibility

When you purchase a Reserved Instance, you can choose to optimize for instance size flexibility which means that the Reserved Instance isn't tied to an exact virtual machine type anymore, but rather to a family of virtual machines. This means that if a business' requirements for their virtual machines change within a family, the Reserved Instance is still applied automatically to different virtual machines, via the use of ratios.

This is the Dv3 family with its associated ratios:

Instance	Ratio
D2 v3	1
D4 v3	2
D8 v3	4
D16 v3	8
D32 v3	16
D48 v3	24
D64 v3	32

Figure 140: Dv3 family ratios

Let's imagine that World of Magnolia have acquired a D16 v3 Reserved Instance; we can see from the table that this equates to 8 units of the Dv3 family. Presumably they purchased this Reserved Instance because they were intending to run a D16 v3 virtual machine and, indeed, we know that this Reserved Instance will automatically be applied to that virtual machine and completely cover the base compute cost.

However, World of Magnolia's business requirements change, and they need to run two D8 v3 virtual machines instead of the original D16 v3. If we calculate the units of base compute required, we see that it would again total 8 units and the Reserved Instance would again cover the base compute costs of both of these virtual machines. So, finally, what happens if they want to use a D32 v3 virtual machine which is 16 units? Well, the Reserved Instance will cover half of the base compute costs and the remainder will be charged on a consumption basis on the relevant base compute meter.

If World of Magnolia need to change the term, the billing frequency, the virtual machine family, or the Azure region, then they would need to exchange the Reserved Instance as described above, in the **Exchanging Reservations** section.

5-year Reserved Instances

There are 5-year Reserved Instances available for a handful of virtual machines – the HBv2 and HBv3 series for example. The 1- and 3-year Reserved Instances give an estimated 25% and 50% saving on the compute costs of the VM, and the 5-year Reserved Instances increase this to approximately 67%. The early termination fee for 5-year Reserved Instances is 35% rather than the usual 12%.

Azure Dedicated Host

There are two parts to licensing Azure Dedicated Host: the infrastructure of the Azure Dedicated Host solution which hosts the virtual machines, and then the software for whatever is running inside the virtual machines.

Reservations are available for the infrastructure part of the Azure Dedicated Host and they always exactly match the Type of Azure Dedicated Host: if you have chosen a Dsv3 – Type 1 Azure Dedicated Host Type, then that is what you would buy a Reservation for. An Azure Dedicated Host Reservation pays fully for the infrastructure of the Azure Dedicated Host solution regardless of the number of virtual machines running.

You make the usual choices with regards to the term, billing frequency, and Azure region, and can expect up to about 60% savings. You can read more about licensing Azure Dedicated Host solutions on page 352.

Azure SQL: Reserved Capacity

Purchasing Reserved Capacity

When you purchase Reserved Capacity to prepay for the infrastructure costs of an Azure SQL Managed Instance or Azure SQL Database solution you make a number of choices. Firstly, you choose the Deployment Type (Azure SQL Managed Instance or Azure SQL Database) and the Performance Tier (General Purpose, Business Critical, or Hyperscale), the Azure region, the scope (single or all Subscriptions, or a Resource Group), and the term (1 or 3 years). The final part of the purchase is the number of virtual cores, or vCores, that you need.

vCore size flexibility

vCore size flexibility enables customers to scale up or down within a Performance Tier and Azure region. If World of Magnolia make a Reserved Capacity purchase of 16 vCores for Azure SQL Managed Instance at the General Purpose Performance Tier in the West US data center, then the Reserved Capacity will automatically be applied if there is a 16-core Managed Instance running in that data center. In reality though, the Reserved Capacity is applied to any General Purpose Azure SQL Managed Instances or Azure SQL Databases running in that data center. This means that it could alternatively cover the full compute costs for 2 x 4-core databases, or cover half of the costs of a 32-core database, the remainder being paid for on a meter.

If World of Magnolia need to change the term, the billing frequency, the Performance Tier, or the Azure region, then they would need to exchange the Reserved Capacity as described above, in the **Exchanging Reservations** section.

Software costs

A Reserved Capacity purchase does not cover the SQL Server software costs of an Azure SQL Managed Instance or Azure SQL Database solution – the most cost-effective way of paying for the software is to take advantage of the Azure Hybrid Benefit as described on page 343. If you don't bring your own licenses via this method, then the software costs will be charged on a meter while the database is running.

Azure Storage: Reserved Capacity

Reserved Capacity purchased for Azure Storage covers both Block Blob and Azure Data Lake Storage Gen2 data. When you purchase Reserved Capacity you choose an Access Tier (Archive, Cool, or Hot), a Redundancy (LRS, ZRS, GRS/RA-GRS, or GZRS/RA-GZRS) and the usual Reservation attributes: term (1 or 3 years), billing frequency (monthly or annual), scope (single or all Subscriptions, or a Resource Group), and Azure region. The final part of the purchase is the number of units of Reserved Capacity that you need, available in units of either 100 TiB or 1 PiB.

As usual, Reserved Capacity is applied automatically to data matching the Access Tier, Redundancy, and Azure region attributes of the Reservation. If World of Magnolia have made a Reserved Capacity purchase and need to change the term, the billing frequency, the Azure region, the Access Tier, or the Redundancy, then they would need to exchange the Reserved Capacity as described above, in the **Exchanging Reservations** section.

SUSE Linux Software Plan

Purchasing a SUSE Linux Software Plan

An Azure virtual machine running SUSE Linux Enterprise Server (SLES) may be purchased as an all-inclusive virtual machine or, as with a Windows Server virtual machine, the components may be paid for separately if a customer is willing to make a duration-based commitment. The compute part of the virtual machine is paid for via a Reserved Instance in the usual way, while a Software Plan allows a customer to prepay for SUSE software usage and get the best rates.

When you purchase a SUSE Software Plan you choose the Type (SLES Standard, SLES for SAP Standard/Priority, or SLES for HPC Standard/Priority), the VM size (1-2, 3-4, or 5+ vCPUs), as well as the usual Reservation attributes: term (1 or 3 years), scope (single or all Subscriptions, or a Resource Group), and Azure region. The only available payment option is upfront, and there are no exchanges or cancelations allowed.

Instance size flexibility

In a similar way to Reserved Instances, there is instance size flexibility within a SUSE Software Plan Type. It all works on a series of tables of ratios – you can find the full list here, https://bit.ly/BOKSUSEInstanceFlexibility but we'll do an example here.

Let's go back to World of Magnolia and imagine that their latest purchase is for a SUSE Linux Enterprise Server for HPC Priority Software Plan. They are running a D4s v3 virtual machine which has 4 cores, so they've chosen the Software Plan with a VM size attribute of 3-4 vCPUs. As you would expect, that Software Plan is assigned automatically to the virtual machine, and the software charges stop.

Let's look at what happens if they choose to run a different-sized virtual machine. Here's the relevant table that I mentioned earlier:

Software Plan	Ratio
SLES for HPC Priority 1-2 vCPUs	1
SLES for HPC Priority 3-4 vCPUs	2
SLES for HPC Priority 5+ vCPUs	2.6

Figure 141: ratios for SLES for HPC Priority Software Plans

We know that they purchased the second Software Plan since their D4s v3 virtual machine has 4 cores. Now, however, they want to deploy in its place a D1 v2 (1-core) and D2 v2 (2-core) virtual machine. Looking at the table, you can see that they purchased 2 units of the Software Plan Type. For 2 virtual machines with either 1 or 2 cores they need 2 x 1 units, so the software costs would be completely covered by their existing Software Plan.

Now let's suppose that they instead want to deploy a D8s v3 virtual machine which has 8 cores. They need 2.6 units of the Software Plan Type and they have purchased 2. This means that their Software Plan purchase will cover 2/2.6 = 0.7692, or about 77% of the software costs, with the remainder being charged on a meter.

AZURE HYBRID BENEFIT

The Azure Hybrid Benefit applies to Windows Server and SQL Server and is essentially a way of being allowed to bring your own licenses to license the Windows or SQL Server software part of solutions in Azure.

Windows Server

Overview

The Azure Hybrid Benefit for Windows Server enables customers to bring their own licenses to license the Windows Server part of an Azure virtual machine.

Customers are eligible for the Azure Hybrid Benefit if they have active Software Assurance on Windows Server Standard or Datacenter Core licenses purchased through any Volume Licensing agreement, or if they have purchased Server Subscriptions for Windows Server Standard Core licenses through CSP.

If you're a customer who has an on-premises server farm which is being migrated to the cloud you may have "spare" Windows Server licenses with SA as on-premises servers are decommissioned and it's ideal to be able to reuse those licenses with virtual machines in Azure. If you're provisioning net new virtual machines in Azure then purchasing Server Subscriptions is likely to be the best choice to license the Windows Server component of the Azure virtual machine.

Licensing with the Azure Hybrid Benefit

Windows Server Standard and Datacenter Core licenses acquired through a Volume Licensing agreement are sold in 2-packs or 16-packs (see page 18) and Windows Server Standard Core licenses sold as a Server Subscription are sold in 8-packs (see page 29). Either of these license types can be used to license on-premises servers following the rules detailed on page 18, and either license type can be used to license an Azure virtual machine, following a different set of rules.

Here we follow the "groups of 8" rule. Licenses must be kept together in groups of 8 and assigned to Azure virtual machines based on the number of cores that they have. Thus, a 1-, 2-, 4- or 8-core virtual machine will all need 1 group of 8 Core licenses, and a 16-core virtual machine will need 2 groups of 8 licenses. Watch out for an E20a v4 virtual machine with its 20 cores – you wouldn't assign 20 Core licenses, but 24 – because the licenses must be kept together in groups of 8.

Note that Microsoft require a minimum of 16 Windows Server Core licenses assigned to Azure to "activate" the Azure Hybrid Benefit. These licenses can be all Volume Licensing licenses, all Server Subscriptions, or a combination of both.

Enabling the Azure Hybrid Benefit

The Azure Hybrid Benefit needs to be manually activated for both new and existing virtual machines.

When you create a Windows Server virtual machine using an image in the Azure Management Portal you can check a box to confirm that you already have appropriate Windows Server licenses. Checking this box will ensure that you can continue with the process of creating a Windows Server virtual machine but that you won't be charged for the Windows Server component because you've confirmed that you have enough licenses for the virtual machine being created.

Note that you don't have to match the edition of the license with the edition of the image – Standard edition licenses can be used with Datacenter edition images, for example.

So how does this work if you have a virtual machine that's already been created and you want to assign some Windows Server licenses to it and thus not be charged for the Windows Server component of that virtual machine? It's a simple matter of going to the **Configure** settings of the virtual machine and then enabling the Azure Hybrid Benefit. This will immediately change the way that the virtual machine is charged with no ongoing charges for the Windows Server component of the virtual machine.

Additional rights for Windows Server Datacenter licenses

There is a difference in rights between a Windows Server 2019 Standard Core license and a Windows Server 2019 Datacenter Core license. With a Standard Core license the Azure Hybrid Use Benefit rights are alternative – an organization can choose to use licenses in an on-premises data center following the rules we discussed on page 18, or use them for Azure virtual machines following the "groups of 8" rule. I think this is how you would expect this benefit to work, so this hopefully feels straightforward.

The rules are different for Datacenter Core licenses though because the Azure Hybrid Use Benefit rights are additive. This means that you can use the licenses in an on-premises data center AND for Azure virtual machines. Take a look at the diagram below: the on-premises servers (bottom left) are licensed correctly with 32 Core licenses each, for a total of 8 groups of 8 licenses. These licenses remain assigned to the servers, but they can also be used to license some base instance virtual machines in Azure. The number of cores of each virtual machine are shown in the circles – do you agree that this customer has enough licenses for this configuration of Azure virtual machines?

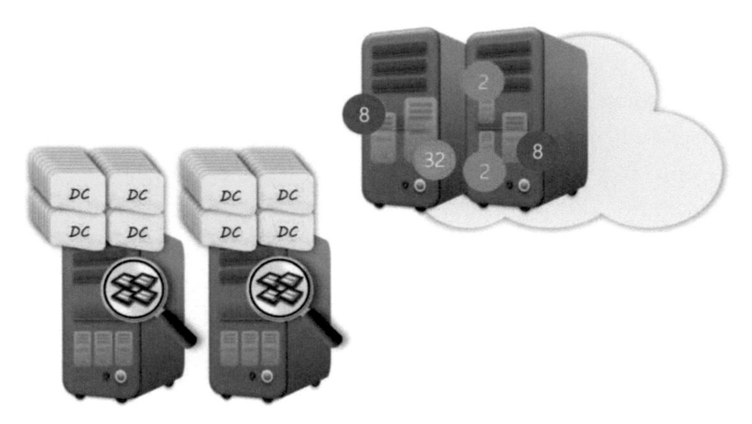

Figure 142: Windows Server 2019 Datacenter Azure Hybrid Benefit

If you count the groups of 8 licenses needed for each of the Azure virtual machines starting at the left (1, 2-3-4-5, 6, 7, 8) then you should find that this is a completely compliant scenario.

Migration rights

Windows Server Standard Core licenses may be assigned to EITHER an on-premises infrastructure OR to Azure. There is, however, an exception to this rule: when customers are migrating existing workloads to Azure then the licenses may be assigned to both environments for up to 180 days.

Extended Security Updates in Azure

If you run Windows Server 2008 or 2008 R2 virtual machines in Azure, they're automatically enabled for Extended Security Updates. You don't need to configure anything, and there's no additional charge for using Extended Security Updates with Azure virtual machines. Extended Security Updates are automatically delivered to Azure virtual machines if they're configured to receive updates.

SQL Server

Overview

The Azure Hybrid Benefit for SQL Server enables customers to bring their own licenses to license the SQL Server part of an Azure virtual machine, or to cover the SQL Server costs for an Azure SQL Managed Instance or Azure SQL Database solution, known as PaaS (Platform as a Service) solutions.

Customers are eligible for the Azure Hybrid Benefit if they have active Software Assurance on SQL Server Standard or Enterprise Core licenses purchased through a Volume Licensing agreement, or if they have purchased Server Subscriptions for SQL Server Standard or Enterprise Core licenses through CSP.

If SQL Server workloads are being migrated to the cloud then there may be "spare" SQL Server licenses with SA as on-premises servers are decommissioned and it's ideal to be able to reuse those licenses with SQL

Server solutions in Azure. If you're provisioning net new SQL Server solutions in Azure then purchasing Server Subscriptions is likely to be the best choice to license the SQL Server software component of those solutions.

Licensing virtual machines with the Azure Hybrid Benefit

SQL Server licenses acquired through a Volume Licensing agreement or CSP are sold in 2-packs. The rules for licensing virtual machines on-premises or in Azure are the same: you count the virtual cores assigned to the virtual machine and assign that number of licenses to the virtual machine, making sure that you meet the minimum of 4 licenses.

However, there are some extra rules when you use the licenses in Azure which give an additional level of deployment flexibility: you can choose to use Enterprise edition licenses to license a virtual machine running SQL Server Standard, or Standard edition licenses to license a virtual machine running SQL Server Enterprise. Let's take a look at the rules.

If you're running SQL Server Standard in a virtual machine and you assign SQL Server Standard Core licenses to it, then each license covers a single virtual core. Thus, an 8-core virtual machine will need 8 SQL Server Standard Core licenses. However, if you use SQL Server Enterprise Core licenses, then each license covers 4 virtual cores. So, the 8-core virtual machine running SQL Server Standard needs just 2 SQL Server Enterprise licenses assigned to it.

Similarly, if you're running SQL Server Enterprise in a virtual machine and you assign SQL Server Enterprise Core licenses to it, then each license covers a single virtual core. Thus, an 8-core virtual machine will need 8 SQL Server Enterprise Core licenses. However, if you use SQL Server Standard Core licenses, then 4 licenses are required to cover each virtual core. So, the 8-core virtual machine running SQL Server Enterprise needs 32 SQL Server Standard licenses assigned to it.

Enabling the Azure Hybrid Benefit for virtual machines

As with Windows Server the Azure Hybrid Benefit needs to be manually activated for both new and existing SQL Server virtual machines.

Enterprise Agreement customers can provision a Bring-Your-Own-License SQL Server image from the Azure Marketplace when they create a virtual machine. This creates a SQL Server virtual machine but does not charge for the SQL Server component.

Customers without an Enterprise Agreement need to provision a virtual machine using a Pay-As-You-Go SQL Server image from the Azure Marketplace and then activate the Azure Hybrid Benefit in the configuration settings of the virtual machine. This method can also be used to stop the SQL Server charges on an existing virtual machine.

Extended Security Updates for virtual machines

If you run SQL Server 2008 or 2008 R2 virtual machines in Azure, you'll automatically receive Extended Security Updates, free of charge, through existing SQL update channels.

Licensing PaaS solutions with the Azure Hybrid Benefit

Existing SQL Server Standard or Enterprise Core licenses cover a certain number of vCores for either Azure SQL Managed Instance or Azure SQL Database solutions, dependent on the tier that is chosen, as shown below:

Edition	General Purpose/ Hyperscale	Business Critical
Standard	1 license = 1 vCore	4 Core licenses = 1 vCore
Enterprise	1 Core license = 4 vCores	1 Core license = 1 vCore

Figure 143: Azure Hybrid Benefit rights to Azure SQL vCores

To help with the licenses required for all of the Azure SQL solutions there's an Azure Hybrid Benefit Savings Calculator which you can find here: https://bit.ly/BOKAHBCalculator.

In the screenshot below you can see that Tangerine Truckers have 16 SQL Server Standard and 16 SQL Server Enterprise licenses and want to assign them to 8-core General Purpose Managed Instances. The calculator helps them to see that these licenses would cover 10 instances:

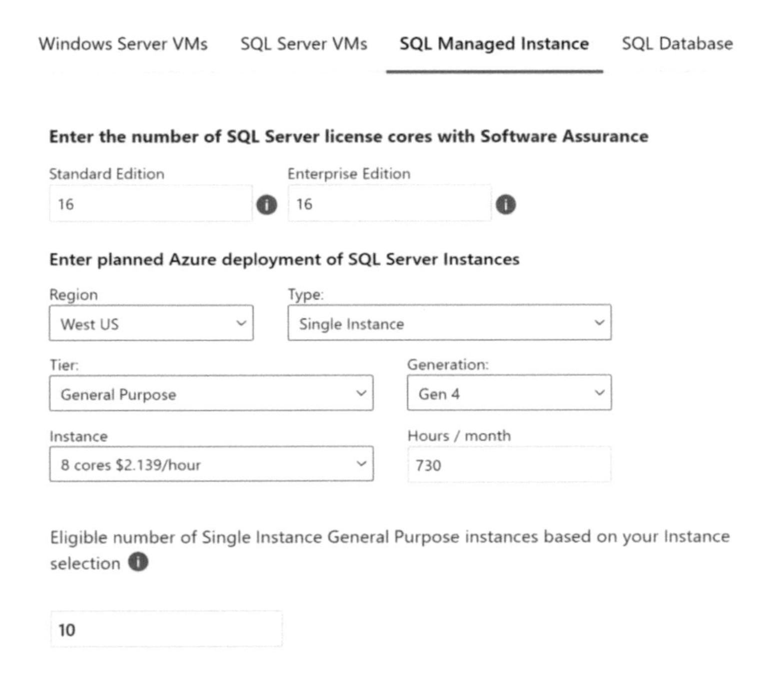

Figure 144: Azure Hybrid Benefit Savings Calculator

Enabling the Azure Hybrid Benefit for PaaS solutions

As we have seen before, the Azure Hybrid Benefit is not enabled automatically. However, it's a simple task for an administrator to adjust a database's configuration settings to turn this option on for any database.

Migration rights

The Azure Hybrid Benefit allows a customer to use their licenses in an on-premises instruction OR in Azure virtual machines OR with Azure SQL PaaS solutions. There is, however, an exception to this rule: when customers are migrating existing workloads to Azure then the licenses may be assigned to both the on-premises and Azure infrastructures for up to 180 days.

LICENSE MOBILITY THROUGH SA

This, as its name suggests, is a Software Assurance benefit, and it allows customers to use their server application licenses on third party hardware.

Hardware options

Customers can choose to use their licenses in Azure, and the following Azure options are permitted:

- Azure multi-tenant servers
- Azure Dedicated Host

Alternatively, customers can choose to use a partner's hardware, and the following options are supported:

- Shared hardware managed by an Authorized Mobility partner
- Dedicated hardware managed by a Listed Provider

If you're not familiar with these terms, then take a look at page 358.

Eligible products

Licenses with active Software Assurance acquired through any Volume Licensing agreement for the following products include this benefit:

- System Center 2019
- SQL Server 2019
- BizTalk Server 2020
- Project Server 2019
- Exchange Server 2019
- SharePoint Server 2019
- Skype for Business 2019
- Dynamics 365 for Operations Server
- Azure DevOps Server 2020

Notably, Windows Server does not include this benefit.

Licensing rules

Licenses may be used either on-premises or with virtual machines running on the authorized hardware detailed above. The licensing rules (for the most part) don't change and for the products licensed with the Server/CAL licensing model, for example, a single license allows the software to be run in one virtual machine, and customers must have Software Assurance on the CALs as well as the Server license.

When System Center 2019 Standard or Datacenter MLs are used with third party hardware, a Standard ML allows the management of 2 OSEs, a Datacenter one allows the management of 10 OSEs.

Processes

When eligible licenses are assigned to a partner's shared servers or to Azure multi-tenant hardware there is a process that needs to be followed. There's a form called the License Verification Form which must be completed, and this confirms that the licenses will be used in an Authorized Mobility partners' infrastructure, or on Azure shared servers, and states the number of licenses that are being assigned. The form is sent to Microsoft to be verified, and when Microsoft returns the form, the customer should retain this document.

Multiple benefits for SQL Server

SQL Server Standard and Enterprise Core licenses with Software Assurance are eligible for both the License Mobility through SA benefit AND the Azure Hybrid Benefit. This gives a bit of an overlap as far as Azure is concerned since both benefits allow the licenses to be used in Azure. However, the Azure Hybrid Benefit gives more flexibility and more options, so for these licenses it's probably worth considering the Azure Hybrid Benefit the main benefit as far as Azure deployment is concerned.

LICENSING AZURE DEDICATED HOST SOLUTIONS

Azure Dedicated Host is an Azure service that provides physical servers, able to host one or more Azure virtual machines for Windows or Linux, which are dedicated to a single organization and their workloads. The fact that the server capacity is not shared with other customers means that this is an attractive solution for organizations who need direct visibility and control over the underlying Azure infrastructure, or who have corporate policies requiring host level isolation or a dedicated host.

Choosing the Azure Dedicated Host

First of all, an organization chooses the right type of Azure Dedicated Host for their business. In May 2021 there were 24 to choose between, and the choice is dependent on the type of virtual machine you want to run (the Dsv3 series, for example), and the resources you want to support it – the available vCPUs, RAM and CPU type that's best for you.

The available vCPUs dictate how many virtual machines you're able to run. Let's take an example to illustrate this. Taupe Telecoms want to have an Azure Dedicated Host solution based on the Dsv3 family of virtual machines. There are three types of Azure Dedicate Host for them to choose between:

Azure Dedicated Host	Available vCPUs
Dsv3 – Type 1	64
Dsv3 – Type 2	76
Dsv3 – Type 3	80

Figure 145: Dsv3 series Azure Dedicated Host choices

The virtual machines in the Dsv3 family have the number of virtual cores in their name, so the D2s v3, for example, has 2 virtual cores and the D16s v3 has 16. They can run any virtual machines in the Dsv3 family up to the total amount of virtual cores in the Azure Dedicated Host. So, for example, they could choose the Type 2 solution and run 4 x D16s v3 + 1 x D8s v3 + 1 x D4s v3 virtual machines because (4 x 16) + (1 x 8) + (1 x 4) = 76.

Azure Dedicated Host is charged at the host level and you're billed as soon as you provision the host, regardless of the number of virtual machines you've got running. There is Pay-As-You-Go pricing available as well as 1 and 3-year Reservations which give up to about 60% savings.

Licensing the virtual machines with a meter

Let's imagine that Taupe Telecoms want to run Windows Server and SQL Server in their 6 virtual machines that they chose in the last section. There are a couple of different ways of doing this, and the first is to pay for Windows Server and SQL Server on a meter basis. There are meters for 2 core, 4 core, 8 core etc. virtual machines that would be automatically charged for virtual machines running the software in their Azure Dedicated Host solution. Since this is a metered service, Taupe Telecoms will only be charged when the virtual machines are up and running Windows Server and SQL Server. Note that they still pay the underlying Azure Dedicated Host charges regardless of whether their virtual machines are running.

There are meters for other software too including BizTalk Server, as well as Linux offerings.

Meters are great for flexibility, but they are usually the most expensive way of paying for anything in Azure, including the software component of virtual machines so, as you might expect, there are options to bring your own licenses to save money.

Licensing individual virtual machines

If customers are eligible for the Azure Hybrid Benefit for Windows Server and SQL Server then they can bring those licenses to virtual machines in an Azure Dedicated Host solution. The rules in terms of how many licenses are required are exactly the same as detailed on page 343 for Windows Server and page 346 for SQL Server.

So, for the machines that Taupe Telecoms chose earlier (4 x D16s v3 + 1 x D8s v3 + 1 x D4s v3) they would need (4 x 16) + (2 x 8) = 80 Windows Server Core licenses and (4 x 16) + (1 x 8) + (1 x 4) = 76 SQL Server Core licenses, both with active Software Assurance, or purchased as Server Subscriptions.

Licensing for unlimited virtualization

An alternative to licensing at the virtual machine level is to license for unlimited virtualization. To do this, you need Windows Server Datacenter Core licenses with active Software Assurance and SQL Server Enterprise Core licenses with active Software Assurance or SQL Server Enterprise Core Server Subscriptions, and you need to license all of the available physical cores of the Azure Dedicated Host.

In our earlier example, Taupe Telecoms chose the Dsv3 – Type 2 Azure Dedicated Host which has 76 virtual cores. How do you know how many available physical cores there are? Well, there's a table here https://bit.ly/BOKADHRatios which shows the ratio of physical cores to vCPUs, and for the Dsv3 family the ratio is shown as 2:1, meaning that for this Dedicated Host there are 38 available physical cores. Thus, if Taupe Telecoms choose this route then they'll need just 38 Windows Server Datacenter Core licenses and 38 SQL Server Enterprise Core licenses.

There is just one difference to be aware of – Windows Server Datacenter Core licenses with active Software Assurance can't be used on-premises AND for licensing unlimited virtual machines in an Azure Dedicated Host.

Extended Security Updates

If you run Windows Server/SQL Server 2008 or 2008 R2 virtual machines in Azure Dedicated Host, they're automatically enabled for Extended Security Updates. You don't need to configure anything, and there's no additional charge for using Extended Security Updates with Azure virtual machines.

LICENSING SPECIALIST VIRTUAL MACHINES

In this section we'll take a look at two specialist types of virtual machines which can be used to save money for particular types of workloads.

Azure Spot virtual machines

Introduction

When Microsoft has unused virtual machine capacity, they offer special pricing for the particular virtual machine types in the specific regions with the spare capacity. This is "spot" – at that moment in time – pricing, and thus the virtual machines that take advantage of this special pricing are known as Azure Spot virtual machines. As an example, here are the different prices for a particular virtual machine type (F2s v2), in the East US region, in May 2021:

Payment option	Cost per hour
Pay-As-You-Go	$0.1630
1-year Reserved Instance	$0.1420
3-year Reserved Instance	$0.1231
Spot	$0.0280

Figure 146: comparing VM pricing

Workload types

Although Azure Spot virtual machines are created in the same way as other virtual machines, they are defined as a Spot VM in the creation process and thereafter behave differently. When Azure needs the capacity back, the Azure Spot virtual machines are evicted with 30 seconds' notice. Thus, this type of virtual machine is ideal for a workload that can handle interruptions (batch processing jobs or Dev/Test environments etc.) but probably not for the regular workloads that support the day-to-day running of a business.

Eviction options

When you create an Azure Spot VM you can choose whether the virtual machine will be stopped/deallocated or deleted when it's evicted. Deallocating allows you to redeploy the VM later, and while you're not charged for the VM when it's deallocated, you are charged storage costs for the underlying disks. Choosing the delete option will delete both the VM and its underlying disks upon eviction.

The other choice you make is when you want the VM to be evicted. Spot pricing is often attractive, but changes, and you can set a maximum price that when it's reached the VM is evicted. Alternatively, you can choose to accept a maximum price equivalent to the Pay-As-You-Go rate. In both cases, even if the maximum price isn't met, but Azure needs the capacity, the VM will be evicted.

Constrained core virtual machines

Introduction

Sometimes a SQL Server workload has high memory, storage and I/O bandwidth requirements but isn't core intensive. There are special virtual machines available in Azure where the virtual core count is constrained; this reduces the cost of the software licensing, while maintaining the same memory, storage, and I/O bandwidth.

Example of savings

Let's take a look at an example to see what this means in real life. The figures in the table below are for virtual machines in the West US region in May 2021. The first row is for the regular E32s v4 virtual machine which has 32 cores, and the second row is for the constrained core version of the same virtual machine. This second virtual machine uses 32 cores for the compute and Windows Server components of the virtual machine, and just 8 cores for the SQL Server part. Thus, the figures are the same for the compute and Windows Server components for both virtual machines, but there are significant savings on the SQL Server component since just a quarter of the cores need to be licensed for SQL Server:

	Compute	Windows Server	SQL Server	Total
E32s v4	$1,635.20	$1,074.56	$8,760.00	$11,469.76
E32-8s v4	$1,635.20	$1,074.56	$2,190.00	$4,899.76

Figure 147: example cost savings of constrained core VMs

To find the list of constrained core virtual machines you can go to Microsoft's virtual machines pricing page here: https://bit.ly/BOKVMPricing and just search for the word **constrained**.

LICENSE DEPLOYMENT OPTIONS

30 years ago, customers bought their server licenses with, or without, Software Assurance through a Volume Licensing agreement and then deployed the products on their own on-premises servers. They acquired device licenses for Windows and Office in the same way and installed the products locally on their users' devices.

Fast forward to today and the choice expands – there are now user licenses for Windows and Office, and Server Subscriptions are available in CSP. As for the deployment options, virtualization plays a big part and there's a whole host of partner offerings for all types of managed services with, sometimes, the option of taking your own licenses to those solutions.

The aim of this section of the book is to bring all of these alternatives together so that you can see either what choices you have with certain types of licenses, or indeed what licenses you need to achieve a particular deployment option.

Dedicated hardware options

A dedicated hardware option is one where the hardware is completely dedicated to a single customer. Customers might want to run the server applications in virtual machines, or to run Windows 10 and Office virtual desktops to deliver to their users, or to stream the Office applications.

Customer-owned and managed

The simplest dedicated hardware option is the traditional, customer-owned server that sits on the customer's premises and is managed by them.

Listed Providers

Customers may choose to use hardware that is dedicated to them but is owned and managed by a third party. Microsoft categorize partners that offer this type of solution either as Listed Providers or Authorized Outsourcers, and the licensing rules differ dependent on the partner type. The Listed Providers, at May 2021, are the following organizations: Alibaba,

Amazon, Google, and Microsoft. If there were to be changes to the list of Listed Providers, you can always find the up-to-date list here: http://aka.ms/listedproviders.

Authorized Outsourcers

All other organizations offering dedicated hardware solutions are known as Authorized Outsourcers.

Azure Dedicated Host

Microsoft is classed as a Listed Provider as far as the licensing of dedicated hardware solutions goes, but, as you might guess, the rules are a bit different from the other Listed Providers. Microsoft's dedicated hardware solution is called Azure Dedicated Host. See page 352 for more details on the licensing of this solution.

Shared hardware options

Shared hardware solutions, also known as multi-tenant solutions, are where partners offer end-customer solutions hosted on hardware that is shared between customers. Again, customers might want to run the server applications in virtual machines, or to run Windows 10 and Office virtual desktops to deliver to their users, or to stream the Office applications.

Microsoft authorize partners to offer one or more of these types of solutions.

Authorized Mobility partner

An Authorized Mobility partner is a SPLA partner who has signed a License Mobility Addendum, and offers solutions based on the server products. In May 2021 there were around 1,800 of these partners all over the world.

Qualified Multi-Tenant Hosting (QMTH) partner

A QMTH partner is both a SPLA partner and a Direct CSP partner and is authorized to offer solutions based on the desktop products. In May 2021 there were around 750 of these partners all over the world.

Microsoft Azure

Azure is a multi-tenant offering and here Microsoft acts, in effect, as both an Authorized Mobility partner and a QMTH partner from a licensing perspective.

Windows Virtual Desktop service

The Windows Virtual Desktop service running in Azure is another option for a customer who wants to deliver virtual desktops to their users or to stream the Office applications.

Summary of deployment options

So far we've talked about choices for both server and desktop solutions across a range of hardware options. Here's the summary of what's possible if you've got the right licenses:

	Dedicated options				Shared options			
	Customer-owned	Authorized Outsourcer	Listed Provider	Azure Dedicated Host	Azure multi-tenant	Authorized Mobility partner	QMTH partner	Windows Virtual Desktop
Server	✔	✔	✔	✔	✔	✔	N/A	N/A
Desktop	✔	✔	✔	✔	✔	N/A	✔	✔

Figure 148: summary of deployment options

Server options

Customers with licenses, with or without Software Assurance, bought through a Volume Licensing agreement or through CSP, may use those licenses to install and run products on their **own servers** or those of an **Authorized Outsourcer**.

To use licenses on a **Listed Provider's** or **Authorized Mobility partner's** servers you need the License Mobility through SA benefit. See page 350 for full details on this benefit.

To use licenses on **Azure multi-tenant** hardware or **Azure Dedicated Host** you need either the Azure Hybrid Benefit (see page 343) or the License Mobility through SA benefit (page 350).

QMTH partners and the **Windows Virtual Desktop** service facilitate desktop solutions and are thus marked N/A in the table.

Desktop options

Let's start with the easy one – an Authorized Mobility partner provides server solutions, and so is marked N/A in the table.

For all of the other options, what you're allowed to do depends on whether you have user or device licenses, what program you've purchased them through, and, for Windows, whether you have a Qualifying Operating System or not. You can find out more on page 365 onwards.

Get the detail!

The following sections focus on each of the different products giving you the complete story for that product on the different hardware options:

- Windows Server
- SQL Server
- All other server applications
- Office 2019 device licenses
- Windows 10 and VDA device licenses
- Microsoft 365 Apps user licenses
- Windows 10 user licenses

Windows Server

Azure Hybrid Benefit ✔

The following licenses include the Azure Hybrid Benefit:

- Windows Server Standard and Datacenter Core licenses with SA acquired through any Volume Licensing agreement (L&SA)
- Windows Server Standard Core licenses acquired as Server Subscriptions through CSP (SS)

License Mobility through SA benefit

Windows Server licenses never have the License Mobility through SA benefit and can thus never be used in a Listed Provider's or Authorized Mobility partner's infrastructure.

Deployment rights

Customers may use their Windows Server licenses as shown below:

	Dedicated options				Shared options			
	Customer-owned	Authorized Outsourcer	Listed Provider	Azure Dedicated Host	Azure multi-tenant	Authorized Mobility partner	QMTH partner	Windows Virtual Desktop
L-only	✔	✔					N/A	N/A
L&SA	✔	✔		✔	✔		N/A	N/A
SS	✔	✔		✔	✔		N/A	N/A

Figure 149: Windows Server deployment options

SQL Server

Azure Hybrid Benefit ✔

The following licenses include the Azure Hybrid Benefit:

- SQL Server Standard and Enterprise Core licenses with SA acquired through any Volume Licensing agreement (L&SA)
- SQL Server Standard and Enterprise Core licenses acquired as Server Subscriptions through CSP (SS)

License Mobility through SA benefit ✔

The following licenses include the License Mobility through SA benefit:

- SQL Server Standard and Enterprise Core licenses with SA acquired through any Volume Licensing agreement
- SQL Server Standard Server licenses with SA acquired through any Volume Licensing agreement

Deployment rights

Customers may use their SQL Server licenses as shown below:

	Dedicated options				Shared options			
	Customer-owned	Authorized Outsourcer	Listed Provider	Azure Dedicated Host	Azure multi-tenant	Authorized Mobility partner	QMTH partner	Windows Virtual Desktop
L-only	✔	✔					N/A	N/A
L&SA	✔	✔	✔	✔✔	✔✔	✔	N/A	N/A
SS	✔	✔		✔	✔		N/A	N/A

Figure 150: SQL Server deployment options

Other server applications

License Mobility through SA benefit ✓

The following licenses with active Software Assurance acquired through any Volume Licensing agreement include the License Mobility through SA benefit:

- System Center 2019
- SQL Server 2019
- BizTalk Server 2020
- Project Server 2019
- Exchange Server 2019
- SharePoint Server 2019
- Skype for Business 2019
- Dynamics 365 for Operations Server
- Azure DevOps Server 2020

Deployment rights

Customers can use their server licenses as shown below:

	Dedicated options				Shared options			
	Customer-owned	Authorized Outsourcer	Listed Provider	Azure Dedicated Host	Azure multi-tenant	Authorized Mobility partner	QMTH partner	Windows Virtual Desktop
L-only	✓	✓					N/A	N/A
L&SA	✓	✓	✓	✓	✓	✓	N/A	N/A

Figure 151: other server applications deployment options

Office 2019 device licenses

Server usage rights

The following device licenses include rights to remotely access Office running on a server:

- Office 2019 Standard or Professional Plus licenses without Software Assurance acquired through the Open License program or CSP
- Office 2019 Standard or Professional Plus licenses with Software Assurance acquired through a Volume Licensing agreement

Deployment rights

Customers can use their Office 2019 device licenses as shown below. There is no option to take licenses to any kind of shared hardware:

	Dedicated options			
	Customer-owned	Authorized Outsourcer	Listed Provider	Azure Dedicated Host
Office 2019 Standard/ Professional without SA	✔	✔		
Office 2019 Standard/ Professional with SA	✔	✔		

Figure 152: Office 2019 device license deployment options

Windows 10 and VDA device licenses

VDA rights

The following device licenses acquired through any Volume Licensing agreement include rights to remotely access desktops running on a server:

- Windows 10 Enterprise with active SA
- VDA Device SL

Qualifying Operating System requirements

Windows 10 Enterprise licenses must be assigned to a device with a Qualifying Operating System (see page 99). VDA licenses may be assigned to any device.

Deployment rights

Customers can use their Windows and VDA device licenses as shown below. There is no option to take these licenses to any kind of shared hardware:

		Dedicated options			
	QOS?	Customer-owned	Authorized Outsourcer	Listed Provider	Azure Dedicated Host
Windows 10 Enterprise	Yes	✔	✔		
VDA Device SL	No	✔	✔		

Figure 153: Windows 10 and VDA device license deployment options

Microsoft 365 Apps user licenses

Shared Computer Activation rights

The following User SLs include Shared Computer Activation rights for the Office apps:

- Microsoft 365 Apps for enterprise
- Office 365 E3/E5
- Microsoft 365 E3/E5
- Microsoft 365 Business Premium

The notable exception here is the Microsoft 365 Apps for business User SL – SCA rights are only included when the apps are licensed via the Microsoft 365 Business Premium User SL.

Deployment rights

The licenses listed above may be purchased through CSP or a Volume Licensing agreement, and the apps may be used on servers as shown below, where you'll notice the rights are the same regardless of how the licenses were acquired:

	Dedicated options				Shared options			
	Customer-owned	Authorized Outsourcer	Listed Provider	Azure Dedicated Host	Azure multi-tenant	Authorized Mobility partner	QMTH partner	Windows Virtual Desktop
CSP	✔	✔		✔	✔	N/A	✔	✔
VL	✔	✔		✔	✔	N/A	✔	✔

Figure 154: Microsoft 365 Apps deployment options

Windows 10 user licenses

Licenses that include rights to Windows

Rights to install Windows 10 Enterprise on some or all dedicated or shared servers are included in these User SLs:

- Windows 10 Enterprise E3/E5
- Microsoft 365 E3/E5
- Microsoft 365 F3
- VDA E3/E5
- Microsoft 365 Business Premium

Qualifying Operating System requirements

A Windows 10 Enterprise E3/E5 User SL must always be assigned to a user whose main device has a Qualifying Operating System (see page 174). A VDA E3/E5 User SL, on the other hand, may be assigned to any user using any device. The Microsoft 365 E3/E5/F3 licenses can be assigned to a user with or without a primary device with a Qualifying Operating System, but the deployment options are reduced if there is no Qualifying Operating System. There are no Qualifying Operating System requirements for the Microsoft 365 Business Premium User SL regarding use of Windows 10 Enterprise.

VDA Add-on for Microsoft 365 E3/E5

This VDA Add-on User SL is an interesting one. It's used for users who are licensed with a Microsoft 365 E3/E5 User SL who don't have a primary device with a Qualifying Operating System, and it adds on for them a whole host of deployment options equivalent to those included with a VDA User SL. It's only available to purchase through the Enterprise Agreement.

License availability

The licenses that include rights to Windows are available through the ways to buy shown in the following table. It's important to know how a license has been acquired since the deployment rights are sometimes different, dependent on the purchasing mechanism:

	EA	MPSA	CSP
Windows 10 Enterprise E3/E5	✔	✔	✔
Microsoft 365 E3/E5/F3	✔	✔	✔
Microsoft 365 Business Premium			✔
VDA E3	✔	✔	✔
VDA E5	✔	✔	
VDA Add-on	✔		

Figure 155: availability of licenses that include some Windows 10 Enterprise rights

The summary table

So, we've seen which licenses include rights to install Windows 10 Enterprise on some or all servers, we've talked about the need, or not, for Qualifying Operating Systems, and we know that different licenses are available in different programs. It's time now to bring everything together and to see exactly what options are available for which licenses through the different ways to buy, and that's what the summary table on the next page shows. As you use the table, remember that only VDA E3 is available through CSP, and the VDA Add-on is only available through the EA.

	QOS?	Dedicated options				Shared options			
		Customer-owned	Authorized Outsourcer	Listed Provider	Azure Dedicated Host	Azure multi-tenant	Authorized Mobility partner	QMTH partner	Windows Virtual Desktop
Windows 10 Enterprise E3/E5 Microsoft 365 E3/E5 Microsoft 365 F3	Yes	✓ (EA/MPSA)	✓ (EA/MPSA)		✓ (EA/MPSA) ✓ (CSP)	✓ (EA/MPSA) ✓ (CSP)	N/A	✓ (EA/MPSA) ✓ (CSP)	✓ (EA/MPSA) ✓ (CSP)
Microsoft 365 E3/E5 Microsoft 365 F3	No						N/A		✓ (EA/MPSA) ✓ (CSP)
VDA E3/E5	No	✓ (EA/MPSA)	✓ (EA/MPSA)	✓ (EA/MPSA)	✓ (EA/MPSA) ✓ (CSP)	✓ (EA/MPSA) ✓ (CSP)	N/A	✓ (EA/MPSA) ✓ (CSP)	✓ (EA/MPSA) ✓ (CSP)
Microsoft 365 E3/E5 + VDA Add-on	No	✓ (EA/MPSA)	✓ (EA/MPSA)	✓ (EA/MPSA)	✓ (EA/MPSA)	✓ (EA/MPSA)	N/A	✓ (EA/MPSA)	✓ (EA/MPSA)
Microsoft 365 Business Premium	No						N/A		✓ (CSP)

✓ (EA/MPSA) Licenses purchased through the EA/MPSA ✓ (CSP) Licenses purchased through CSP

Figure 156: Windows 10 user license deployment options

AZURE DEFENDER

Microsoft Defender is Microsoft's extended detection and response (XDR) solution for threat protection, and it's comprised of two products: Microsoft 365 Defender and Azure Defender. Azure Defender provides threat protection for workloads running in Azure, on premises, and in other clouds, while Microsoft 365 Defender works across endpoints, identities, email, and applications providing integrated protection against attacks. The licensing of the Microsoft 365 Defender components is covered on page 205.

There's a whole host of services that make up Azure Defender: Azure Defender for Servers, Azure Defender for App Service, Azure Defender for SQL on Azure, Azure Defender for SQL outside Azure, and the list goes on. All of these services are charged on a consumption basis, so, for example, Azure Defender for Servers is a cost per server per hour, Azure Defender for SQL on Azure is a charge per instance per hour, and Azure Defender for SQL outside Azure is a cost per vCore per hour.

The only licensing point of note is that Azure Defender for Servers includes Microsoft Defender for Endpoint Server, the licensing of which is detailed on page 208. If you find yourself looking through technical documentation, it's probably also worth knowing that Azure Defender for Servers is the new name for Azure Security Center Standard edition.

WINDOWS VIRTUAL DESKTOP

The Windows Virtual Desktop service in Azure allows customers to take advantage of a secure remote virtual desktop and app experience. Customers can choose a Windows client or Windows Server desktop.

Purchasing Windows Virtual Desktop

Customers who want to deploy Windows Virtual Desktop solutions need to pay for two distinct parts of the solution: user access rights, and Azure infrastructure costs.

User access rights

Rights to use Windows 7 or Windows 10 virtual desktops are included in the following licenses acquired through a Volume Licensing agreement or CSP:

- Windows 10 E3/E5
- Windows 10 VDA E3/E5
- Microsoft 365 E3/E5, F3, Business Premium

Rights to use Windows Server virtual desktops are included in the following licenses:

- RDS User CAL with SA
- RDS CAL User SL
- RDS Device CAL with SA (for users using the licensed device)

Azure infrastructure

Azure infrastructure costs will typically include virtual machines, storage and networking costs, and are charged on a consumption basis.

Extended Security Updates

Windows 7 virtual desktops include free Extended Security Updates until January 2023.

LICENSING DEV/TEST SOLUTIONS

You can think of the Microsoft developer tools as being in two categories: Visual Studio subscriptions, and the Azure DevOps tools.

Visual Studio subscriptions are assigned to an individual user who is typically a developer and needs tools to create and test applications. A Visual Studio subscription gives these users access to the Visual Studio software and a whole host of benefits. There are two ways of buying these Visual Studio subscriptions. Firstly, they can be purchased as a license with Software Assurance through a Volume Licensing agreement, and these are known as Standard subscriptions. Secondly, they're available as Cloud subscriptions which are monthly subscriptions and are purchased against an Azure Subscription. Cloud subscriptions are the focus of this section, and if you need information on the Standard subscriptions, you can find details on page 91.

The Azure DevOps tools form an Application Lifecycle Management solution which provides an environment where software developers, testers, project managers, and other members of a software development team can communicate and collaborate throughout the process of designing, building, testing, and deploying software. These tools are available either as an on-premises solution called Azure DevOps Server 2020 which is covered on page 96, or as a cloud-based solution simply called Azure DevOps which is covered on page 376.

VISUAL STUDIO

Visual Studio Cloud subscriptions

There are just two Visual Studio Cloud subscriptions, both aimed at developers:

- Visual Studio Professional
- Visual Studio Enterprise

Both of these subscriptions give access to the Visual Studio IDE, but the rights to the Visual Studio tools are not perpetual and end when the subscription ends. Both subscriptions also include an Azure DevOps Server CAL for the licensed user and the rights to install Azure DevOps Server 2020, as well as licenses for Azure DevOps in the cloud: a Basic plan license for Visual Studio Professional users, and a Basic + Test plan license for Visual Studio Enterprise users.

Visual Studio Cloud subscriptions don't include the wide range of subscriber benefits, such as rights to install software for Dev/Test purposes, as the Visual Studio Standard subscriptions do, but licensed users do have access to Azure Dev/Test pricing.

Buying Visual Studio Cloud subscriptions

Visual Studio Cloud subscriptions behave in a different way to their Visual Studio Standard subscription cousins, and also differently to Online Services licensed with User Subscription Licenses. First of all, they are monthly subscriptions which automatically renew each month – there's no commitment to a 12-month term as there is with most subscriptions, and you can cancel whenever you like, which just turns off the automatic renewal.

Secondly, they are only available through the Visual Studio Marketplace, and they have to be purchased through an active Azure Subscription (see page 320 to learn about Azure Subscriptions). It's normally Azure consumption services that are paid for through an Azure Subscription, so this is indeed slightly odd.

From an EA perspective these Visual Studio Cloud subscriptions can't be paid for out of Azure Prepayment funds; the purchase triggers a monthly overage invoice. The first monthly payment for all customers is pro-rated dependent on when the subscription was purchased – if The Cobalt Bolt Company purchase a subscription half-way through a month, they'll just be charged half a month on that first invoice.

And the final noteworthy licensing point is the discounts that are available: you get a 5% discount on the 6th and all subsequent subscriptions each month. Note that this is within each type of subscription – so there would be no discount if 3 Visual Studio Professional and 3 Visual Studio Enterprise subscriptions were purchased, only if 6 (or more) of either individual one were purchased.

AZURE DEVOPS

There are two parts to the Azure DevOps service from a licensing perspective. Firstly, user licenses are assigned to individual users to allow access to the environment where software developers, testers, project managers, and other members of a software development team can communicate and collaborate throughout the process of designing, building, testing, and deploying software. Secondly, there are individual services (Azure Pipelines and Azure Artifacts) which are purchased on an as-needed basis.

Azure DevOps user licenses

There are three user licenses available for Azure DevOps users: Stakeholder, Basic plan, and a Basic + Test plan.

Stakeholder licenses are assigned to users who need access to a limited set of functionality for tasks within Azure DevOps related to checking project status and providing direction and feedback to a team. These licenses are free and there is no limit to the number that may be assigned to users.

Basic plan licenses are aimed at the majority of users and enable them to create and review delivery plans, as well as access tools such as Azure Boards, Azure Repos, Azure Pipelines and Azure Artifacts. The first 5 licenses for a customer are free, and then there's a charge of $6 per user per month. So, 10 users would cost $30 – calculated by (5 x $0) + (5 x $6) = $30, for example. The Basic Plan also includes an Azure DevOps Server CAL for the licensed user and the rights to install Azure DevOps Server 2020.

Basic + Test plan licenses include all the Basic plan features as well as test planning, tracking and execution capabilities. These licenses are priced at $52 per user per month and include licenses for the Azure DevOps solution as per the Basic plan. Prices are taken from Microsoft's public website here: https://bit.ly/BOKDevOpsPricing.

Licenses assigned to Visual Studio subscription users

Users with existing Visual Studio Standard or Cloud subscriptions are already licensed with either the Basic or Basic + Test plans as per the table below:

Visual Studio subscription	Azure DevOps plan
Visual Studio Professional	Basic
Visual Studio Enterprise	Basic + Test
Visual Studio Test Professional	Basic + Test
MSDN Platforms	Basic + Test

Figure 157: Azure DevOps plans for Visual Studio subscribers

When a Visual Studio subscriber signs in to Azure DevOps their license is automatically detected, so there is no license assignment to do. These included licenses do not count against the 5 free included Basic plan licenses.

Setting up billing

Creating an Azure DevOps account is free. Within that account you need to have at least one Organization which is a mechanism for organizing and collecting groups of projects. An Organization could represent the whole company, a regional division, or a business unit, for example. Each Organization gets its own free tier of services which includes, for example, a certain amount of minutes for Azure Pipelines, storage for Azure Artifacts, as well as the 5 Azure DevOps Basic plan user licenses.

In common with the Visual Studio Cloud subscriptions, Azure DevOps licenses are billed through an Azure Subscription and so, when you've created the Azure DevOps Organization, an Azure Subscription needs to be associated with it before you can start acquiring Azure DevOps user or individual services licenses.

Assigning Azure DevOps user licenses

In 2019 Microsoft changed the billing for Azure DevOps user licenses so that rather than completing a purchasing process for a license, you add users to your Organization, assign them an access level (Stakeholder, Basic, or Basic + Test), and then you're billed according to those assignments. As a concept, this is known as user assignment-based billing.

Azure DevOps user licenses don't have a 1-month or 12-month term associated with them, and billing is on a daily basis. If The Cobalt Bolt Company have assigned a Basic + Test plan access level to 3 of their users and then 1 of those users leaves the company, they simply remove the user from their Azure DevOps Organization and the billing stops for that user.

When you assign an access level to an individual user it's known as direct assignment, and billing starts for a user as soon as an access level is assigned to them, even if they don't use Azure DevOps. An alternative, and more cost-effective, mechanism is to create a group rule where you create a group, add members, and define the access level for members of the group. When these users without direct assignments sign in to Azure DevOps the relevant access level is assigned to them and billing only starts then.

Multi-Organization billing

As we discovered above, an Azure DevOps Organization is a way of organizing groups of projects and, as such, it's entirely possible that The Cobalt Bolt Company may have multiple Organizations. The Cobalt Bolt Company use a single Azure Subscription for the billing of all of their Azure DevOps. With multiple Organizations, The Cobalt Bolt Company need to make a choice as to how they are billed – via Single Organization or Multi-Organization billing.

With Single Organization billing, each Organization is considered completely separately. This means that each Organization receives the 5 free Basic plan licenses, but if a user is assigned the Basic + Test plan access level in 3

Organizations, then The Cobalt Bolt Company need to pay for 3 licenses for him.

With Multi-Organization billing, billing works across all Organizations within an Azure Subscription. This means that The Cobalt Bolt Company will only receive the 5 free Basic plan licenses once, at the Subscription level, but if users are added to multiple Organizations, then the relevant licenses are only paid for once.

You can imagine that customers will make a billing choice based on their particular situation: when most users access only one Organization then 5 free users per Organization is attractive via the Single Organization billing option, whereas if many users access multiple Organizations, then it's likely that Multi-Organization billing is the right choice.

DEV/TEST SUBSCRIPTIONS

An Azure Subscription is a container to which Azure resources are assigned as they are created. There are different Subscription types associated with the ways that a customer buys – an Azure Subscription for CSP is different to the one for an Enterprise Agreement, for example. All of these "regular" Subscription types are used for production workloads supporting the day-to-day business of an organization.

However, there's another type of Azure Subscription which is used for dev and test purposes. The benefit for organizations is that there are discounted rates on some of the Azure services when they are assigned to a Dev/Test Subscription. For example, a Windows Server virtual machine is charged at the rate for a Linux VM of the same size and type. As you would expect, these Subscriptions can only be used for Dev/Test workloads and, unless it's for UAT purposes, may only be used by users with active Visual Studio Standard or Cloud subscriptions.

A Dev/Test Subscription is only available through an Enterprise Agreement or the Enterprise MCA, or via azure.com.

AZURE MARKETPLACE

The Azure Marketplace is where Microsoft and partners sell solutions that are built on Azure. Partners who build these solutions are often known as Independent Software Vendors, or ISVs. Consultancy services based on Azure may also be listed on the public Azure Marketplace, although customers don't transact anything through Marketplace, they contact the partner directly to engage their services.

Offer types

When a customer buys an ISV solution through the Azure Marketplace they need to pay for two things: firstly, for the "solution" part – the Intellectual Property that the ISV has built, and secondly, for the Azure services that will be consumed as part of the solution. There are various ways that these parts are paid for, dependent on the type of solution.

Bring-Your-Own-License (BYOL) offers

With a Bring-Your-Own-License offer a customer buys a license for the IP part of the solution outside of Marketplace in the form of a software license. The associated consumption services are then billed against the Azure Subscription that they choose when they transact the BYOL offer.

Usage-based offers

With a usage-based offer a customer pays Microsoft for the IP part of the solution according to prices that the ISV has set. Microsoft then pay the ISV for their part of the solution, retaining an agreed transaction fee. As with the BYOL offers, the associated consumption services are then billed against the Azure Subscription that the customer chooses when they transact the Marketplace offer.

SaaS subscription offers

A SaaS offer is typically available with both monthly and annual subscription options. Here a single fee is paid by the customer – perhaps as a User Subscription License – which covers both the IP part of the solution AND the associated Azure services. In these offers, Microsoft again pay the ISV directly for the IP part of the solution, and this time, it's the ISV who pays for the underlying Azure consumption services via their own Enterprise Agreement, or through azure.com, for example.

Availability

When an ISV partner publishes their offer, it is available through the public Azure Marketplace at https://azuremarketplace.microsoft.com. In addition, a partner can choose to make their offer available through CSP, which they do as part of the solution publishing process.

This is a summary of which sorts of offers are available through the different ways to buy Azure:

Program or agreement	Marketplace offers available
Enterprise Agreement	All offers
MPSA	None
Select Plus	None
Open programs	Bring-Your-Own-License offers only
CSP	Offers opted in by publishing partners
Enterprise MCA	All offers

Figure 158: Marketplace offer availability

BUYING AZURE SERVICES: EA

Customers can buy the Azure services in an Enterprise Agreement through either the two Enterprise Enrollments or the Server and Cloud Enrollment

Azure components availability

In terms of Azure, the following components are available through the EA enrollments:

Azure components	
User plans	✔
Consumption services	✔
Reservations	✔
Marketplace solutions	✔
Dev/Test Subscriptions	✔

Figure 159: availability of Azure components in the EA enrollments

Azure User plans

The Azure services licensed via User Subscription Licenses, such as Azure Information Protection, follow the same rules as the Online Services as described on page 293 onwards. The only additional thing to mention here is that you can't use Azure Prepayment funds (see below) to pay for them.

Buying Azure services through the Enterprise Enrollments

In November 2019 Microsoft made some changes to buying Azure through the Enterprise Enrollments which affect commercial customers in countries where Microsoft bill Enterprise Agreement customers directly rather than through partners. As part of the initiative to move to the New Commerce Experience governed by the Microsoft Customer Agreement, these customers who have never bought the Azure consumption services through an Enterprise Enrollment may now not add them to the enrollment. They must purchase them through one of the New Commerce Experience channels: either direct from azure.com, via a CSP partner, or direct from a Microsoft salesperson using the Enterprise MCA.

Consumption services: Azure Prepayment

To buy Azure consumption services in an Enterprise Enrollment, a customer must already have made a commitment to either the Enterprise Products or Enterprise Online Services. The consumption services are then paid for upfront with an Azure Prepayment and then, as the services are used, the relevant amount is decremented from this Azure Prepayment amount each month. Until quite recently, Azure Prepayment was known as Monetary Commitment.

Azure Prepayment: Annually Prepaid

There are two types of Azure Prepayment, and the first one we'll look at, the Annually Prepaid option, works in the same way as Monetary Commitment used to. Azure Prepayment is sold in multiples of a single SKU costing $100, and a customer must make an upfront payment for at least one of these SKUs per month. In the Annually Prepaid option therefore, a customer places an Azure Prepayment order of at least $1,200 at the start of the year.

As the services are used this amount is decremented. Of course, it's extremely unlikely that a customer will have precisely estimated what they will spend on the Azure consumption services and their Azure Prepayment may be too large or too small. If it's too small, then when the Azure Prepayment funds are exhausted the customer is simply invoiced monthly for the overspend which is known as overage. If, however, there are funds remaining at the end of the year, this money does not roll over to the following year – with the Annually Prepaid option a customer makes a payment at the start of each year of the Enterprise Enrollment and the funds expire at the anniversary.

Azure Prepayment: Fully Prepaid

The Fully Prepaid option for Azure Prepayment is an alternative for customers who want the Azure Prepayment funds to be available for the full three-year term of the Enterprise Enrollment. In this option the customer's first Azure Prepayment must be for a minimum of $100 per month for the full 36 months, so $3,600 of course. They make a single payment at the start of the Enterprise Enrollment and the Azure Prepayment funds don't expire at the anniversary but at the end of the enrollment. Again, if funds are exhausted, then overage invoices are issued monthly.

Azure Prepayment: changes

Customers who want to make additional Azure Prepayment orders or change the amount they are due to pay at the next anniversary engage with Microsoft or their reseller to work through the relevant processes.

Consumption services: pricing and price protection

There are no price levels for the Azure consumption services in the Enterprise Enrollments, so a price per hour for a Windows Server virtual machine is the same regardless of which price level the customer is entitled to for his Enterprise Products or Enterprise Online Services.

Customers who buy the Azure consumption services through an Enterprise Enrollment get best price protection for these services. This means that every month when the Azure systems are deciding how much to decrement the Azure Prepayment total by for a particular service, they check the following sources and charge the customer the best price of all three:

- Baseline price – the price of the service when the Enterprise Enrollment was signed
- Negotiated price – any special price for the service that was agreed when the enrollment was signed
- Current price – from the current month's pricelist

This means that an Enterprise Enrollment customer knows that they will never pay a higher price than an Azure service was when their enrolment was signed.

Paying for Reservations

The full range of Reservations is available in the Enterprise Enrollments. Typically, the term of a Reservation is 1 or 3 years, and customers can choose to pay upfront or monthly, and there are no penalties (in terms of higher costs) for choosing a monthly option.

All Reservations are paid for from the Azure Prepayment funds, unless these are exhausted, in which case the charges for any Reservations will appear on the next monthly invoice. If a Reservation is canceled, it is refunded to the original mechanism used to purchase it: if Azure Prepayment was used, it is returned to the available balance, and if overage was used then it shows as a credit on the monthly invoice.

Note that Reservations are not aligned to the enrollment anniversary, nor are they pro-rated in any way – they have a 1- or 3-year term regardless of when they were purchased.

Paying for Marketplace solutions

The vast majority of Azure Marketplace solutions are charged for on an Enterprise Enrollment customer's monthly invoice. In March 2018 there were some changes made so that some Linux Support and Linux virtual machines offerings do consume Azure Prepayment funds. You can find the list here: https://bit.ly/BOKEAMarketplace.

Dev/Test Subscriptions

Dev/Test Subscriptions are available in the Enterprise Enrollments and are designated as this type of Azure Subscription when they are created. See page 380 to learn about the advantages of Dev/Test Subscriptions.

Buying Azure services through an SCE

The Server and Cloud Enrollment gives two ways for a customer to pay for the Azure consumption services dependent on whether or not they have already signed an SCE for another product. Regardless of which option the customer chooses, Reservations, Marketplace purchases and Dev/Test Subscriptions work in exactly the same way as the Enterprise Enrollments.

Azure as an additional service

When a customer signs an SCE for any of the three components detailed in the section starting on page 133 they are automatically provisioned for Azure. This means that technically they're ready to use any of the Azure services and they're just invoiced monthly in arrears for whatever services they consume. The customer does not have to make any sort of commitment and there are no minimum purchasing requirements.

Azure-only SCE

Alternatively, a customer can sign a Server and Cloud Enrollment by making a commitment to Azure via an Azure Prepayment. This works in exactly the same way as in the section on Enterprise Enrollments with just a difference in the minimums: for the SCE there is a required minimum of 10 Azure Prepayment SKUs per month which equates to 10 × 12 × $100 = $12,000 per year. The same Annually Prepaid and Fully Prepaid options are available.

On page 383 I explained the changes that Microsoft made in November 2019 for customers purchasing the Azure services through the Enterprise Enrollments. They also made some changes which affect Server and Cloud Enrollment customers: from that date no new Azure-only SCEs can be signed or existing ones renewed for commercial customers in the countries where Microsoft bill Enterprise Agreement customers directly.

BUYING AZURE SERVICES: MPSA

Azure components availability

Only the Azure User plans are available through the MPSA, and they are transacted in the same way as Online Services such as Office 365. Find out more on page 303.

Azure components	
User plans	✔
Consumption services	
Reservations	
Marketplace solutions	
Dev/Test Subscriptions	

Figure 160: availability of Azure components in the MPSA

BUYING AZURE SERVICES: SELECT PLUS

None of the Azure components are available through a Select Plus agreement.

BUYING AZURE SERVICES: OPEN PROGRAMS

We'll consider the Open License program, and the Open Value and Open Value Subscription agreements in one section here, since the Azure services work the same way in all of them.

Azure components availability

In the Open programs, licenses for the Azure User plans are available and transacted in the same way as Online Services such as Office 365. Customers can purchase the Azure consumption services and can transact a subset of the Marketplace offerings, those sold on a Bring-Your-Own-License (BYOL) basis:

Azure components	
User plans	✔
Consumption services	✔
Reservations	
Marketplace solutions	✔
Dev/Test Subscriptions	

Figure 161: availability of Azure components in the Open programs

Paying for Azure consumption services

In the Open programs Azure Prepayment credits are purchased to pay for the Azure consumption services. A customer pays upfront for $100 worth of credit which must be used within a 12-month term – it cannot roll over from one 12-month period to the next.

Azure Prepayment credits are typically purchased via a partner and a customer will receive an Online Services Activation, or OSA, key for the amount they have purchased. They could just purchase $100 worth and would receive a key for that, or they could purchase, for example, $600 worth and would also receive a single key. The 12-month period during which the credit must be used does not start until the key is activated and that must happen within 5 years of the purchase date. This could mean that the original agreement through which the Azure Prepayment credits were purchased has expired. That's no problem at all – although the credits have been purchased through an agreement they are not tied to that agreement and must simply be activated during the 5-year window.

The first key that the customer purchases will be used to activate an **Azure in Open** Subscription and subsequent purchases will simply be added to that Subscription. If a customer buys further credit and assigns it to a Subscription before the credit with a previous key has been exhausted, then the credit on the older key is used before the newer one. The prices that a customer pays for the Azure consumption services are those advertised publicly on azure.com.

If an Azure in Open Subscription reaches a zero balance, the services will be suspended. The data will be retained for 90 days, and once funds are added to the Subscription the services can be reinstated; however there could be some services that would need to be redeployed after this interruption. Thus, there is another way for a customer to purchase these Azure Prepayment credits and that is via a credit card. This is, if you like, an emergency option for a customer in case they can't reach their partner to buy credits, and helps them to avoid service disruption when Azure Prepayment funds are almost exhausted.

Customers use the Azure Management Portal to add their Azure Prepayment credits, supplying either the key that they have received from their partner or adding Azure Prepayment funds via a credit card.

Paying for Azure Marketplace solutions

Only Bring-Your-Own-License Marketplace offers are available for customers buying through the Open programs. The underlying Azure consumption services are charged against the Azure Subscription that is chosen when the offer is transacted.

Transitioning out of the Open License agreement

Customers won't be able to purchase Azure Prepayment credits through an Open License agreement after 31 December, 2021, so what should businesses who have purchased their Azure consumption services through an Open License agreement do after this date?

Well, it's all good news really. The services running inside an Azure in Open Subscription aren't affected by the status of the Open License agreement and will continue using Azure Prepayment credits from activated keys. Any keys that haven't been activated aren't affected either – they must still just be activated within the 5-year window. When customers need more Azure Prepayment credit they can start a new Open Value agreement with the purchase of just 1 x $100 worth of credit. Equally they could purchase more Azure Prepayment credit through an existing Open Value or Open Value Subscription agreement since the type of Subscription is consistent through all the agreements as are the Azure Prepayment keys. Equally, the customer could opt to purchase more Azure Prepayment credit via the credit card option in the Azure Management Portal.

BUYING AZURE SERVICES: CSP

As usual, we'll cover what's available to the partner to sell and how they are invoiced for it, knowing that it's up to the partner what solutions and payment terms are actually offered to the customer.

Azure components availability

The Azure User plans, purchased as User SLs, are transacted in exactly the same way as the Online Services such as Office 365.

ISV partners who create solutions for sale in the Azure Marketplace publish to the public Marketplace and then can choose whether they also make their offerings available through CSP – hence the gray tick indicates that not all Marketplace solutions are necessarily available through CSP:

Azure components	
User plans	✔
Consumption services	✔
Reservations	✔
Marketplace solutions	✔ (gray)
Dev/Test Subscriptions	

Figure 162: availability of Azure components in CSP

Paying for the Azure consumption services

When a CSP customer wants to start using the Azure consumption services, their partner transacts the Azure plan for them. This sets up the customer's first Azure Subscription, which means that Azure resources (like virtual machines) can be created. In CSP it's the partner who will go to the Azure Management Portal and create the resources, although they can give customers access to the Azure Subscription(s) if that suits everyone better.

There is no commitment required within CSP to purchase the Azure consumption services; the partner is simply invoiced at the end of the month for whatever services the customer has consumed. Again, the partner can invoice the customer in this way, or may impose their own terms and conditions.

The partner is invoiced according to a monthly price list and thus there is no notion of price protection in CSP. There's also just one price level in CSP. The pricing of the Azure consumption services to the customer is, of course, determined by the partner, but Microsoft's intention is that it equals both EA pricing and the public prices on azure.com. Naturally this changes if the Azure consumption services are part of a wider solution which include partner services for which an all-inclusive price has been agreed.

Paying for Reservations

The full range of Reservations is available in CSP and the payment options for partners match those available to customers buying direct through azure.com. Typically, the term of a Reservation is 1 or 3 years, and you can choose to pay upfront or monthly, and there are no penalties (in terms of higher costs) for choosing a monthly option. Monthly payments are not an option for third-party Software Plans such as SUSE Linux and Red Hat Plans.

Reservations for Azure services, such as Reserved Instances and Reserved Capacity, may be canceled, but those for the Software Plans may not. Credit is calculated for the remaining term and an early termination fee of 12% is deducted, and then the balance is refunded. At the time of writing (May 2021) Microsoft are not currently charging the early termination fees for refunds. However, refunds are capped at $50,000 per partner per rolling 12-month period.

Customers who want to purchase their own Reservations in CSP can only do this if it's specifically enabled by their partner. There are two requirements that must be met: first of all, the customer user must be assigned the Owner role for an Azure Subscription, and then the partner must adjust the relevant Customer Permissions setting so that Reservations may be purchased by the customer. It's important to note that even though the customer can buy

Reservations they can't change the scope, or exchange or cancel Reservations after purchase.

Paying for Marketplace solutions

Partners pay for Azure Marketplace transactions on their monthly invoices. Note that if a customer has been assigned the Owner role on an Azure Subscription, they are able to make purchases for BYOL and usage-based Marketplace offers without reference to their partner.

BUYING AZURE SERVICES: ENTERPRISE MCA

When a customer decides to buy the Azure consumption services from Microsoft in this way, the internal salesperson will typically carry out two tasks: they will initiate the creation of the Microsoft Customer Agreement for the customer to accept in the Microsoft 365 Admin Center, and they will provision a regular Azure plan and perhaps the Azure plan for Dev/Test as well. The initial Azure Subscription is created for the customer in both cases. Customers are then free to assign resources against those Subscriptions in the Azure Management Portal and to purchase Reservations and Marketplace solutions, the full range of which are available.

Azure components availability

The Online Services such as Office 365 are not yet available through this way to buy, and since the Azure User SLs are transacted in the same way, this particular Azure component is not available in the Enterprise MCA:

Azure components	
User plans	
Consumption services	✔
Reservations	✔
Marketplace solutions	✔
Dev/Test Subscriptions	✔

Figure 163: availability of Azure components in the Enterprise MCA

Paying for the Azure consumption services

In the Enterprise MCA there's a choice of how customers pay for the Azure consumption services. The default option is to receive an invoice at the end of the month for the services that have been consumed that month. Alternatively, customers can make an Azure Prepayment, where the amount and term are agreed directly with Microsoft. The Azure Prepayment amount is decremented monthly as services are used, and all unused Azure Prepayment expires at the end of the term.

For both options, pricing for the individual services is the same as the rates publicly available on azure.com, and there is no notion of price protection or multiple price levels though this way to buy.

Index

B

C

D

F

G

H

I

L

M

N

O

P

Q

R

S

T

U

V

W

Acknowledgements

Thanks to Simon Taylor for proof reading with the beadiest eyes in the business; if there are still errors then the fault is mine as I had the final say. Thanks also to Simon for coming up with all the fictional company names that are used throughout.

Thanks to Simona Millham, the creative brain behind the graphics used in this book. Again, if any are less than perfect it's due to my tweaking.

A special thank you to Paul Burgum, a business partner in a million; endlessly generous with his time, always supportive, and full of good ideas – if you love the index in this book, then that was one of his great suggestions.

Louise Ulrick